C000133803

A WIGAN CHILDHOOD

A Wigan Childhood

JOHN SHARROCK TAYLOR

PALATINE

To my sons and the Richards and Williams
of twelve generations

A Wigan Childhood

Copyright © John Sharrock Taylor 2010

First edition, 2010

Published by Palatine Books,
an imprint of Carnegie Publishing Ltd
Carnegie House,
Chatsworth Road,
Lancaster, LA1 4SL
www.carnegiepublishing.com

All rights reserved
Unauthorised duplication contravenes existing laws

ISBN 978-1-874181-71-2

Designed and typeset by Carnegie Book Production
Printed and bound in the UK by Short Run Press, Exeter

Contents

WIGAN PIER.

Acknowledgements

BECAUSE OF ITS BEAUTIFULLY EERIE gothic style I have quoted verbatim from William Roughead's *The Dunecht Mystery* from *Twelve Scots Trials* published in 1913 by William Green and Sons, though extensive research has failed to find the copyright holder. In drawing on James Fairhurst's account of the Button Pit in *Wigan's Worst Victorian Murders* (Book Clearance Centre 2001) I have made free use of his quotations from the original transcript of the trial of Thomas Grime. *Wigan Coal And Iron*, a positively encyclopaedic work by Donald Anderson and AA France (Smiths of Wigan 1994) gave me some valuable insights into the working life of my colliery overlooker great-grandfather and my farmer-turned-miner grandfather. MD Smith's *About Haigh and Aspull* (2000) told me more about that complex amalgam of industry and agriculture where my most patriarchal of ancestors, John Taylor, farmed for almost fifty years, while Tony Smith's award-winning Boothstown website set the scene for John's early life as a young gamekeeper in 'Botany Bay'. John Benn's spoof *Festival of Lessons and Carols*, quoted in Chapter 15, made me laugh when I first read it forty years ago and it still does.

I should like to acknowledge the invaluable help given to me by the following:Brian Elsey, whose *Wigan World* website is an absolutely indispensable resource for anyone researching Wigan history. Joyce Bell, for her eyewitness account of the Wellington bomber crash and permission to quote from our correspondence about her childhood in wartime Leytonstone. Linda Edwards of Seattle, for introducing me to her pioneering great-grandfather, William Taylor, and his many descendants in Washington State, and for sending me copies of valuable Taylor documents and family photographs.

Brian Sharrock, for encouraging my first faltering steps in genealogy and raising the intriguing possibility of our Chirac ancestry. Lawrence Sharrock, for poring with me over the problem of our elusive great-great-grandfather, Henry. Marty Smith of the Ridware Historical Society, and the staffs of the Stafford and Lichfield Records Offices, for helping me to discover the Taylor family's unexpected Staffordshire origins. My first cousin David Taylor, for the loan of family photographs and the touching letter written to his father Jim by our uncle Jack shortly before he was killed on active service with the RAF in 1942. Leanne Turner of Michigan, for her enormous generosity in entrusting me permanently with the whole of her Hart family photo archive. Christine and Simon of the History Shop in Wigan, for guiding me through its labyrinths and those of the Archives at Leigh Town Hall. And most of all my wife Val for much more than I could ever express.

PREFACE

A Plague of Aunts

'NOT ANOTHER BLOODY AUNT!' I muttered irritably to myself, but not loudly enough for my grandmother to hear. When I was a boy practically any female over the age of consent and under the age of death was an aunt. There were far too many aunts in the world and I found it confusing. This latest specimen was particularly worrying. She had the kind of figure that used to be described as portly, her several chins wobbled nervously and her cheeks were tinged with an unhealthy puce. She subsided into one of my grandmother's antimacassared armchairs and gasped: 'Ee, Annie! Your Jack!'

I looked at her resignedly across the Algebra homework which was spread out on the kitchen table.

'Jack!' she repeated, as if mesmerised.

'Yes,' I replied, irritated but by no means puzzled.

By the time I was in my teens I had already played this scene several times with different partners, so I knew what to expect. My resemblance, physically, vocally and in terms of mannerisms, to my uncle and namesake, who had been killed when his Wellington bomber crashed in the Second World War, was an accepted fact within the immediate family but visitors who had known my uncle, John Sharrock Taylor, and did not know me, were always shocked. My grandmother, who apart from my wife and children is the person in the whole of my life with whom I have most closely identified, was convinced that I had been sent to her as a replacement for her lost son. For obvious reasons I could sympathise with her feeling but I found it disturbing and I still do. Finally I took pity on the visitor and said to her:

'I'm Jack, but I'm not THAT Jack.'

And that, together with the Wiggin Tree, illustrates the main theme of this book.

My ancestors play a large role in this book, partly because their genes and experiences have determined to a greater or lesser extent what has happened to my parents, to me and to my children. I was dimly aware of this fact from the beginning, but even so, during the process of writing, I was surprised at how often I found myself interpreting my forebears' doings in the light of my own actions and feelings. And vice-versa. Somebody once wrote that we live life forwards but understand it backwards. It is nowhere near as simple as that. The past is not just another country where they do things differently. It is a country which coexists with the present and the future and continually interacts with them. This realisation has radically affected the form of my narrative and, however much I wanted to keep things simple, starting at the beginning and continuing straight on to the end was just not possible.

When I began to investigate my origins I assumed that I was Lancastrian through and through, but I soon discovered that my mother's grandfather Albert Norcliffe had been a West Riding wool-stapler married to a Welsh girl, transplanted like my Welsh rowan tree to the industrial north of England. Several of my lines of descent were Lancashire enough, though one researcher claims that even my grandmother's family, the Sharrocks, active in the County Palatine since at least the 13th century, were actually Chiracs of Norman origin. Most surprising of all, I found that we Taylors had been in Lancashire for a mere 150 years. John Taylor, my great-grandfather and a major character in this story, had cared more about Old Testament genealogy than about his own family tree. He was vague about his place and date of birth. His own children thought he had been born at Worsley near Manchester, an error perpetuated in his obituary in the *Wigan Observer*, but he too had been uprooted at an early age from Staffordshire, where his grandfather, Old William, had been the model John later adopted when he set out to re-root his own life. In his turn, John's son, another William, transplanted himself from Lancashire to the United States of America during its last great period of expansion. As my own sons continue to add to the forty-odd countries we have already lived or travelled in, the image of the Wiggin Tree, its roots burrowing and branching underneath the ground to emerge in unexpected places, seems all the more potent.

Writing this book has often seemed to me to be more a matter of necessity than of choice. I might have begun my belated literary career with a book about our experiences in El Salvador, Chile, India or Spain, all fertile fields for reminiscence, but I found that the story of my family kept dragging me back to the word processor in a way that no other was capable of doing. By a happy coincidence, genealogy and local history are currently a growth industry in the western world, fuelled by TV programmes such as *Who Do You Think You Are?* and *So You Think You're Royal?* I treasure the stunned expression on Olympic oarsman Matthew Pinsent's face when the genealogist showed him the tables of his descent from William the Conqueror and, perhaps less convincingly, Jesus Christ.

It is reasonably easy to follow an unusual surname back to the beginning of Civil Registration in 1837 and sometimes even as far as the start of parish records in the mid 16th century. In order to go beyond that one needs to be fortunate enough to find a 'somebody', a person belonging to a family sufficiently important to have had their pedigree recorded by the professionals of the day. Working recently on the maternal line of my Minnesota daughter-in-law I discovered such a 'gateway ancestor' and was able to establish beyond doubt that my tiny grandson is descended not only from Owen Glendower, Prince of North Wales and Elihu Yale, endower of the great university, but also from a man hanged drawn and quartered at Tyburn in 1660 as a regicide of King Charles I.

Not everybody can find his pedigree in Debrett or the College of Arms, so with the beginner in mind I have included in this book some of the steps by which I traced my own family's history. Genealogy sometimes seems to present enormous obstacles to those with 'common' names but if I can follow my paternal line back to John Taylor in the 17th century almost anybody can do it.

So researching this book has helped me to make sense of my own life and see something of the patterns which link it with the lives of my ancestors. My wife and sons will read it with a sense of ownership but I hope it will also find some resonance with other readers, not least because though national historians write of the 1950s as a period of decline and austerity, growing up in Wigan during that decade was as rich and exciting to me as Laurie Lee's Gloucestershire childhood was to him fifty years earlier. I have done my best to give an accurate account of our story and where possible I have found independent verification of my facts, but it will be just as well for me to paraphrase Laurie's disclaimer from *Cider With Rosie*: This book is a recollection of early boyhood (and of times much earlier than that) and some of the facts may be distorted by time.

John Sharrock Taylor
Cortijo del Rector, Andalucía, April 2009

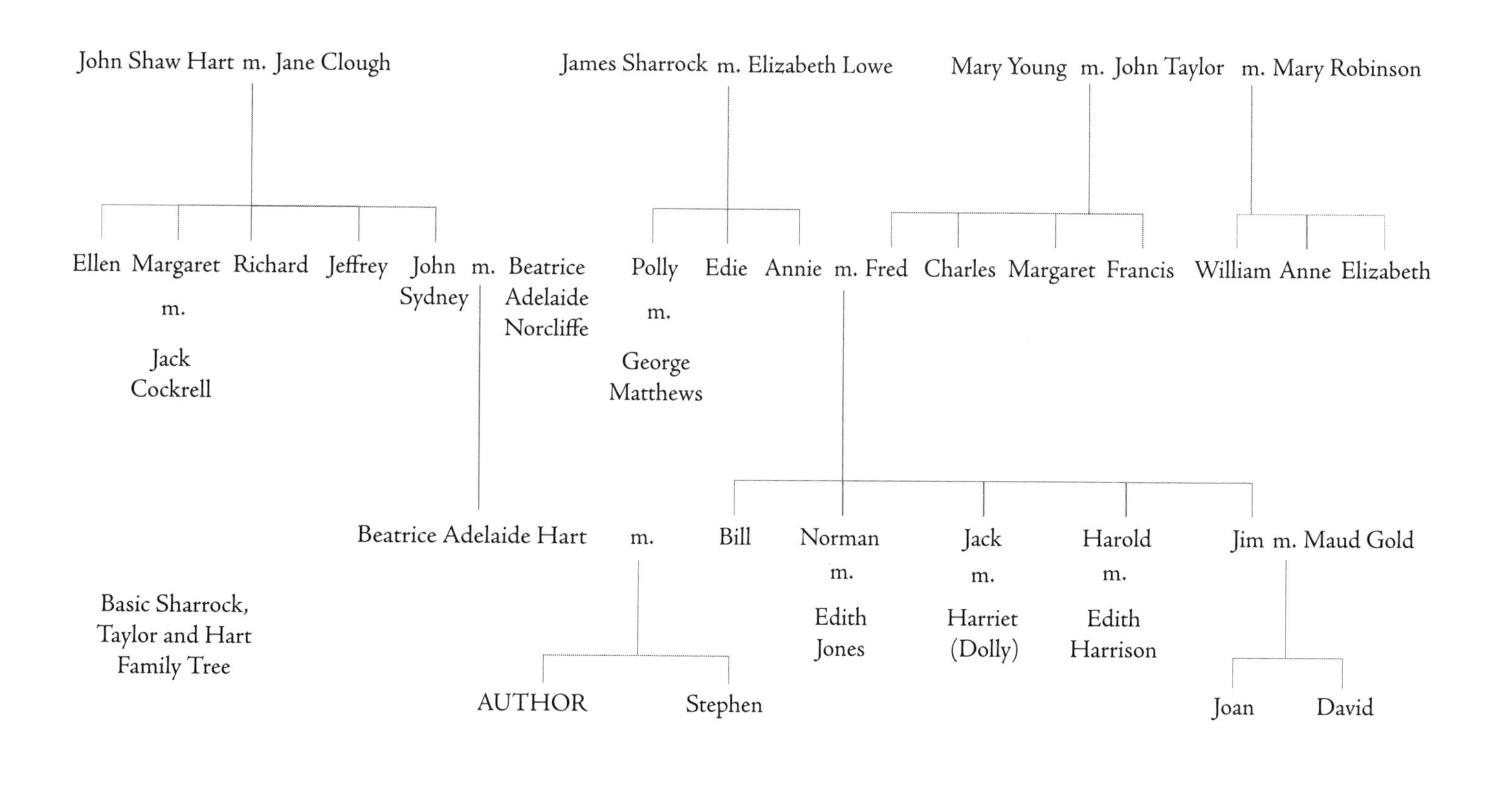

Basic Sharrock, Taylor and Hart Family Tree

The Wiggin Tree

MUCH AS I LOVED WIGAN, the town where I was born and brought up, a major highlight of my childhood were frequent trips to Garth Ucha near Ruabon in North Wales, where Jack and Margaret Cockrell, my mother's uncle and aunt, had a timber bungalow in the corner of a remote upland field overlooking the Vale of Llangollen. On one of these visits when I was about eleven years old I dug up a two foot rowan sapling from the coppice below the house, took it home and presented it to my mother Beatrice who planted it in our garden in Pemberton. At the time of her death in 1998 the rowan had several trunks reaching well over twenty feet and its blaze of red berries contrasted vividly with the more muted autumn colours of the neighbouring suburban gardens. My mother always referred to it as her 'John tree' and as I travelled on four continents it became for her an image of my eventual return. As an eleven year old I had not known that the rowan, or mountain ash, was also the Wiggin Tree in the Ancient and Loyal Borough's coat of arms, nor that in Celtic mythology the rowan is a magic plant protecting the home. Almost fifty years later when I was searching for a key image for this book it occurred to me that this almost-forgotten symbol was ideal for the purpose.

SAVE
THE
KING
37

CHAPTER 1

The Village Stream

OUR VILLAGE, OR TO BE MORE ACCURATE our cluster of villages, was in South Lancashire two and a half miles to the north-east of the County Borough of Wigan. It was a district in a process of transition which still goes on today. There were actually four settlements in all. At Aspull, which means 'aspen hill', mining was well established by Tudor and Stuart times, with local landowners quarrelling over the ownership of various coal pits and magistrates continually complaining about the rowdy village ale house. Haigh, which means 'enclosure' in Old English, grew up around its ancient manor house and it was well into the 19th century that the name gradually transferred itself to the village. The first Ordnance Survey map from about 1840 identifying Haigh as Lane Ends shows the medieval stocks, but there are many industrial sites, including a forge, a foundry, a sawmill, coke kilns, a bleach works, a brick works, a copperas smelting furnace, a paper mill and a brewery. There are also several coal pits, such as King Coal, Arley, Crawford, Scot Lane and the Lindsay and Alexandra Collieries where my great-grandfather, James Sharrock, would later be the Overlooker. In 1838 John Sumner, the proprietor of Haigh Brewery, successfully petitioned William Peace, Chief Mining Agent to the Earl of Crawford, to install a wind pumping plant to supply water for the brewery. A wind pump was preferred because it cost little to run and avoided the smoke pollution caused by a steam engine (Lord Crawford had already complained about the 'vast column of black smoke' emitted from the brewery chimney). The wind pump was

Above: Mary Young Left: Makinson Arcade
© Wigan Archives Service

built and proved so efficient that there was enough water to supply Haigh Hall and some of the estate cottages. Raw materials for brewing were delivered by the mineral railways which crossed the area and linked up with the main lines, and in its heyday the brewery employed forty-five shire horses.

The ground rises towards the east and north and at about 520 feet above sea level the village of Haigh is one of its highest points, with views towards Winter Hill and the West Pennine Moors. Today it is a picturesque warren of woodlands, deep steep secret leafy lanes, farms and stone houses clustering around St David's Church, the Balcarres Arms and the long-ruined brewery wind pump in the Windmill Field, where as a child I gazed eagerly at the farm animals of the annual Haigh Foal Show. The coal pits and iron mines are long-disused. The workings are overgrown and only the dimly discernible line of a dismantled narrow-gauge railroad shows where coal and ore tubs once plied busily.

Astley's Farm, on the northern bank of the Leeds and Liverpool Canal at Haigh, was the home of my paternal great-grandfather, John Taylor, and here my grandfather Fred and his adventurous eldest brother William were brought up with a numerous clutch of other brothers and sisters, the children of John's successive marriages to two Marys. In the mid 19th century Haigh's nearest neighbour developed as one of the first modern pit villages grouped around the high and Tractarian new red-brick church (improbably dedicated to St Elizabeth of Hungary) on the wide and windy space of Aspull Moor, and here in one of the little terraces of limestone cottages Fred's future wife Annie was born in 1881 to James and Elizabeth Sharrock. Descending the main Wigan–Bolton road from the Aspull finger-post the traveller passes through New Springs, a fairly featureless narrow ribbon development of brick houses crossed by the great water-highway of the canal, eventually arriving at Whelley where her father James worked as a colliery overlooker and Annie, a young widow, would eventually raise my father Bill and his four brothers.

In medieval times the manor of Haigh and much of the adjoining territory had been owned by the turbulent Bradshaigh family. In 1295 Sir William de Bradshaigh, a scion of the Bradshaighs of Turton, had acquired the property by marrying an heiress, Mabel le Norreys of Blackrod, and when I was a child my great-aunt Edie told me a romantic story about them which had formed the basis of a novel by Sir Walter Scott. According to the legend, Sir William went off to the crusades and was missing for ten years, during which time Lady Mabel, presuming him dead, had married a Welsh knight. In 1324 Sir William suddenly returned disguised as a palmer, or Holy-Land pilgrim, and discovered that the new husband had not only usurped his place but was abusing Lady Mabel. Sir William promptly hunted down the abuser and killed him at Newton-le-Willows. In penance for her bigamy Mabel was obliged for the rest of her life to walk barefoot in her shift once a week from Haigh Hall to the monument in Wigan's Standishgate which still bears the name of Mab's Cross.

As told by Aunty Edie it made an excellent story, but although Sir William and Lady Mabel's tomb in Wigan parish church shows her kneeling at a wayside cross, the truth is somewhat different from the legend. There are many indications that Mabel loved William and remained faithful to his memory even after his death and there are none at all that she ever took a second husband. English knights were not involved in crusades in the early 14th century and in reality Sir William's extended absence from Haigh was due to his banishment by King Edward II for the crimes of rebellion and murder in 1315. This was the lawless age of the original robber barons, great nobles with their own private armies of retainers, who often defied the sovereign and lived by murder and pillage. Edward II, the effete and bisexual son of the great Edward Longshanks, Hammer of the Scots, had antagonised his nobility by handing over much of the business of government to his commoner favourite Piers Gaveston. Thomas Earl of Lancaster, enthusiastically supported by his feudal vassal, Sir William de Bradshaigh, was one of the ringleaders of a rebellion against Edward, which succeeded first in banishing and later in executing Gaveston. By 1315 Lancaster was the effective ruler of the country but at this point, having successfully rebelled against the king, he in turn suffered a revolt by his own supporters. Two of the principal renegades were Sir Adam Banastre and Sir William de Bradshaigh, who were resentful of the favour shown by Lancaster to Robert de Holland, head of the powerful family of the same name who lived at Upholland to the west of Wigan. The Banastre–Bradshaigh faction began a campaign of violence and intimidation against Holland supporters, plundering Norley Hall and Clitheroe Castle, imprisoning Adam de Radcliffe and murdering Sir Henry de Bury (and stealing his horse, the chronicles rather quaintly add) before eventually being defeated at the Battle of Deepdale near Preston. Sir William escaped, probably to Wales, and was outlawed. The Hollands were in control of Lancashire for next five years or so but on 16 March 1322 Lancaster was beaten by the king's forces at Boroughbridge and beheaded. Holland had deserted him before the battle in order to ingratiate himself with the king, but Edward understandably distrusted him and had him imprisoned. With his main enemies out of the way, Sir William returned to Lancashire to carry on his feud with the lesser fry for ten violent years of sieges, skirmishes, robberies, murder and mayhem. Finally on 16 August 1333, he was killed in a fight at Newton-le-Willows with members of the Radcliffe family whose manor he had attacked eighteen years before. So it was not Lady Mabel's mythical second husband who was killed at Newton but Sir William himself. After his death his wife founded a chantry at Wigan parish church to pray in perpetuity for his soul. After such a turbulent life he obviously needed all the intercession he could muster. Although the manor of Haigh had been assigned to another claimant during Sir William's outlawry, Lady Mabel had done her best to hang onto it and after a legal tussle the Bradshaigh lands remained in the family. The Bradshaighs were slow to learn their lesson and Thomas de Bradshaigh took part in the rebellion of 1403 led by Henry Percy, Shakespeare's Hotspur, and fought on the losing side at the Battle of Shrewsbury, when the formidable Henry IV, the first Lancastrian king, convincingly annihilated his opposers.

By my great-grandparents' time the Bradshaighs, with their lances and chain mail, had given way to their gentler descendants the Lindsays, Earls of Crawford and Balcarres in Scotland in addition to their title of Baron Wigan, who had enriched themselves by developing the many deposits of high-grade coal and iron on their Lancashire estate.

The Haigh Foundry was initially opened in 1810 for manufacturing winding engines and pumping equipment for the mining industry and it was here that the famous Laxey Wheel of the Isle of Man was cast. From 1835 the foundry also built railway locomotives for such organisations as the Great Western and South Devon Railways and in 1855 two engines were built for use in the Crimean War against Russia. We have little idea of how the old Haigh Hall looked because in the heyday of their wealth the Lindsays demolished it and built an opulent if rather characterless new hall, which was completed in 1840. The extensive plantations were laid out in the 1860s to improve a landscape disfigured by coal mining, giving work to unemployed Wiganers during the cotton famine caused by the American Civil War. Abundant fuel and the humidity of the coastal plain in the shadow of the Pennines provided ideal conditions for the growth of the cotton-spinning industry during the Industrial Revolution of the mid 19th century, when Lancashire supported the Confederacy against what both called northern aggression. During the heyday of the Industrial Revolution the brooks of the Haigh estate ran yellow with rust and the great smoke-belching steelworks of Top Place dominated the eastern skyline and became a target for the zeppelin raids of the Great War.

The vast economic movements changed but did not obliterate the ancient way of life and when I was a child the Harvest Festival gifts at St Stephen's Church in Whelley included both the traditional sheaves of corn and also glistening lumps of cannel coal. The view from the scrubbed and donkey-stoned front doorstep of my grandmother's little terraced house at 169 Whelley, across the main Bolton road, was of the headgear and fan-housings of the Lindsay and Alexandra Pits. From the back garden I looked across a deep, narrow, well-watered valley to the slag heaps of Top Place, but if I descended into the valley in springtime the industrial workings disappeared behind clouds of fragrant hawthorn and luxuriant pasture grass in which brown and white cows browsed hock-deep.

The stories and legends on which I grew up came from the lanes and fields, from the castle and the cottage, from the church, the school and the pub, from soldiers serving in France, Germany, North Africa, Palestine and Italy, from girls working in the cotton mills and tailoring shops, from men in the mines and the steel works and a dozen other sources. Some of the tales had already been half lost to local memory. The most imposing of the several Whelley pubs had a sign proclaiming it as The Alexandra, after Edward VII's long-suffering red-haired Danish queen, but nobody used this name, which had been adopted for patriotic reasons during the First World War. All preferred the original dedication to Von Blücher, pronounced Bomb Bloocher, whom none of us knew had been Wellington's fellow general at Waterloo. Next door to the pub, with its back to rocky Springs Bank, was the derelict boarded-up little sweet shop Aunty Edie had kept in the days when sharing parenting duties with her widowed younger sister, my grandmother Annie, had prevented her continuing with her highly skilled job as a sample hand at Coop and Company's great clothing factory in Wigan's Dorning Street.

CHAPTER 2

The Farmer's Boy

IT IS JUST POSSIBLE that my grandmother, Annie Sharrock, born in the village of Aspull in 1881, was a Lancashire Tess of the d'Urbervilles. In spite of its vigorous branches in the former Confederate States of America, the Sharrock clan's English origins lie in a very closely defined area between south-central Lancashire and the coast. According to a completely erroneous family legend passed on to me as a child, the original Sharrocks were Dutch, or possibly Deutsch, engineers who had come in Stuart times to drain the wetlands around the Martin Mere. In 1998, when I was living in Ecuador, I discovered both the internet and a Sharrock family genealogist, Brian of that ilk, who claimed that the first English Sharrock had been Ralf de Chirac, whose services to William the Conqueror at Senlac in 1066 had been rewarded with the gift of a Lancashire estate eventually called Sharrock or Shorrock Green. According to Brian our humble South Lancashire family were, like Tess, the descendants of minor Norman gentry with a coat of arms and, no doubt, grandly sepulchred 'skellingtons'. There is also a completely opposed theory that the name originates in the term 'shire oak' and points at the original Sharrocks having been denizens of the very centre of Lancashire. I have yet to trace the Chirac or Sharrock line from its earliest English origins, but in the Annals of Lancashire the family appears at Shorrock Green at an early date. Their original settlement seems to have been in the neighbourhood of Woodfold, where old maps and records give not only Shorrock Green but also Shorrock Hey, Shorrock Hey

Above: Sharrock Family Arms

Fold and Old Shorrock. Shorrock Green appears on local maps until about the 1830s and even today Higher, Middle and Lower Shorrockhayes are very close to the site. The alternative name Sharoe Green survives in the name of a large hospital just outside Preston. Throughout the Middle Ages, Sharrocks had their ups and downs and rather oddly one of the downs resulted indirectly to the adoption of a coat of arms. One branch of the family eventually settled in the West Country and the 'Visitation of Cornwall' which dates from the early 17th century tells of the

> Sharrockes of Ribbelsdale in Com. Lanc. first of wh. was Ralph Shorrock of Shorockhayes wch in the Barrons' Wars was advanced to be a Captaine and therein lost his life, his descent grewe poore, and when the Scotts overan the Northern borders & parte of Lancashire and Chesheire the most part of this familie fled into Dublyn in Ireland, where by the Corruption of the Irish Ideoam they were termed Sharlock wch name of necessitie they were constrained to hold in the time of King Henrie the Seventh.

The Barons' War took place between 1258 and 1267 during the reign of Henry III, and Henry VII was on the throne from 1485 to 1509. Obviously the 13th-century Ralph was not the first Sharrock, nor even the first Ralph if Brian's thesis holds true. What does seem clear is that it was the Irish branch of the family which was the first to be granted the Sharrock coat of arms, 'a blue shield with a gold pile and a fret and two stars in base'.

While Ralph's descendants were having a rough time in Ireland the English Sharrocks were in a reasonably prosperous condition back home in Lancashire, though some of them occasionally sailed fairly close to the wind, as in 1292, when Alice de Shorrok, Adam de Hunteleye and Henry de Sholley were sued for felling three hundred oak trees worth forty shillings in woodland belonging to the Lords of Mellor. This seems to have been larceny on a rather stupendous scale and Alice and her accomplices did not simply walk off with three hundred forest giants in one job lot. The tree rustling took place over a period of ten years or more. Why the Lords of Mellor took so long to twig what was going on will probably forever remain a mystery. To lose one oak tree may be regarded as a misfortune, my Lord. To lose three hundred looks like carelessness. When I came across this piece of information I wondered, slightly facetiously, if the proto-feminist Alice had been capitalising on the 'shire oak' interpretation of her surname.

William and Henry, sons of Roger de Shorok, presumably from a collateral line, also flourished about the time Alice was busily taking advantage of her neighbours' inattention. The family continued to make money and Richard de Shorrok was one of the biggest contributors to the subsidy of 1332 under Edward III, while William his son appears as a freeholder in 1336. John de Shorrok contributed to the Poll Tax of 1379 and his son and heir, another William, was in possession of 'Old Shorock' in Mellor in 1411. Geoffrey Shorock made his will before witnesses in 1459 during the unsettled times leading up to the Wars of the Roses. In 1682 George Shorrock held the estate at Shorrock Green and by the early 18th century branches of the family held lands at Preston and Fulwood. For a long period the descent of the Sharrock Green estate cannot be traced, but ultimately it passed to the Clayton family.

I have always assumed that my grandmother knew very little about chivalry and absolutely nothing about heraldry, but in the light of Brian Sharrock's claim that we are descended from a man who fought at the Battle of Hastings it is slightly startling to recall that she named her first two sons Norman and Harold, labels which had not previously appeared in either the Sharrock or the Taylor family trees. She gave due respect to the monarch but whether or not she suspected that their remote ancestors' lives might have been linked in the mutual brigandage from which all ancient nobility and gentry stem will probably forever remain a mystery. Lesser 'nobs', the county's aristocracy, she viewed with satirical tolerance. She was comfortably aware that she herself, though her means were modest, was part of our villages' aristocracy of merit.

James Sharrock, born in the village of Lathom, near Ormskirk on the fertile West Lancashire coastal plain, was the much-loved father of my grandmother Annie and her elder sister my great-aunt Edie. He was a tall, lean man with a square-cut grizzled beard, who rose from being a teenage vagabond to become a much-trusted servant of another James, James Ludovic Lindsay (1847–1913), 26th Earl of Crawford and 9th Earl of Balcarres. When I was a boy and the old ladies were in their seventies and eighties I spent many a rapt hour in their little terraced National Coal Board house at 169 Whelley, listening to stories of events which are now a hundred and fifty years distant in time. As they told it their father's history was a folk song in its own right. Whatever their remoter origins, our Sharrocks had been established in the Lathom area for at least a century before James's birth on 25 November 1845. His great-grandparents, John Sharrock and Ellen Southward, had been wed at Croston church on 26 December 1791 and, in traditional Lancashire fashion, had anticipated their marriage vows, because their son Richard, the first of their eleven children, was born in neighbouring Rufford on 11 March 1792. This Richard and his wife Mary, James's grandparents, raised only three children of their own, which was perhaps fortunate because they were to play a crucial role in the upbringing of six grandchildren virtually orphaned by their mother's early death and their unstable father's prostrating grief.

Henry Sharrock, the second child of Richard and Mary, born in 1821, was married on 24 October 1842 at the parish church of Saints Peter and Paul in Ormskirk to another Mary, the daughter of James Ollerton, a Newburgh stonemason whose forebears had been christened, married and buried in the same church for at least the previous three centuries. Employed as a dryster in the corn mill at Lathom, Henry's father Richard had managed to arrange for his son to learn the whole mystery of milling and by the time of his marriage Henry had served his seven years' apprenticeship with an Ormskirk miller and ought to have been well set for a lucrative and respected career. The first two of Henry and Mary's children were born in Lathom, Richard in 1843 and James in 1845, but by the time Elizabeth and John arrived in 1847 and 1850 respectively the family was living in Liverpool's booming new twin port of Birkenhead, established in 1843 on the Cheshire bank of the River Mersey. An important centre for corn-milling, it ought to have been fertile ground for Henry's developing career.

Henry may have been the breadwinner in both the literal and the metaphorical sense, but Mary's was the strength which held together the growing family. Her early death shattered it forever and ensured that the Sharrock children would never again live together under one roof. Henry fell into despair. He took to the bottle and became, in our Sharrock mythology at least, the archetypal drunkard of Victorian melodrama. Unstable and grief-stricken, he broke up the family home and left his younger children in the care of his parents at Lathom. Richard and James, at eighteen and sixteen, were deemed old enough to make their own way in life. Richard, bred to the trade, found an apprenticeship with Peter Longton, a wealthy young corn merchant and miller with an extensive establishment at Woolton near what is now Liverpool's John Lennon Airport. There he married a local girl, Elizabeth Stevens, and there his sister Ellen eventually found a home with the young couple until her own marriage. Meanwhile James had headed back to south-west Lancashire in search of work and lodging. At least there he would have his dependable grandparents to fall back on if all else failed. Times were hard for farmers and the blockade of Confederate ports by the Union Navy had hit Lancashire's cotton trade and made them even harder. James suffered refusal after refusal as he tramped the lanes around his native Lathom. Then he had a stroke of luck when he knocked on the door of Mount Pleasant Farm. William Sephton did not in the strictest sense have need of an additional worker on his 160-acre holding but his softer-hearted wife Mary was standing behind him at the front door as he was about to turn the young vagrant away, and both she and her daughter Elizabeth were captivated by the blue eyes, the black shaggy mane of hair, the sharp planes of cheek and forehead and the air of awkward integrity. At this point in the story Aunty Edie, her voice still true at eighty, would break softly into song:

> The farmer's wife said 'Try the lad!
> Let him no longer seek.'
> 'Yes, Father, do!'
> The daughter cried,
> And the tears rolled down her cheek.

Needless to relate, the farmer relented and James found himself employment as a carter at Mount Pleasant Farm. 'The Farmer's Boy' remained his favourite song and, though he hardly ever touched alcohol, his daughter Annie, my grandmother, recalled that he once celebrated the satisfactory outcome of a local parliamentary election by singing it at the top of his voice while striding through New Springs village in an unprecedented state of inebriation, arm in arm with his son-in-law, my grandfather Fred Taylor. It was the only time James ever succumbed to his father's weakness and he retained a lifetime's horror of drunkenness.

Securing his first paid employment was not to be the last time James's enterprise would land him on his feet. A farm labourer's wage together with board and lodging kept the wolf from the door but there were no prospects for advancement and James was ambitious. 'Where there's muck there's brass' was a Lancashire truism and both muck and brass were to be found in plenty on the coalfields further east. One of the great coal owners was the Earl of Crawford and Balcarres, whose estate was at Haigh near Wigan, and it was for Haigh that James Sharrock set off eight years after charming the farmer's wife and daughter. Finding surface work in one of the Earl's mines, he lodged with the family of John Lowe in Copperas Lane, the very name redolent of the complex mineral wealth of the district. Lowe was an engineer or engine-tenter looking after the great static steam pumping engine that drained one of the many coal mines on the estate. He and his wife Betty had raised seven children, two of whom were still at home. Their eldest son, Alexander, named after the 25th Earl of Crawford, had been apprenticed to a blacksmith before going off to make money in the booming steel mills of Sheffield. A daughter, Mary, perhaps influenced by friends on the Haigh Hall staff, had become the personal maid of Bessie Vans Agnew, the young second wife of Inner Temple barrister Edward Salvin Bowlby, whose numerous Debrett connections included Viscount Hugh Trenchard, future Marshall of the Royal Air Force. Aunt Mary would return periodically to fascinate her nieces with her beautiful clothes and tales of travel and high Victorian society and as a child sixty years later I would insist that her curved-lidded cabin trunk, in the corner of Aunty Edie's bedroom at 169 Whelley, was a pirate chest full of golden sovereigns.

James now had a secure job but something important was still missing. As I know from personal experience, children of conflict-ridden homes can react to domestic turmoil in very different ways. My parents fought every day of their married life, mentally lacerating both themselves and their children in the process. My mother did her best to brainwash us into never descending into the hell of wedded bliss and for whatever reason my brother has never married, whereas I was wed just after my twenty-second birthday and in forty years of married life have had no reason to regret it. When he was in his mid-teens, James's family life had fallen to pieces and in spite of their grandparents' loving care his vulnerable younger brother John was permanently damaged by the experience. It would not have been surprising if James himself had declined to risk the adventure, but if ever a man was destined by temperament to be the father of a family it was James Sharrock. He and John Lowe's daughter Elizabeth rapidly came to an understanding and were married in St David's Church, Haigh, on 15 November 1869, ten days before James's twenty-fourth birthday. Initially, they lived with Elizabeth's parents before eventually setting up home at Lindsay Terrace in nearby Aspull. The word was not part of their understated vocabulary, but love was the warp and weft of the family in which their children were to grow up. A hundred years after James courted Elizabeth beneath the beech trees of Copperas Lane I sat on the fireside peg-rug and listened to their daughters softly reminiscing about an idyllic childhood.

'You know, Edie, my father really *liked* my mother.'

'He did that!' my aunt would reply, hushing her voice to a whisper I was not supposed to hear, 'and he looked after our George like his own.'

Forty years after these conversations, when I was beginning to put them down on paper, a penny dropped. When I was a child my long-dead great-uncle George Lowe had existed to me only in the dry murmured recollections of these old ladies, in a name on an earthenware mug in the lean-to pantry and in an immaculate copperplate school copybook, kept with a pile of Victorian Sunday school prizes in the ornate walnut-veneered parlour sideboard in the front room. With hindsight I realised that George had been the old ladies' eldest sibling, born to my great-grandmother Elizabeth Lowe before she met James. The parents had no doubt been impressed by the young man's determination, good looks and intelligence but, with sound common sense and practicality, had also seen him as the answer to a fallen maiden's prayer. He proved to be a good investment. As a child I had imagined my grandmother's brother George as a frail little boy who had died young. When I began to research our family history I was glad to discover that I could not have been more wrong. On the Internet the censuses leap into focus like closed-circuit TV images, showing the interior of James and Elizabeth's family home. There are their daughters, Polly, Edie and my future grandmother Annie as children in single figures. And there is George, a teenage telegraph-messenger, with a bicycle and a peaked cap, whom James in his census return describes simply as his son. By the time of the 1901 Census, George is well-established with a wife and two daughters in a very select villa in the poshest tree-shaded part of Victorian Wigan, and I realise with a start of recognition that his nine-year-old Edith is the plump and stately sixty-year-old Aunty Edie Lowe who used to visit her aunts at 169 Whelley when I was growing up in the 1960s. And it was she whom I shocked almost into apoplexy by appearing to be the reincarnation of my dead uncle.

Henry Sharrock's career never recovered from the trauma of his wife's death. He continued to live a solitary life as an employee in a corn mill just outside Preston and for many years James knew little or nothing of him. Then one day while James and Elizabeth were still living with Elizabeth's parents in Copperas Lane, there was a tentative knock at the door. Elizabeth went to answer it and returned grave-faced.

'James, it's your father.'

'I'll not see him!' exclaimed James.

'Yes, you will,' replied Elizabeth firmly, and the reconciliation was so complete that when their first child was born in 1870 he was named Henry after his grandfather.

CHAPTER 3

The Missing Corpses

LIKE HIS CHILDREN, his grandchildren, his great-grandchildren and my sons, his great-great-grandchildren, James Sharrock lived in rapidly changing and unpredictable times. In the 21st century we are inclined to talk glibly about Victorian respectability. A glance through the assize court records of mid-19th-century Wigan gives a vastly different impression. Lancashire was desperately poor and despair breeds crime and violence. With an engine-tenter for a father-in-law it is not surprising that James felt particularly strongly about the notorious murder of James Barton, his friend and neighbour and also the night-furnaceman at Bawk House Pit next to Astley's Farm on the Crawford estate. This infamous crime, which became known as the Button-Pit Murder, occurred on the night of Friday 2 January 1863. The local press described it as:

> A murder rivalling in its atrocity and revolting character the most cold-blooded and horrifying deed recorded in (that) well-known volume the Newgate Calendar and putting in the shade the most improbable incidents and sensations …

The Haigh pits were honeycombed with underground streams and the steam pumping engines had to be kept going night and day. In those long-ago days before the advent of electricity, when moonless winter nights were pitch black, James Barton was accustomed to light a fire on the pit bank to guide the early shift. James Whatmough, arriving first to prepare the pit ponies for the day shift, was puzzled to see no light. When he arrived at the pit he found the furnace untended and the pump motionless. At around 6 a.m. he alerted Barton's son John, who initiated a fruitless search of the mine galleries before calling the police. By the time they arrived it was fully light and they were able to see blood on the boiler house floor and walls. A bloodstained crowbar lay on the floor. The cinders at the edge of the ash-pit were coagulated. The ashes were sieved and a belt buckle and boot nails were found together with fragments of burned bone and teeth. There was no sign of Barton's expensive pocket watch, which was assumed to have been stolen by the murderer.

The gruesome nature of the murder appalled even a community accustomed to violence. Lord Crawford, himself destined to become the victim of a macabre crime, offered a reward of a hundred pounds for the capture of the murderer, and this enormous sum was subsequently increased to two hundred pounds by the Home Secretary. Captain Elgee, the Chief Constable of Wigan, personally took charge of the investigation, but for a while, as in every good crime novel, the police were baffled. Then in April 1866, more than three years after the event, a local publican reported to the Aspull bobby, Elias Worthington, that one of his customers, Thomas Walton, had been boasting drunkenly of his part in a murder. Arrested, Walton made several statements which were found to be so inaccurate and inconsistent that he was eventually discharged on grounds of insufficient evidence, but one of his claims rather surprisingly led to the conviction of a third person. Walton told the police that after the murder the victim's watch had been thrown into the Leeds and Liverpool Canal. The Pendlebury reach of the canal was duly drained and nothing was found but a Chorley man, James Grime, reading a description of the watch in a newspaper report of the investigation, realised with a jolt that it was the same watch he had been given by his brother Thomas in 1864 just before Thomas had begun a sentence at Dartmoor Prison. James Grime took the watch to the police and Thomas was duly interrogated in Dartmoor. According to Grime, the actual killer had been a certain William Thompson, whom James Barton had reported for poaching on the Earl's land. During an extended drinking bout at the Castle Inn at Chorley Thompson had persuaded Thomas Grime, John Healey and another acquaintance, Joseph Seddon, to accompany him to Haigh to confront James Barton. During the altercation Thompson had struck Barton twice on the head with a crowbar and he and Seddon had put him in the firehole, thrown some shovelfuls of slack on him and closed the door. It is not clear whether the victim was dead or merely stunned when he went into the fire. Apart from this allegation by a convicted felon, the police investigation uncovered no evidence to implicate Seddon and Thompson, who were known to be men of good character. Walton, shifty, vainglorious and unreliable, had already been discharged. Possession of the victim's watch provided a solid link between the murder and Grime, who had also given a convincing picture of how the crime had been carried out. The jury at the Liverpool Assizes took only a few minutes to convict him. In passing sentence, Judge Baron Martin told Grime that he had not the slightest doubt that he had been implicated in the murder:

> It is probable that you did not strike the blow but you are just as guilty as the man who did. You went there with the purpose of murder and you took part

> in the proceeds of the watch that was taken from the murdered man. A more cruel and barbarous murder was never proved in a court of law and if the punishment of death is to be inflicted at all, an occasion more worthy of it was never proved.

On Saturday 1 September 1866, James Sharrock stood in front of a scaffold erected outside Kirkdale Jail in Liverpool to watch William Colcroft hang Thomas Grime in one of the last public executions ever to be held in England. I was going to write the cliché that he saw justice done, but I am not so sure about that, and before we leave the execution scene and its silent crowd of 30,000, many of whom had walked the twenty miles from Wigan, we should perhaps reflect for a moment on the case and on the judge's opinion that Grime had probably not struck the death blow but was just as guilty as the man who had done so. Victorian rules of evidence were not as strict as those applied today. Did James think the right man had been hanged?

Public and private feelings about murder and capital punishment are complex. That we are fascinated by violent death and official retribution is witnessed by hundreds of detective novels and TV crime series. James's daughters Annie and Edie were the gentlest souls imaginable but in old age they loved to read stories of mayhem in the News of the World. For ninety years after James Grime's hanging, the public's fascination with ritual death continued to be fed with periodic executions, some of which have become famous landmarks in the history of jurisprudence. My mother's grandparents told her of the capture and trial of Dr Crippen, the first murderer to be apprehended through the use of wireless telegraphy, and as a teenager she hoped fervently and vainly that the handsome Anglo-Indian wife-murderer Dr Buck Ruxton would escape the noose. When I was a student in Lancaster in the 1960s, Ruxton's house on Dalton Square was still boarded up, though no doubt its seclusion succumbed to rising property values not long afterwards.

Macabre incidents were not reserved solely for the deaths of the poor and obscure. James Sharrock's first aristocratic employer, the 25th Earl of Crawford, Alexander William Crawford Lindsay, for whom James's brother-in-law Alexander Lowe had been named, achieved sensational notoriety some months after his death in 1880, and rather than trying to retell the story in my own words I shall leave it to a contemporary writer who clearly revelled in all the requisite gothic touches. I have edited his account to remove the repetitions and less interesting minutiae of the court proceedings:

> When the readers of the daily journals learned, some twelve months after the death and burial of the late Earl of Crawford and Balcarres, that his remains had been stolen from the family vault at Dunecht House, near Aberdeen, in circumstances inexplicable and mysterious, the excitement throughout the country was intense. The dead earl had been in his day a notable nobleman. Born in 1812, he succeeded to the title in 1869 as eighth Earl of Balcarres and twenty-fifth Earl of Crawford. He was a man of many tastes and talents; much of his time and money

was devoted to astronomical research, and he was a capable theologian as well as an erudite antiquarian and genealogist. He published much, and the great library at Haigh Hall, near Wigan, his Lancashire seat, is a monument to his industry and learning.

In the winter of 1879 the Earl of Crawford, whose health had begun to fail, visited Egypt and afterwards Italy, where he died at Florence on 13th December 1880. His body, which for removal to his native land was embalmed by a Florentine chemist skilled in the art, was placed within three coffins, the inner one being of soft Italian wood, the middle one of lead, and the outer one of polished oak, elaborately carved and mounted with fittings of chased silver. These three coffins were deposited within a huge walnut shell, on the top of which was a cross carved in high relief, the weight of the whole amounting to nearly half a ton. The conveyance of the remains across the Alps was attended with great difficulty, but under the care of a trusted family servant they reached France in safety. A special steamer was chartered to convey the body to London, and in crossing the Channel she encountered so heavy a gale that the coffin had to be lashed to the deck. The removal to Aberdeen on 24 December was more easily effected, but there an unexpected obstacle arose. No hearse large enough to contain the coffin was procurable, and the outer shell had to be removed. It was afterwards deposited in the crypt beside the three coffins in which the body was encased. The last stage of its long journey, that from Aberdeen to Dunecht, was undertaken in one of the most violent snow-storms ever experienced in Scotland, and it is recorded that the hearse, when returning to Aberdeen, was snowed up by the wayside for several days. These inauspicious happenings, however, were but the prelude to a misadventure yet more remarkable.

On Sunday, 29 May 1881, exactly five months after the interment of Lord Crawford's body, the housekeeper at Dunecht, coming home from church through the grounds, perceived a pleasant aromatic smell issuing from the vault. Next day the gardener also noticed the odour, which he attributed to the arbor vitae used as a background to the flowers of the numerous wreaths left upon the coffin. He thought that it came through the ventilator, but though he had been in the habit of passing the vault daily, he had never observed the smell before. On 8th September Mr. William Yeats, the family's local solicitor, received an anonymous letter in the following terms:

> SIR: The remains of the late Earl of Crawford are not beneath the chaple at Dunecht as you believe, but were removed hence last spring, and the smell of decayed flowers ascending from the vault since that time will, on investigation, be found to proceed from another cause than flowers.
> NABOB

A search party subsequently descended to the crypt and were horrified at the sight which awaited them. The floor of the vault was strewn with planks and sawdust, the three coffins were lying open and empty side by side in the middle and the body of the dead earl had disappeared. The lid of the outer coffin had been unscrewed in a tradesman-like manner, after which it had been turned over on its side and the leaden coffin rolled out and cut open. The inner coffin had then been opened with some sharp instrument sufficiently to admit of the body being drawn out. Its silver handles, plates, and mountings were untouched. From the scented sawdust with which the coffin had been filled came the peculiar aromatic odour that had been remarked in the previous May. The fact that the sawdust was mildewed and the leaden shell, where cut, oxidised, indicated that a considerable time had elapsed since the commission of the outrage.

An inquiry into the mysterious circumstances of the case was at once commenced by the procurator-fiscal and all persons connected with the estate were closely examined. The new earl, who had been absent from home at the time of the discovery, was at once informed of what had occurred, and returned forthwith to Dunecht. An exhaustive search of the surrounding district was instituted, and was continued diligently for a fortnight, but without result. It was interrupted by a severe snowstorm which began at that date, and as the snow remained upon the ground until well on into the following spring, the search had to be abandoned for the time. A sensational feature of these attempts to discover the body was the employment of the celebrated bloodhound Morgan, which in 1876 had successfully run to earth Fish, the Blackburn murderer. Owing, however, to persistent frost the experiment proved unsuccessful. Weeks passed, and all sorts of rumour circulated in the press. It was said that the outrage had been committed the day before the discovery of the rifled tomb, under cloud of a tempestuous night, by Florentine desperadoes who had tracked the corpse from Italy. Alternatively, the body had never been in the vault at all, having been abstracted before the coffin left Florence. According to other accounts, the deed had been done by certain Italian painters employed in decorating the interior of the mansion-house, or by some medical students from Aberdeen for professional purposes. Meanwhile, on 4th December the procurator-fiscal published in the local newspapers an advertisement earnestly requesting anyone, who during that year had observed anything bearing reference to the removal of the remains, to communicate with him or with the Chief Constable of Aberdeen. The result was a second letter from the mysterious 'Nabob'.

> SIR: The late Earl of Crawford
>
> The body is still in Aberdeenshire, and I can put you in possession of the same as soon as you bring one or more of the desperados who stole it to justice, so that I may know with whom I have to deal. I have no wish to be assinated by rusarectionests, nor suspected by the public of being an accomplice in such dastardly work, which I most assuredly would be unless the gulty party are brought to justice. Had Dr. Yeats noted on the hint I gave him last Sept., he might have found the remains as though by

axedand and hunted up the robers at lsure, but that chance is lost, so I hope you will find your men and make it safe and prudent for me to find what you want.

P.S.—Should they find out that an outsider knows their secret it may be removed to another place.
NABOB

On 17th July 1882 the police apprehended a man named Charles Soutar, forty-two years of age, who followed the occupation of a vermin killer, and resided in Schoolhill, Aberdeen. He had been employed for five or six years as a rat-catcher at Dunecht, but on account of his poaching proclivities had been dismissed some three years before the earl's death. The same day the prisoner was judicially examined and admitted that the two letters signed 'Nabob' were both written by him. He told the following remarkable tale:

> One night about the end of April 1881, after eleven o'clock, he was poaching with a net in the Crow Wood, near Dunecht House. On hearing a rustle in the brushwood he thought the keepers were trying to surround him, so he took to his heels, making for the thickest part of the wood. After running about twenty yards, he was tripped up by someone and thrown on his back to the ground, where he was held down by two men who seemed to be gentlemen, and spoke like educated men. Both wore masks. One of them presented a large plated revolver at his breast, and said 'Remember what I am going to tell you; you're known to our party, and if you breathe a syllable of what you have seen, I will have your life if you're on the face of the earth.' He was then released and told to leave the wood by the way he came. After hunting for an hour or two he returned at daybreak to the spot. The four masked men were gone, but looking about, he noticed a heap of rubbish where they had concealed something. On opening this up he saw a blanket, which he lifted, disclosing the dead body of a man, whom he thought at the time had been murdered. He looked at the face, and covered the body up again as he had found it. There was a strong smell like benzoline, from which he inferred that an attempt had been made to destroy the corpse with chemicals. The same smell stuck to his hands for half a day afterwards. He returned on foot to Aberdeen by the turnpike.

Following Soutar's deposition a search party was sent to explore the area of the wood where he had reported seeing the corpse. At the bottom of an old ditch, about a foot below the surface, lay wrapped in a blanket, the missing body of the earl. The place was some five hundred yards from the house, close by a gravel-pit. Before its removal from the grave, the body was inspected by Dr. Ogston of Aberdeen. From the state of the wrappings and of the surrounding soil, he formed the opinion that the body, which had suffered no injury, had been buried for a considerable time, and had not since been disturbed. The face was quite recognisable. The remains of the late earl were in due course removed to Haigh Hall, and were afterwards reinterred in the family vault beneath the Lindsay Chapel in the parish church of Wigan.

The police did not believe Nabob's fanciful story of his accidental encounter with the four masked men and when the case eventually came to trial in High Court of Justiciary in Edinburgh, Charles Soutar appeared in the dock accused of the crime of 'violating the sepulchres of the dead and the raising and carrying away dead bodies out of their graves. In sentencing the accused to penal servitude for a period of five years the justices stated their view that the Dunecht mystery was only half solved by the verdict of the jury. That Soutar was not alone concerned in the crime is certain; and while it is satisfactory to know that one of the miscreants who inflicted upon a noble house such long mental agony, did not escape retribution, the failure of Justice to detect and punish the other actors in the execrable plot must be a matter of regret. It does not appear that Soutar ever disclosed the identity of his accomplices, but some of these at least were probably his superiors in station and intelligence, for it is difficult to believe that a scheme of this elaborate sort, devised with diabolic ingenuity and executed with a skill and success unequalled in the annals of crime, was the product of the brain and hand of an obscure and illiterate ratcatcher.

Why did the supposed gang steal the earl's body in the first place? Did they all have grievances against the family, such as the ratcatcher's dismissal for poaching? The fact that the valuable silver fittings of the outer coffin remained intact showed that this was not the work of a common thief. Were the kidnappers intending to hold the corpse to ransom and if so why was no demand ever received? Were they deterred by the statement issued by the family that in no circumstances would they offer a reward for the recovery of the body? Were they simply frightened off by the hue and cry which followed the discovery that the body was missing, with hordes of policemen trampling about the Dunecht woods and even spiritualists from London declaring that they had 'seen' the body carried from the vault to a house on the estate? Why did Nabob write his two letters? He was quite obviously more terrified of his accomplices than he was of the Law, so why not simply keep quiet and let sleeping earls lie? Did his conscience trouble him so that he slept less soundly than the deceased nobleman in his improvised grave? None of these questions has ever been answered. What is certain is that once again our little village of Haigh, and with it the Earl's faithful retainer, James Sharrock, had been touched by gothic horror on a national scale.

CHAPTER 4

God's Almighty Hand

WITH A GROWING FAMILY James and Elizabeth felt the need to move out of her parents' house in Copperas Lane and establish their own home. On a bright, sunny spring day in 2005 I visited their cottage in Lindsay Terrace on the edge of Aspull Moor. The picturesque slate-roofed row of four houses has been meticulously restored. The outside walls, smoke-blackened in James and Elizabeth's time, have been rendered and painted white and the houses look out over the broad sweep of a village green. Initially employed as a porter, James had been encouraged to live rent-free in accommodation provided by his employer in the grounds of the Hall. His friendly colleagues could not understand why he declined, until one night a couple of them trailed him to Lindsay Terrace and peeped in through the window. What they saw was very like the idealised scene described in Grey's *Elegy*: the young mother preparing supper, the father relaxing by the fireside with a churchwarden pipe while his children clambered onto his knee the envied kiss to share.

Family life was not always tranquil. One winter evening James arrived home to find the house in semi-darkness, supper unmade, his young wife paralysed with distress and clutching the children to her. In response to his concerned enquiries she told him that for the past two hours weird cries and keenings had been penetrating the party wall between the Sharrock house and the house next door, where the Molloys, an immigrant Irish family, had recently suffered the loss of the paterfamilias. Eventually she had peeped

Above: Lindsay Terrace

in fearfully through a chink in the drawn window curtains. The pallid corpse of Michael Molloy, pennies on his eyelids, lay in his best suit in an open coffin on the parlour table surrounded by the flickering light of candles, while the Molloys and the Murphys stood around toasting the deceased in generous libations of Irish whiskey and apostrophising him in tones of extravagant grief:

'Oh! Feyther! Whyyyyy did ye die?!!!'

It was culture shock more than a century before the term was invented. Brought up at the height of the British Empire, in the tradition of the stiff upper lip, my great-grandparents had no experience of a culture which assuaged its grief by venting it. The English way was to draw the curtains, stop the clocks and dress in black and purple mourning whose degree, depth and duration depended on the closeness of the relationship to the deceased.

Medical science was limited, human beings were heir to a plethora of ailments and life expectancy was short. Before the process was packaged and sanitised for us by modern funeral directors, the trappings of death were ever present and in addition to the panoply of mourning the Victorians evolved a considerable folk literature of macabre jokes and stories which helped them come to terms with the grim reaper. Lancashire cottages frequently had narrow twisting staircases. Bending the deceased to carry him down from the death chamber often displaced trapped air and Aunty Edie liked to tell how her neighbours had dropped a corpse and fled after it had emitted a hollow groan on being carried round a particularly difficult corner. The practice grew in middle- and working-class families of putting on a substantial funeral meal with copious libations of whisky, brandy and port, not only because these were occasions of family solidarity when relatives might travel long distances in order to be together, but also because the grieving immediate family, sharing a small house for several days with a coffined corpse, might have had little inclination to eat. 'We buried him with ham!' said working-class families, relieved and proud that they had been able to entertain the extended family with proper hospitality.

James and Elizabeth's family gradually took shape with the arrival of Mary, always to be known as Polly, in 1873, Edith in 1878, Annie in 1881 and finally John, the musician of the family, in 1883. As the family grew, the cottage at Lindsay Terrace began to seem even smaller and James and Elizabeth decided to move to a bigger home at Bark Hill. Even so the house was always full, especially when Elizabeth's sister Mary Jane Lowe, the lady's maid, came home on holiday to impress her nieces with her beautiful dresses and tales of social grandeur.

At the village school Edie developed a confident mezzo-soprano and sang 'seconds' in the choir but Annie was the abler scholar, deputed by her teacher to help the others with their reading, writing and arithmetic. She would dearly have loved to stay on at school as a pupil-teacher but working-class girls seldom had that privilege and soon after her ninth birthday she was sent to join Edie at the huge Wigan clothing factory of Coop and Son. To begin with she did odd jobs, sweeping up scraps of fabric and making tea. She was a friendly, confident child and a willing worker. The other girls made something of a pet of her and when the onset of her periods brought agonising cramps they hid her from the supervisor under the long work-table, clutching a comforting hot-water bottle while they did her work for her. Gradually she learned the skills of both hand and machine work and was eventually promoted to be a mantle-maker, sewing the cloaks and tippets worn by fashionable late-Victorian ladies.

Annie was a good needlewoman but Edie was a star who shone at every aspect of the tailoring trade, including the fiddly button-holing which she cordially detested. Coops aspired to make London fashions available to well-off Lancashire ladies within a few days of their appearing in the West End. As a Coops 'sample hand' Edie would be presented with a glossy fashion-plate which she would have to translate into a finished garment for the inspection of the directors who could then decide whether or not to duplicate it for the mass market. The linings of her cloaks and jackets were particularly superb, with impossibly complex arabesques created on her small Singer treadle machine.

A child in the 1950s, I listened to the old ladies' stories of home life in Aspull when they were young girls. Inevitably at some point one of them would add '... And there was no wireless nor television in them days.' Social life in the village revolved around the family, St David's Church and the Christian Year as set forth in the *Authorised Version of the Bible*, the *1662 Book of Common Prayer* and *Hymns Ancient and Modern*. The Industrial Revolution had stimulated a tremendous growth of population in Lancashire which outstripped church accommodation in many areas. Simply designed by Thomas Rickman and built for a total cost of only £3,433, St David's was one of a number of 'Commissioners' churches built after 1819 when the Commissioners of the Treasury were authorised to issue Exchequer Bonds for church building. The church was built on Great Francis Moor and originally consecrated by Bishop John Bird of Chester on 28 November 1833 as a chapel of ease for Wigan parish church, but in 1838 the separate parish of Haigh and Aspull was formed. The Reverend CH James, Vicar of Haigh from 1886 to 1918 personally raised £3,055 for the further expansion of St David's. It was he who married my grandparents Fred Taylor and Annie Sharrock in 1908 and conducted Fred's funeral less than ten years later. Poor man, he was accustomed to tragedy. Four of his sons were killed in the First World War.

In 1890, when Annie and Edie were nine and thirteen respectively, from late November through all of December a severe frost and temperatures down to fifteen degrees below zero provided the best skating weather for three years, especially in the lower-lying areas where there were many shallow lodges and flashes caused by centuries of mining subsidence. A group of Scots exiles even managed to demonstrate their national sport of curling. There were many duckings and one near-fatality when PC Betts heroically rescued young James Latham who had fallen through the ice on a pond in Lower Ince. The *Wigan Observer* told the story in graphic detail.

> He went on the ice to rescue the boy who was about forty yards from the bank. When the officer had covered that distance with the exception of about ten yards, the ice gave way, and he went overhead into the water. Coming to the surface he got into a standing position, and nothing daunted broke the ice for about ten

> yards with his hands and knees until he reached the boy. He hoisted him on his shoulders and prepared to make the return journey, but had not gone very far before he stepped into a hole, and both rescuer and rescued were once more submerged. The officer gallantly struggled to his feet again, never once having lost his hold upon the boy, and a rope was then thrown to him which he fastened round the boy's body, and by that means the spectators drew him along the top of the ice to the bank. For some reason or other the officer was unable to follow the lad, but he made his way to an old tree stump which projected out of the water, and remained there for three-quarters of an hour. By that time another rope was procured and was thrown to him. He fastened it round his body, and more dead than alive with cold and exhaustion he was hauled through the ice and water to terra firma.

A week later, on Sunday 13 December, just before midnight, a short but heavy shower of rain took place. The ground was quickly covered with a treacherous coating of smooth ice and on the Monday morning, Edie, arriving early for work in the winter darkness, was obliged to go on her hands and knees down the slippery slope of Dorning Street to reach Coop's factory.

The penitential season of Advent gave way to a Christmas totally unlike the angst-ridden, commercialised, secular festival of today. For one thing, it did not begin until Christmas Eve, when the children decorated the house, festooning the low beams with holly, ivy and chains made with paper cut from newspapers or magazines and pasted into links with flour and water. Elizabeth, occasionally hindered by James, was busy in the kitchen with the many tasks of preparation: roasting the goose and making the mince-pies whose spicy contents were a symbol of the gifts of the Magi. Queen Victoria may have had her unamused moments, but Victorian children were children. The famous parody about the three kings travelling by taxi, car and scooter had not yet been invented but Edie had her own favourite which poked gentle fun at the kitchen chaos.

> Christians awake!
> Me mother's baking cake
> Me father's putting corrans in …

Meanwhile, in nearby St Helens, the musically talented son of a humble Wigan family whose product had become a household name was challenged by his father to contribute to the firm's seasonal publicity drive and came up with:

> Hark! The herald angels sing:
> Beecham's pills are just the thing.
> Two for an adult
> One for a child.
> Peace on earth and mercy mild!

On Christmas Eve stockings were hung from the mantelshelf and somehow, eventually, the children were hustled off to bed, and though they were convinced that they would lie awake until dawn the next sound they heard was James raking the fire back to life in the Christmas dawn. As a child in the 1950s, when they thought I was absorbed in solitary play, I would listen to my grandmother and great-aunt softly reminiscing about their Victorian childhood. When my parents were making frantic and expensive preparations for our modern Christmases, Annie and Edie contentedly recalled the contents of their Christmas stockings long ago: an apple, an orange, a new half penny and a sugar pig. At Mattins the age-old Christmas story read by a church warden in 16th-century English and the resonant accents of Haigh took on a special authenticity:

'Thurr wurr sheperrts abidin' in th' fields, keepin' watch ovurr thurr flocks by neet ...'

New Year was celebrated at the Lowes' with midnight ushered in to the sound of church bells and the traditional double-barrelled discharge of Slappy Boardman's muzzle-loader. James, a dark-browed first-footer, brought in the traditional cob of coal, toasts were drunk and the teenage Edie had her first and only encounter with inebriation. Elderberry wine can be very potent when mixed with the frosty night air. Arriving back home she climbed onto a tall cupboard, owlishly following a fly as it walked up the kitchen wall. As she told me fifty years later, all might have been well if the fly had not then decided to walk across the ceiling.

Unlike Anglo-Catholic St Elizabeth's in Aspull, a 'low' church like St David's did not put the Eucharist at the centre of its worship, but for all Anglicans Easter Sunday was the principal holy day of obligation when all confirmed members had to receive Communion. It also gave village maidens such as Edie and Annie the opportunity to show off the Easter bonnets they had so carefully decorated with artificial flowers and fruits during the previous couple of weeks. But the greatest opportunity for displaying finery was Whit Sunday, when the whole parish turned out in a procession of Christian witness which had originated in medieval Catholic times.

First came a crucifer carrying the processional cross, then the vicar's and people's wardens with their brass-tipped wands of office, then in two files the surpliced choir of men and boys, then the vicar himself, Van Dyke bearded, in his caped cassock, mortarboard and university hood, accompanied by his curate and the guest preacher. Young girls in white dresses and flowered bonnets held with white gloved hands the ribbons of St David's banner, its heavy gold-fringed dark blue brocade lifting lazily in the spring breeze; young boys in knee-breeches carried shepherds' crooks wound with flowers; the Mother's Union, dedicated to Mary and secure in parochial pre-eminence, were followed by the young wives, conscious of their more recent matronly dignity; the Sunday School carried posies with its flower-like maiden teachers and the men's Bible Class, with its jaunty swagger, followed. Haigh Brass Band played 'Poet and Peasant' and 'Guide Me, O Thou Great Redeemer' as the procession beat the bounds of the parish, finally pausing in the Windmill Field where the Vicar invoked a blessing before the choir led the multitude in 'Lead us Heavenly Father' and the guest preacher, his white surplice billowing, clambered aboard a farm cart to speak of the tongues and fire of that first Whit Sunday. Like many well-loved incumbents, the Rev. James was popularly supposed to be in direct communication with the Almighty and to be able to ensure fine weather for the great day.

'It's Vicar's weather reet enough!'

'Aye it is that!'

The sermon over, the congregation could devote itself to a sumptuous Lancashire tea laid out on white-clothed trestle tables under the elms of the Windmill field, while thirsting after righteousness, members of the Haigh Brass Band retired red-faced and exhausted to the Balcarres Arms to restore their depleted energy with copious libations of Old and Mild.

Autumn's Harvest Festival was another great St David's occasion, with the aisle and chancel arches decked with greenery and the window bottoms rich with displays of russet and gold autumn fruits. Unlike John Betjeman's church mouse, the St David's regulars had no occasion to stare disapprovingly at churchgoers who materialised only for great festivals. Cities such as London and Manchester had teeming under-classes who were seldom touched by religion unless some great evangelist awakened their imaginations and seized their souls, but almost everybody in Haigh attended church on a regular basis. On the surface, Harvest Festival was wholly a service of thanksgiving for the bounty of the earth, and the packed congregation sang lustily as the choir processed round the church, the organ pealing triumphantly with a superannuated choirboy red-faced at the bellows.

Come, ye thankful people, come,
Sing the song of harvest home.
All is safely gathered in
Ere the winter storms begin.
God, our Maker doth provide
For our wants to be supplied
Come to his own temple, come,
Sing the song of harvest home.

Alone of all the Church's great occasions Harvest had no rubric specifically allocated to it in the 1662 Prayer Book used by all Anglican churches, and in addition to being a Christian service of thanksgiving it was also rooted in the tradition of propitiating pagan deities, a practice established centuries before Christianity had come to our islands. Like the Israelites of old, inhabitants of Haigh and Aspull approached their God with a sense of awe and a lively understanding of what he might or might not do for them or to them.

Thou, O God, art praised in Zion
And unto thee shall the law be performed in
Jerusalem.
Thou that hearest the prayer,
Unto thee shall all flesh come.
My misdeeds prevail against me.
O be thou merciful unto my sins ...

As a child listening seventy years later to the same psalm I had not been particularly conscious of my sins or of pleasing a potentially perilous God who might just be persuaded to provide me with enough food for the coming winter. I skimmed impatiently over those nervous bits and arrived happily at the entertaining part where the mountains skipped like rams, the little hills rejoiced on every side and the fields of corn were so delighted with their golden ripeness that they laughed and sang. Just after the Third Collect, the Choir sang Greene's graceful little anthem *Thou visitest the earth and blessest it. Thou crownest the year with Thy goodness* and then it was time for a little ecclesiastical joke to launch a three-quarter-hour sermon on the theme of God's partnership with Man:

'My word, Thomas, you and the Lord have made a wonderful job of this garden!'

'True enough, Vicar, but you should have seen th' reet mess it were in when 'e had it to 'imself.'

However they may occasionally have cut loose with their peers, in the presence of their elders Victorian children were expected to be seen and not heard, and seen to be perfectly behaved. Munching toffees during the sermon or doing anything but listening, or at very least appearing to listen, was strictly prohibited. The service ended with another ancient harvest hymn with a rousing tenor line in which the baritones sometimes joined, much to the annoyance of the real tenors.

We plough the fields and scatter
The good seed on the land
But it is fed and watered
By God's almighty hand.

When I was a church choirmaster in Cambridgeshire in the 1980s more than a hundred years after the newly married James and Elizabeth celebrated their first Harvest at St David's I had cause to laugh aloud when I suddenly saw this hymn quoted in a very unusual context. Over the years, Mid-Anglia has combined its smaller fields into huge prairies that can easily be worked by such heavy machinery as combine harvesters. One such monster field, sporting a lush crop of winter wheat, faced the house of a family who attended our village church. The father, a lecturer at the University of Cambridge, was a devout Evangelical with a dry sense of humour and first-class calligraphic skills. The agricultural conglomerate responsible for the field had erected a hoarding with the statement:

GROWN ENTIRELY WITH GRAMOXONE

As I passed it on my way to work the morning after it appeared I noticed that an addition, not scrawled but neatly stencilled, had appeared overnight below the original inscription:

BUT FED AND WATERED BY GOD'S ALMIGHTY HAND

CHAPTER 5

Rabbits & Revelations

UNLIKE JAMES SHARROCK, my paternal great-grandfather John Taylor, born in 1843 on the borders of Staffordshire and Shropshire, was a man of property with social pretensions and a sense that the Taylors had come down in the world during his parents' move to Lancashire in 1850. The certificate of his second marriage on 23 June 1880 to my great-grandmother Mary Young gives his own profession and that of his bride's deceased father as 'farmer', while John's late father Daniel is described as a 'gentleman'. In Victorian times this designation could still carry connotations of lineage in addition to those of wealth but if the document raised any hopes in me that the Taylors might have exalted connections, these were soon dashed by a little more genealogical digging.

The fact is that we Taylors spring from stout Staffordshire yeoman stock. The son of Ralph Taylor and his wife Mary Saunders, John Taylor's grandfather, Old William, was born in 1772 in the village of Chebsey, a couple of miles from the bustling little market town of Eccleshall and not far from the cottage of Izaak Walton of *Compleat Angler* fame. The Taylors had been settled in Chebsey since the 1600s but during the first half of the 19th century they had become surprisingly mobile. In the first decade of the 1800s Old William, then in his thirties, was farming at Pirehill, between Eccleshall and Stone, and was already of sufficient consequence to occupy a private family pew at Stone parish church. It was a late marriage and William's wife Anne was six years older than himself. Nevertheless all their five children, Sarah (1802) Mary (1803) William

Above: John Taylor, 1843–1924

(1804) Daniel (1806) and Edward (1809), would survive infancy, and all except the fiercely independent Sarah would marry and have children of their own. Old William had eventually shifted his growing family to the south of the county, and as a child in the 1840s his grandson John, my future great-grandfather, lived at Manor Farm in Mavesyn Ridware near Lichfield, as part of an extended clan with numerous labourers and servants, some of whom had served the Taylors over several generations. With its cottages, barns and mill, Manor Farm was almost a village in its own right, and as my own son Richard is now a brewer with Wells-Young of Bedford, it gave me a pleasing sense of continuity to learn that there was also a maltings, where John Peters, a Kentish man from Rochester and almost as venerable as Old William himself, had passed on his skills to Edward, who had set up as a maltster at nearby Hill Ridware.

The last quarter of Old William's life had frequently been touched by sadness. Mary, his second daughter and the wife of John Cliff, a farmer of Ashmore Brook in neighbouring Burntwood, had died in 1840 at the age of only thirty-seven. Old William's own wife Anne, his senior by six years, had died aged seventy-eight in January 1843, to be followed two years later by their infant grandson William, the son of William Junior, Old William's eldest son and heir and his wife Elizabeth Brownson.

The moment his infant son had been born, William Junior had sent for his father's old friend, Mavesyn's elderly rector, the Reverend Thomas Grove. The Taylors were not only persons of consequence in the parish but also devout and active members of his congregation and whether or not the baby had in the strictest sense been alive when he was privately baptised will never be known. Infant William was buried the following day and the parish register duly recorded that he had lived for 'one hour'. Finally, William Junior himself was laid to rest at the age of forty-six in April 1850 in the yew-shaded graveyard just outside the porch of St Nicholas's Church. Like Richard Sharrock, a hundred miles away in Lancashire, Old William and his unmarried daughter Sarah took in the children orphaned by these tragedies and the Ridware ménage in the 1840s and 1850s includes several of these young Taylors and Cliffs.

The phrase is overdone, but Mavesyn Ridware, with its ancient farmsteads, venerable oaks and beeches and Old Hall with its massive medieval gatehouse, is a picture-postcard village. Having crawled unsuccessfully round an overgrown Lancashire graveyard only a few days before, Val and I went there for the first time on a rainy, blustery day in the late summer of 2006, pushed open the iron gate of the village church and were immediately confronted by the gravestones of Mary, Anne, William Junior and infant William, cut in slate and looking as if they were erected yesterday instead of a hundred and fifty years ago. Arriving back in Andalucía I told my neighbour José, himself a farmer, about the experience of seeing my great-great-great-grandmother's grave.

'A solemn moment,' he said, 'to think that this woman's blood runs in your veins.'

Old William's second son Daniel, born in 1806, had married twenty-year-old Mary Barlow at Eccleshall parish church in 1833, and during the next ten years they had successively scraped a living on small tenant farms at the nearby hamlets of Bradley and Sugden Parva before moving in the mid 1840s to High Offley, where my great-grandfather's brother Septimus was born. Between 1834 and 1852 Mary gave birth to ten children, of whom only half would reach their majority. The name Septimus was sometimes given to the traditionally fortunate seventh child of Victorian couples and the fact that Daniel and Mary's Septimus was only their fourth surviving child is an indication that three others had already died in infancy. In his late sixties, Old William decided to retire from farming and Daniel shifted to the Ridwares to take over his extensive establishment. It was not a successful move. Times were hard for farmers and perhaps Daniel did not have the tenacity of his father. To invoke a historical cliché, he had grown up as the spare and not the heir. His elder brother, William Junior, had been destined to take over the complex Mavesyn ménage, but William Junior and his little son were both dead.

In 1850 a momentous decision was made which was to have major repercussions for the future of the Taylors, when Daniel and Mary transplanted their growing family from the lush fields and leafy lanes of rural Staffordshire to start a grocery business in Tyldesley near Wigan among the belching chimneys, headgears and dark satanic mills of industrial Lancashire. It was not a move that could be made precipitately. Mary went on ahead to Tyldesley to establish the new family home at Mosley Common, taking with her Daniel, eleven, Septimus, five, and Mary Ann, aged just two, while Daniel stayed behind in the Ridwares to hand over the family farm to his sister Sarah. The whole tenor of my great-grandfather John Taylor's later life shows that the move away from the land was certainly not to his taste and it is significant that the only one of Daniel and Mary's children who did not accompany his mother to Lancashire was seven-year-old John, who remained in Staffordshire so that he could spend as much time as possible with his grandfather.

Though nominally retired, Old William remained fit and active for a further ten years. In January 1860, at the age of eighty-eight, he made his will at the chambers of a Lichfield solicitor. The witnesses noted that he appeared to be of sound mind and body and there is no doubt he was both, because in the following spring he felt fit enough to travel the hundred or so miles to Lancashire to attend the wedding of seventeen-year-old John Taylor to Mary Robinson on 28 April at St George's Church, Tyldesley. A year later they were to name their firstborn son William after his great-grandfather.

Even given the tremendous expansion of the railways in the mid-Victorian period it was a considerable journey from Lichfield to Tyldesley and Old William stayed on for a while in Lancashire enjoying the company of his son and grandchildren. Suddenly, in September 1861, he died, aged almost ninety. Faithful to his last wishes, Daniel and Mary brought his body back for burial in St Nicholas's churchyard, Mavesyn Ridware, where he lies with his wife Anne, their children Mary and William and his grandson, infant William, who had lived for just one hour. Like the Old Shepherd in *The Winter's Tale*, Old William had been the weather-beaten conduit of many kings' reigns, having been born at the time of George III and lived through the reigns of both George IV and William IV to die when Victoria had already been on the throne for twenty-four years.

Like that of his grandson John, sixty-three years later, the theme of Old William's last will and testament is that of looking after his survivors. His wife Anne and his two sons William and Edward had predeceased him, as had his daughter Mary Cliff. A codicil confirms the previous conveyance of thirteen acres of farmland near Stone to Mary's widower John Cliff. After the death of William Junior, Old William had always regarded John Cliff as a son and he and his son Robert joined Daniel as the Executors of the will. There is a bequest to Anna, Edward's surviving daughter, of half the rental income of two houses in Stone. The rest of the property is divided equally between Daniel, Sarah and John Cliff. Oddly there is no mention of the other surviving grandson, Thomas William Taylor, the son of William Junior. Perhaps Old William thought his mother Elizabeth's wealthy Brownson connections were enough to secure his future.

Old William's unmarried daughter Sarah continued farming at Court Fields in Pipe Ridware and brought up Anna Elizabeth, the daughter of her brother Edward and his wife, another Sarah, who, like Young William, had both died young. After several years of struggle on their small farm at King's Bromley, young William's widow Elizabeth and their son Thomas William also moved to Pipe to assist Elizabeth's formidable mother, Margaret Brownson, in running the family farm at Gold Hay Fields, a considerably bigger holding than Old William's 120 acres at Mavesyn. Our last sight of Thomas William is as a gardener at Uttoxeter in the first year of the 20th century, with a wife, Miriam, and a numerous brood of children, so it is very likely that we wandering Taylors still have many Staffordshire 'cousins'.

Eventually Daniel and Mary managed to establish a solid if unspectacular business in Lancashire, but at first it was certainly touch and go, with Daniel having to work at day-labouring rates on neighbouring farms to balance the family budget. Two more sons were born in Tyldesley, first Thomas and finally Frederick who would eventually follow his parents into the grocery business, but the family was struck by double tragedy with the deaths, first of eighteen year old Daniel Junior in 1858 and then of Septimus, who died in 1871 at the age of twenty-four leaving a young widow, Martha, and an infant daughter Alice who would eventually keep house for her uncle John Taylor at Astley's Farm, Haigh, a farm which was to be in many ways a replica of Old William's establishment in the Ridwares.

The 1861 census found John Taylor, like my other great-grandfather James Sharrock, living and working as a farmer's boy outside the family home, but there was a crucial difference in their circumstances. For James, charming the farmer's wife and daughter into persuading the head of the family to take him on had been a simple matter of survival and a stepping-stone to a responsible and well-paid post in industrial Lancashire. For John, finding farm work in Lancashire was both a way of continuing with the life he loved and a means of escaping from a family home tainted by failure and establishing himself as an independent man in his own right. In April 1861, at barely seventeen years of age, he married Mary Robinson, several years older than himself and the daughter of George Robinson, a collier whose family were neighbours of the Daniel Taylors. Mary had also been born in Mosley Common and like most working-class girls in the neighbourhood she worked in a cotton mill. In marrying her in his own family's local church of St George in Tyldesley John was breaking with the strong tradition that weddings take place in the bride's parish; this was by no means to be the last time he would fly in the face of convention. In another break with tradition, his best man was not one of his brothers but Samuel Edge, the younger brother of James Edge the fellow farm worker with whom John was lodging at the time of his marriage.

The outskirts of Manchester in the middle of the Victorian era were by no means wholly industrial and Mosley Common supported many working farms well into the 20th century. Coal mines and cotton co-existed with areas of unspoiled natural beauty, one of which was the area of woodland called Botany Bay, planted in the late 18th century on an area used to dump earth from the construction of the Bridgewater Canal. The name had been given to the wood by the canal workers, who felt so remote from civilisation that they might have been transported to New South Wales. Botany Bay is drained by Shaw Brook which is fed by a stream called the Sniggly Ditch because it once abounded in the young eels known in Lancashire as snigs. Even today it is only possible to see this secret landscape from the canal at Boothstown. There are no roads other than the roughest tracks and no public access to the two farms or to Botany Bay Wood, which is protected by a gamekeeper and fierce dogs. The area has become a wildlife sanctuary, with foxes, deer, rabbits, hares, water voles, both common black and rare white moles, and a rich variety of birdlife.

In the middle of the 19th century Botany Bay was owned by Lord Francis Egerton, who had established Malkins Wood Farm as a rabbitry and Grange Farm as a model dairy farm, and the gamekeeper who kept the world at bay was my great-grandfather, John Taylor, who had so resented his enforced removal from rural Staffordshire to industrial Lancashire. No doubt being able to observe the working of the model dairy farm stood him in good stead in the next phase of his life and, as I know from a photograph of him taken in his seventies, he retained an abiding affection for rabbits. It was at Botany Bay that John Taylor and Mary Robinson raised their family through the 1860s in a gamekeeper's cottage on the canal bank: first William, born in 1862 and destined to found a dynasty and make his contribution to pioneering history in the farthest north west corner of Washington State, then Anne, the soft-spoken, who was to become my father's favourite Taylor aunt, then Elizabeth and three others who died in childhood. Mary herself died in 1878, a month after giving birth to yet another stillborn baby. By this time John had taken on the tenancy of Astley's Farm, on the Crawford Estate at Haigh near Wigan. A vigorous man in his late thirties, with a dairy farm to run and teenage children to support, in less than two years he was ready to consider the possibility of a second marriage.

Research into John Taylor's claim that his father Daniel had been a gentleman had revealed the truth that he had been a grocer. Similarly, there was no foundation in his fanciful assertion that John Young, the deceased father of his new bride, had been a farmer. In fact he had been something of less social consequence but far more interesting from a local historian's point of view. Throughout the 19th century the Youngs' home village of Lowton near Leigh had been the centre of the silk industry, and the ten-yearly censuses reveal that John Young had spent the whole of his working life practising the skilled home-based trade of an independent hand-loom silk weaver.

Eighteenth century Leigh and its satellite villages had a thriving domestic textile industry. Most workers wove in their own homes, but there were one or two factories for hand-loom weavers. It was a local man, Thomas Highs, who was the inventor of the spinning-jenny and the water-frame in the 1760s rather than James Hargreaves and Sir Richard Arkwright, the men who patented them and subsequently made fortunes from the royalties. Arkwright had worked on the spinning-frame with a Warrington clockmaker called John Kay who had previously assisted Thomas Highs, and there is strong evidence that Kay and Arkwright were able to plagiarise the invention because Highs had been too poor to develop and patent the idea. Arkwright patented the water-frame in 1769, but in 1775 he also tried to patent the complete process of cotton-thread production, craftily attempting to pass off the water-frame as an entirely new machine called a roving-frame. This caused a major legal battle with other manufacturers and inventors and a series of witnesses, including Thomas Highs, testified that Arkwright had systematically stolen their ideas. The result was that Arkwright's patents were revoked. Even so, he died in 1792 one of the richest men in England, with a fortune in excess of £500,000.

Silk weaving had arrived in Leigh in 1827 as a result of a wage dispute in the Middleton silk trade. Leigh's muslin weavers, who were already used to fine work, were easily able to adapt to weaving the silk yarn supplied by the spinners of Macclesfield, and by 1835 there were as many as 10,000 silk weavers employed in the Leigh area. There were some local manufacturers, such as Bickham and Pownall (from 1833) and le Mare's (from 1851), but the industry was mainly organised by the agents of Manchester manufacturers who put out work and receive finished pieces or cuts of cloth from the domestic hand-loom weavers. The industry was just about surviving in the years immediately preceding the First World War, but changing fashions and the lifting of the import duty on French silk had caused a gradual decline from about 1870. The introduction of powered weaving from the 1850s also meant that less work was available for the domestic weavers who suffered great poverty. There are still a few surviving houses of the type in which my great-great-grandfather John Young and his wife and children once pursued their trade: low two-storey, wide-windowed buildings with loom shops either on the rear ground floor or in the cellar with a short flight of steps up to street level.

With the exception of Mary, who was naturally gentle and had her own reasons for being genteel, the Youngs were a rough and ready lot, and John Taylor, at thirty-eight already a man of consequence in his own small community, may have wanted to distance himself from them. John Young's family life had followed a typical Lancashire working-class pattern. Men frequently refused to marry until their prospective wives had demonstrated that they could produce healthy children. Couples would mark the start of their liaison with a lively party at which two neighbours would hold the ends of a broom while the protagonists leapt over it. John Young and Ellen Gregson had 'lived over th' brush' in what the Church of England would have called sin until three of their children had reached school age. The parents had only then officially tied the knot.

Jane Austen writes satirically of mothers whose main objective in life is to marry off their daughters to wealthy men, however unsuitable in terms of age, looks or temperament. Mary Young, the silk weaver's daughter, had a special friend of her own age who had 'caught' a well-heeled retired businessman some thirty years her senior. When William Whatmough took his young bride off to their new seaside villa in fashionable North Meols, near Southport, Mary Young, a pleasant, petite, soft-spoken spinster of thirty who may have been thinking that she was well and truly on the shelf, went with them as Ellen Whatmough's trusted friend and companion. The Whatmoughs had relatives in Haigh, where John Taylor, recently widowed, was struggling to run a dairy farm and bring up his motherless children. Within a short time he and Mary Young had come to an understanding and were married in Mary's village church of Christ Church, Lowton, with Ellen Whatmough standing as witness and matron of honour. Astley's Farm, the home to which John took his new bride, was one of those great sprawling Lancashire farmsteads with its own massive barn and group of satellite labourers' cottages loosely grouped around a massively built double-fronted farmhouse of honey-coloured limestone, with a heavy, iron-studded door and low, mullioned windows. After two years without a mistress, it needed a woman's hand.

Like her predecessor, Mary Robinson, my great-grandmother Mary Young was illiterate and signed her marriage 'lines' with a cross. In contrast, her new husband John Taylor was a fine graphic artist and an eloquent speaker and writer. As he had been working on farms since his middle teens it is clear that he was largely self-educated. He was also an amateur theologian whose studies took him to conferences as far afield as London, and as he never bothered to learn the art of tying his cravat, it was on these rare formal occasions that Mary would tie his necktie for him before he left Astley's; John would not untie it until he returned home. Presumably he removed the tie at night by slackening it and slipping it over his head. I remember as a child finding in the sideboard cupboard at 169 Whelley one of his published works dating from this period, an exquisitely drawn illustration of *The Beast and its Rider* from the Book of Revelation, together with a pamphlet interpreting St John's apocalyptic vision in the light of contemporary 19th-century history. The Beast was the Church of Rome and its Rider the Whore of Babylon. Like St John's vision on Patmos, John Taylor's exegesis was end-time theology. In his book the impending fall of the Roman Catholic Antichrist and the beginning of Heaven on Earth was presaged by Garibaldi's victories in Italy, the collapse of the Papal States and the discrediting of the forces of reaction under Pope Pius IX. The theology and the rhetoric were hard, protestant and uncompromising. In John's theology alcohol, like papistry, was also the work of the Devil. At a later stage, when he discovered that the doctor had prescribed Mary a tonic containing a distilled spirit, it was immediately flung through the window into the farmyard.

CHAPTER 6

Go West, Young Man

AFTER LIFE AS A CHERISHED FRIEND and companion in the genteel and childless North Meols household, arriving in June 1880 to be mistress of Astley's Farm cannot have been easy, for domestic conflict was in the air. Mary Robinson had been dead for barely two years and her eldest son William was eighteen years old and already chafing at his father's curb.

If James Sharrock had been the incarnation of a folk song, William Taylor, born in the isolated Botany Bay cottage on 22 November 1862, was to become a pioneer of the American West and a minor legend in his own lifetime. William was an early child, born when his father John was only eighteen. As a young man, brimming with talent and energy and with several younger siblings, he must have been aware that he faced decades under his father's imperious thumb. When I was a child my grandmother Annie told me how William had fretted under John's rigid regime to the point where he could stand it no longer.

One day in 1892, in an era when the three miles to Wigan represented an adventurous journey, thirty-year-old William Taylor packed his trunk and walked out of the door of Astley's Farm with a heavy heart but without a backward glance. The road he stepped onto led to the American West in the last decade of its pioneering age. The carrier's cart took the rutted track downhill, crossing the canal by the hump-backed Pendlebury Bridge. Soon it was lost to view among the overarching trees of Pendlebury Lane. It is a road I came to know well as a child some seventy years later. The waters of the cut reflect

Above: William Taylor, 1862–1923 and family

the sky and there is always a westerly breeze ruffling the cold blue surface. It must have seemed especially chilling on that day. The cart wound down through the woods past the cottage where, twenty years later, the ten-year-old half-brother William was leaving behind would live with his young bride. It passed the mill and slowly ascended steep Brock Mill Lane, eventually entering Wigan by the same Standishgate route taken by the Jacobite rebels in 1745. Some two hours after leaving Astley's it pulled up at the railway station in Wallgate where William's dunnage was loaded onto the Liverpool train.

It did not take long for John to relent. He had a strong conviction of Heaven but a man's children were part of his earthly immortality and an eldest son was especially precious. How could he let him go? He would speak once more with the boy and assure him of his pride of place in the family. Surely a reconciliation was possible. He hitched the pony to his light trap and lashed it into clattering motion. Surely he could overtake the ponderous cart or at least reach the station before the train had departed? He could not.

He took the next train to Liverpool. He interrogated the shipping agents. Which vessels were due to sail for New York? There were several. After an agonising wait, William's name was discovered on the manifest of the *City of New York* bound for Manhattan. The ship had already sailed. My grandmother concluded her story: 'Owd Taylor never saw or heard from his boy again.'

When I first drafted the story of William and John I was almost in tears, for one of my own two dear sons is also a William Taylor. It was only in 2003, thanks to a website, that I managed to connect William with Point Roberts in Washington State, where his own descendants had already carried out some research into their English origins. Over the past few years I have very much enjoyed exchanging Taylor stories with Linda Edwards, William's great-granddaughter, and was relieved to learn that although they never saw each other again William and John had been reconciled and had kept up a friendly correspondence to the end of their lives. When William's own daughters had begun to marry and set up home John had helped them financially just as he had helped my widowed grandmother Annie raise my father and his brothers.

William Taylor was one of the first immigrants to enter the USA via the famous clearing station at Ellis Island, New York. Ellis Island was a stumbling block for those who were considered unhealthy, unproductive or bad bargains, but a strapping young farmer passed the inspection with flying colours. His travels took him to the little Washington village of Point Roberts in Whatcom County, Washington State, where as one of the first homesteaders he 'made settlement' on 4 October 1897, carving his farm out of the wilderness at South Beach within sight of the ocean and the snow-clad peaks of Vancouver. In 1905, at the age of forty-three he married a 29-year-old widow, Lelia Mae Fogg. Born in Ohio, Lelia came from Scotch-Irish stock. Her ancestor, Captain McKeen, was a famous early-19th-century pioneer and her father, who farmed the next homestead to William, rejoiced in the splendid pioneer name of Abner Grimes McKeen. Lelia had previously been married to Clifford Fogg, a fisherman who had drowned, and for that reason she would sit reading in a sheltered spot out of sight of the sea while

William taught their children to swim off South Beach. One of her three children by Clifford had also died in a house fire and because of this tragedy Lelia was always reluctant to make fires. Her daughter Alice remembered in old age that the house was always too cold in winter. I asked Linda why her great-grandparents' wedding had taken place a buggy ride from Point Roberts, across the Canadian border in Ladner, British Columbia. She told me:

'Most of their neighbours were from Iceland and for years the Lutheran church at the Point held its services in Icelandic. It was only after William himself had taught English to the Icelanders that the church instituted an English service.'

The written history of Point Roberts shows William's importance in his little community. For a long time after they established their farms, he, the Thorsteinsens, the McKeens and their other neighbours were squatters with no legal title to their land. When President Theodore Roosevelt sent his representative to regularise the situation, William was elected as the natural representative of his community to negotiate with the visitor.

Linda Edwards sent me the splendid photograph of William's father, John Taylor, taken in the Edwardian era when he was in his sixties. With his piercing eyes and prophetic beard he is every inch the Old Testament patriarch. It was at this stage of his life that my grandmother Annie Sharrock, then a young woman in her early twenties, first met her future father-in-law. She told me:

'Grandma Taylor was a gentle lady but owd Taylor liked his own way in everything. He never changed his old grandfather clock from winter to summer time. He said cows couldn't tell the time but they knew very well when they needed milking.'

Annie recalled that the timing of any summer visit to her parents-in-law had to take this peculiarity into account.

When John eventually retired from Astleys Farm he was wealthy enough to purchase Atherton House, the substantial gentleman's residence which still stands next to the railway embankment just off the main A49 road through Euxton to Chorley. My grandmother recalled John's personally demolishing a redundant wing of the house in order to reduce taxation, and impressing the long-suffering Mary as his labourer. When I visited Atherton House on a rainy day some eighty years after John's death I was able to clear up a mystery for the current owner.

'I've always been puzzled by the fact that the newer wing of the house is single-storey. The break in the cornice quite clearly shows that it was originally intended to be two-storey. But I don't suppose we shall ever know whether the upper floor ever existed.'

'It WAS originally two-storey! My great-grandfather was a man of strong opinions. He was always contentious and didn't believe in contributing unnecessarily to the county exchequer. Although he was not short of a bob or two, he objected to a revised rate assessment on the house and was determined to reduce it. The only way this could be done was to reduce the house itself. And he didn't call in a contractor to do it. He personally dismantled the upper storey of the 'new' wing and he enlisted my great-grandmother as his labourer and handed it down to her brick by brick.'

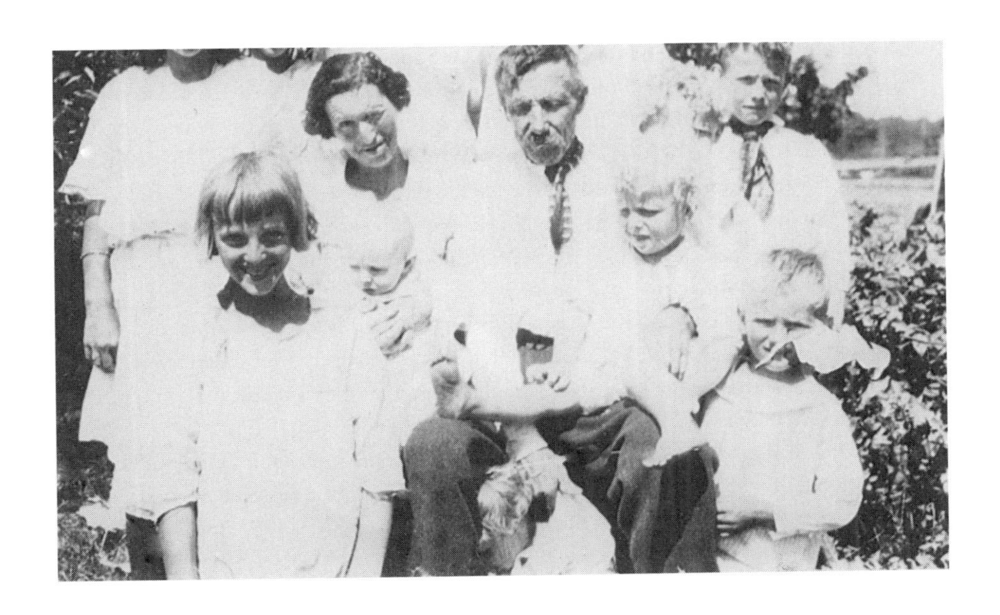

John Taylor died on 24 February 1924. His obituary in the *Wigan Observer* shows him to have been the man of consequence he had always intended to become after circumstances had uprooted him from Staffordshire and the farming life he loved. A representative of the Earl of Crawford and Balcarres, a Knight of the Realm, a Justice of the Peace and no less than nine neighbouring farmers attended his funeral and followed the bier to his graveside. The *Observer*'s erroneous reference to his having been born in Lancashire shows how deeply he had buried the shame of his family's move from the Ridwares. His own children were aware neither of his Staffordshire origins nor of his real age, and even the date on his gravestone is incorrect.

> We regret to record the death of Mr. John Taylor, a former Chairman of the Wigan Board of Guardians, which occurred at Astley's Farm, Haigh on Monday last week. The deceased gentleman, who was 81 years old, was a native of Worsley, but came to Wigan district some fifty years ago, when he became the tenant of Astley's Farm, Haigh, which has remained in the possession of family ever since. Mr. Taylor retired from active farming about thirteen years ago, when he went to reside at Euxton, but two years ago he returned to Haigh, and again took up residence at Astley's Farm, which is now tenanted by his son, Mr. Frank Taylor. In politics Mr. Taylor was a Conservative, and as a member of the Church of England he attended Haigh Parish Church.
>
> Prior to retiring, he had given over a quarter of a century in public service as a Poor Law Guardian. He was first elected a Guardian for Haigh in 1880, and was elected Chairman of the Wigan Board of Guardians in 1907, but he did not seek re-election to the Board at the close of his term of office. When he retired there were only two guardians on the Board who had occupied seats when he was

first elected, and the singular situation prevailed that, although Mr. Taylor did not seek re-election then, he still remained a Guardian for Haigh, as no candidate was nominated to succeed him. In taking his farewell at the close of his year of office as Chairman of the Board of Guardians in April, 1908 when a vote of thanks was passed to him for his services, Mr. Taylor referred to the work of Boards of Guardians in the future, and said he could see things coming that would mean more work, though it was quite possible, he added, that the duties of Guardians might be merged into those of Corporations.

Mr. Taylor leaves a widow and a grown-up family of three sons and one daughter all of whom are resident in the Wigan district. His eldest son, Mr. William Taylor, who pre-deceased him, died in October of last year at Point Roberts, Washington, United States.

The funeral took place on Thursday last week, the interment being at Haigh Parish Church. The Rev. F. L. Marsden, Vicar of Haigh, officiated. Four of the deceased's grandsons, Messrs. William and Tom Churchouse and W. and F. Taylor, J. Smith, and P. Parkinson acted as bearers.

The mourners were: 1st carriage, Mrs. John Taylor, (widow), Mrs. J. Churc-house, (daughter), Mr. James Taylor. Mr. Charles Taylor, and Mr. Frank Taylor (sons): 2nd, Mrs. J. Taylor, Mrs. Fred Taylor, Mrs. C. Taylor, Mr. and Mrs. W. Young: 3rd, Mrs. W. Taylor, Misses Mary and Alice Taylor, and Masters John and Bert Taylor: 4th, Mr. Fred Taylor, Mr. Crook, and Mrs. Buckley. Mr. A.E. Baw J.P. representing the Haigh Estate and also the Wigan Board of Guardians, and Mr. T. Dean Haigh Estate, and Sir. J. Wintersgill, J.P., of Wigan were present at the grave side.

The following neighbouring farmers preceded the hearse to the church: Messrs. J. Barge, R. Mawdsley, R. Eccles, E. Hodge, T. Rowden, J. McCutcheon, J. Walker, T. Collier and J. Mort.

The several references in his obituary to John's work as a Guardian of the Poor intrigued me and I was determined to find more about what had clearly been an important part of his life. In our day, conditioned as we are by such stories as *Oliver Twist*, the Victorian workhouse has rather a fearsome reputation, and I rather feared that I would discover that John had been a combination of Mr Bumble and the Rev. Brocklehurst in *Jane Eyre*. I was both relieved and slightly disappointed to find that this had been far from the case. Certainly he runs true to form when he resists the wish of Fr Power, a local Roman Catholic priest, to install a crucifix as a permanent feature in one of the Infirmary wards, but he is equally firm in informing the Anglican chaplain that he should not expect the Guardians to buy his surplice for him. He is surprisingly emollient when his fellow Guardians want to send an irate letter to the Chief Constable, some of whose minions have been heavy-handed in dealing with a workhouse official, and his amendment that 'the officers were not as civil as they might have been on this occasion' is a model of diplomacy. The work of the Wigan Board of Guardians was an enormous and, as John suggests in his 1907 Chairman's remarks, rather unwieldy operation whose responsibilities went far beyond monetary poor relief. Much of the business transacted at their monthly meetings makes for dry reading, but there are occasional entries in the Minute Book which bring Victorian and Edwardian Wigan vividly to life. On 6 August 1897 the Board resolves

> that Solomon Guest, 52 years of age, of 50 Miry Lane, be allowed a Wooden Leg, cost not to exceed three pounds.

The Wigan Board had a particular interest in the education of the children and young adults in its charge and over many years it maintained a productive link with the captain of the sail training ship *Indefatigable*, who could guarantee to find Royal or Merchant Navy berths for any hardworking boy the Guardians sent him. Whenever the Board discussed the subject of education, John Taylor was a forthright contributor. Living as we do in an age which invented the term 'political correctness' it is surprising to note his Victorian concern for the education of gipsy and vagrant children. A discussion about the relative merits of urban and rural foster homes has him opting for the latter, where children may enjoy fresh air and good food and, while their foster fathers are out at work, avoid running wild with the kind of faginesque street urchins John would not like as companions for his own sons and daughters. He is happy to give financial help to a blind teenager but also insists on sending the boy to a special school where he can learn a trade. Unlike some other Boards and very unlike some of the bodies which supposedly regulate the treatment of old people in 21st century 'care homes', the Wigan Guardians appear to have been sensitive to the needs and feelings of their charges and took pains to find out and respond to what was happening in the workhouse and the infirmary. At Christmas 1896 there was a festive atmosphere thanks to generous public donations of tobacco, snuff, tea, sugar, sweets, toys, apples, oranges, a football, magazines, jam, pickles, nuts, evergreens for decorations and dressed dolls for the children, but

> a complaint was received that the Master had disregarded the request made by one of the Guardians that he should obtain a screen to be placed by the side of a man who was dying in the Imbecile Ward.

The Master duly had his knuckles rapped, not only for this piece of callousness but also for his negligence in other areas of duty. In the depths of winter the temperature in the wards seldom rose much above fifty degrees Fahrenheit and Mr Willis, a ward attendant, informed the Guardians that the Master ignored his requests for coal for the fire and knew nothing about conditions in the ward which he visited hardly once in a month. The Guardians not only instructed the Master to visit each ward every day but also formed a sub-committee to study the problem of heating. It was the work of this group, headed by John Taylor, which rapidly led to the installation of a central heating system. Far from seeing it as a triumph, John regarded his new steam radiators as a second-best solution to the problems of the ancient, poky, overcrowded, dangerous and insanitary workhouse building. His own suggestion in April 1896 had not been to improve it but to knock it down after constructing a brand-new facility on a fifty-acre greenfield site.

AliceTaylor

Unfortunately the majority of the Guardians had quailed at the cost of such an enormous commitment and the workhouse infirmary was to stagger on, increasingly dilapidated, into the late 1950s.

As John's obituary mentions, William Taylor, his eldest son, had predeceased him, dying in Point Roberts, Washington, USA of asthmatic bronchitis, a recurrent feature of the Taylor genetic heritage, at the age of only sixty-one on 21 October 1923. In the photograph his great-grand-daughter Linda sent me he sits outside his South Beach cabin on a sunny day surrounded by most of his twelve children. Like Fred, his half-brother, my grandfather, he is one of the tall fair Taylors with a mop of sun-bleached, curly hair falling across his forehead. His face is lined and weather-beaten and somehow it is simultaneously both serious and humorous. Lelia survived him by almost forty years and her family's success in business, education and many other fields is a credit to her pioneering grit and the potent fusion of Taylor–Grimes genes. After William's death, eldest daughter Alice interrupted her high school studies to help Lelia raise the younger children, but in spite of her domestic chores she was determined to finish school through part-time study. Her graduation picture shows her to have been a pretty, vivacious girl with a halo of chestnut curls. Her grandfather John Taylor left a substantial sum to William's children, out of which Alice was able to buy her first married home. In October 2003 I typed 'William Taylor, Point Roberts' in my browser and came up with Alice's obituary. She had died on Easter Sunday 2003 at the age of ninety-seven and is buried beside her beloved daddy in the cemetery of the Lutheran church.

CHAPTER 7

Annie's Lads

I am like Norman, but I am not Norman.
I am like Harold, but I am not Harold.
I am like Jack, but I am not Jack.
I am like Jim, but I am not Jim.
I am like Bill, but I am not Bill.

IN ADDITION TO MARGARET JANE, born in 1882, Charles in 1884 and Francis in 1886, John and Mary Taylor became the parents of my grandfather, John Frederick Taylor, born at Astleys Farm on 21 April 1881. Unlike the other pattern of stocky, moody, black-browed, deep-voiced Taylor males, Fred was an affectionate, blond, blue-eyed six-foot tenor whom his brother, my great-uncle Charlie, remembered calling the cows home on a ringing top A. He fell in love with Annie, youngest daughter of James Sharrock, on a wagonette trip organised by the Sunday school of St David's Church. Wagonettes were horse-drawn carts in which two rows of country folk would sit facing each other in their best finery. Sixty years afterwards my grandmother recalled how Fred had insisted on sitting opposite her. They were both tall and even if she had wanted to it had been impossible to avoid the pressure of his knees. Sepia tinted photographs showed Grandmother and Aunty Edie as they were in those days, stately in floor-length dresses or buttoned up in their two-piece 'costumes' with the inevitable lace jabot at the throat. With fine, strong bone structure and perfect complexions, they were handsome

Above: Annie Taylor née Sharrock

rather than pretty and there is none of the vulnerability I see in my mother's teenage photographs from the 1930s. There is even a touch of arrogance which proclaims their conviction that in our village and its community Sharrocks were persons of definite consequence.

Fred and Annie were married at St David's Church, Haigh, on 23 September 1908 and set up home in a primitive cottage on the Crawford estate, with a black-leaded range for cooking and heating, and a well in the back garden. A hundred years later the area is still rural. A rustic pocket in the midst of a conurbation, it has been bypassed by the metropolitan sprawl. In time they moved to a two-bedroomed terraced house in Whelley, opposite the Lindsay and Alec Pit gates, with a rambling garden where Fred grew vegetables and fruit and where I had numerous adventures as a child fifty years later. In addition to its proximity to the mine, the great advantage was its closeness to the Sharrock grandparents. Between 1909 and 1917 Annie and Fred produced five sons. When I remember Brian Sharrock's assertion that we are descended from a Chirac ancestor who fought at Hastings I wonder if it was by some kind of historical divination that the eldest came to be christened Norman and the next in line Harold. My grandmother's favourite, John Sharrock (Jack) followed in 1914, James (Jim) in 1915 and my father, William (Bill) in 1917. Even with all the pressures of providing for a growing family on a slender income, Fred was invariably positive and cheerful. In her old age Aunty Edie, though she loved her boys devotedly, was satirically cynical where the generality of men was concerned. Their shows of affection, she said, were all Judas' kisses.

'What about Fred?' I would enquire mischievously, knowing the answer.

'Fred was good,' she would reply. And then, with a sideways glance at my grandmother, 'Too good for *her*.'

Edie herself had been a flirt, played the field and ended up as everybody's aunty. Her last beau had died in the Battle of the Somme. My grandmother had looked seriously at only one man and had snatched the pick of the bunch.

Fred took his responsibilities seriously but enjoyed his recreation, for which he budgeted exactly one shilling a week. This took him every Saturday, via two tram routes, to Haydock Park races, where he would bet up to sixpence on the horses he fancied before taking the tram back to Wigan, where he would stop at the Ship Inn just off the Market Place in Millgate and drink exactly two pints of beer. If he had been successful at Haydock he took the tram home to Whelley, if not, he walked. A modern-day feminist would probably ask what recreation my grandmother enjoyed and the answer would probably be 'very little'. Like most mothers of her era, her focus was the family and when I knew her in the last quarter of her life, preserving its fabric by paying and receiving occasional visits was still the centre of her life. During her short marriage of twelve years she had also enjoyed the company and support of her parents who lived only a few yards away, but apart from that weekly expedition to the races, she and Fred did everything together. Years later she recalled how he would gently bounce querulous babies on the bed until they chuckled and fell asleep.

For whatever reason, after their father John had retired from Astley's Farm in 1911, Fred's relationship with his own brother Charles was an increasingly uneasy one. Fred and Annie had to provide for a rapidly growing family and during the First World War the coal mines were in full swing and paid well, so Fred made the momentous and ultimately fatal decision to become a collier. Perched as they were between the mine and the iron works, the war was a dangerous time for my grandparents. As a miner, Fred was in a reserved occupation and there was no question of enlistment in the armed forces, but there were night-time air-raids during which my grandparents took the children to the garden air-raid shelter. Eventually the all-clear would sound and minutes later they would hear the noise of boots crunching in the broken glass: the Vicar coming to make sure his parishioners had survived the night. As a child I drew my grandmother's attention to the crack which ran through the stone lintel above her parlour fireplace.

'That was done in an air-raid during the war,' she told me.

'What kind of plane was it?' I asked, my mind full of 1940s Dorniers and Stukas.

'Not a plane,' she replied, 'it was one of them balloon things.'

A small boy in 1955, I gazed in awe at this relic of the zeppelin raid of 12 April 1918 in which several people had been killed in the Whelley and Scholes area. The bomb had fallen on a wagon-load of coal in the Alexandra Pit yard just opposite, but the blast had wrecked number 171 next door, where a father had been descending the stairs with his two-year-old son in his arms. Both were killed by the blast, the child's immaculate body being found in the fireplace. No. 171 was never rebuilt and the space it had occupied was later paved with bricks and used as a yard where Annie would hang out her washing. Typically Edie focused on a ludicrous aspect of what must have been a terrible night: the lavatory block belonging to a neighbouring row of terraced houses had been demolished by the bomb blast but all the 'petty' cans remained intact, their wooden seats standing to startled attention.

If James Sharrock had been a farmer's boy who had transferred smoothly into a lifetime career in mining, the same could not be said of his son-in-law. Fred worked hard but was unsuited to life in the dusty gas-filled underground workings half a mile below the fields where he had called the cows home on summer evenings. He suffered from the allergic asthma I was to inherit over thirty years later, though it had bypassed my father and my uncles. Eventually he became a banksman, working on the surface in charge of the cages which carried the colliers to and from their work below ground, but the damage had been done. As I was to do in the early 1950s he contracted a chest infection and then bronchial pneumonia. From my own childhood I vividly remember the agony of the congested lungs, the rasping attempts to exhale, the daggers of pain which lacerated my back and chest and the scalding bite of kaolin poultices. I know something of what my grandfather experienced but for him there was no National Health Service and the penicillin which saved me would not be on the market for another twenty-five years. Fred died aged thirty-seven on 23 June 1918 and my grandmother found herself a widow with five sons, the eldest of whom was barely seven, while the child who would become my father was less than a year old.

There was little time for the luxury of grief. My grandmother, in spite of her five young children, subsequently received several offers of marriage, but Fred's lasting memorial was that she remained celibate until her death over fifty years later. The abrupt disappearance of the breadwinner necessitated an immediate family reorganisation. Before her marriage my grandmother had worked at Coops the tailors in the centre of Wigan. Aunty Edie, at thirty-nine unmarried and living with her parents, still worked there and had risen to be the sample hand, the highly skilled expert who looked at fashion plates and re-created whole ensembles, personally carrying out every process from cutting out, through sewing to finishing and button-holing. Aunty Edie moved her possessions across the road from the Sharrock family home to 169, bringing her optimism, her energy, her salty humour and her weekly wage. Norman, my grandmother's eldest son and the only quiet and unassuming member of her brood, moved in with his grandparents to be raised at their expense until he could contribute to the family exchequer. In addition to her maternal duties my grandmother took in tailoring jobs at home and went across the road every day to scrub the floors of the brick hangars which housed the great steam pumping engines which drained and ventilated the Lindsay and Alexandra pits where her father James was Overlooker.

Annie's father-in-law John Taylor helped his grandchildren with a monthly allowance and Annie, rather over-optimistically, was also expecting her boys to receive a substantial lump sum in his will. But when John died in 1924 her sons each received only a new handkerchief from his estate and note in his will recorded that they had already received the legacies due to them. The allowances had added up to some four hundred pounds, at least four years' wages for a farm worker of the period and considerably more per head than his American grandchildren received, but Annie was furious and never forgave the fancied insult of the five new handkerchiefs. Much as I loved my grandmother, she was no saint and as a child it worried me that she found it impossible to forget an injury. The matter still rankled after fifty years in which she had had little or no contact with her late husband's family, and she was quietly disapproving when I spent a term as a paying guest in great-uncle Charlie Taylor's home when I went up to Lancaster University in 1964. He was then in his eighties and married to his much younger second wife, my Aunty Bella who was cousin to James Cyril Anderton, later to become a charismatic, controversial and much-publicised Chief Constable of Greater Manchester.

My father and his brothers grew up in the brief time of peace between two World Wars. In the photograph of them taken in the late 1920s in the garden at 169 Whelley all wear Norfolk jackets and Eton collars. Norman, bespectacled, lanky and shy, and Harold, grave and confident at sixteen, both sport watch chains in their waistcoats. Jack at fifteen is already the future bomber pilot: handsome in an understated and thoroughly masculine way which transcends the dated ambience of the photograph. My father is touchingly vulnerable at eleven and Jim looks exactly as his son David will look forty years later. All across the near horizon the Top Place ironworks chimneys belch smoke. Whelley in those days, and even in my childhood thirty years later, was a strange blend of the industrial and the rustic. You stepped out of the back garden gate of 169 and, still in view of the ironworks, were immediately in a cow pasture dotted with copses and ponds. Poachers hunted rabbits with lurchers in the woods of the Crawford 'plantation' which began just behind the Alec Pit. In the school holidays my father and his brothers roamed far and wide in this variegated countryside. Before they set out they would each fill lemonade bottles with water and carve themselves 'shalves', generous slices of bread spread with home-made jam. Once a passer-by said to Jack:

'Ah'll gi' thi a tanner if tha con eyt yon shalve.'

It was no contest and Jack earned his sixpence almost without drawing breath.

NORMAN

All the boys showed promise at school. Norman left at fourteen to follow his grandfather into employment with the Crawford collieries and after the Second World War, in which he served in Palestine as a Lance Bombardier in the Royal Artillery, he became a clerk with the newly formed National Coal Board. Tall, gentle and bespectacled, he was viewed by Annie as the least successful of her sons, but not for the first or only time in her life she was wrong. To begin with, he made an excellent choice of life partner. Edith Jane Jones, a buxom, softly spoken country girl from Rainford near Ormskirk exactly suited him. Sadly they had no children of their own but local children were seldom absent from their Victorian terraced house in Wigan's Springfield Road. The first members of our family to own a TV set, in the early 1950s, they could converse knowledgeably about *The Trollenberg Terror* and those other early science fiction programmes that both scared and fascinated us, and I remember Aunt Jane comforting a neighbour's little boy who, after an episode of some such series, unwisely viewed at home, had dreamt of 'space men coming down on him'.

Between the ages of eight and sixteen Norman had been raised by his grandparents, James and Elizabeth, in the Lindsay Pit Overlooker's house just across the road from 169 and, by default, had conceded the premier position in Annie's household to the more assertive Harold. While they dutifully appeared for some of the weekly Sunday gatherings which took place at 169 during the 1940s, 50s and 60s, Norman and Jane preserved a calm detachment and floated serenely above the occasional currents of family controversy in which Harold was more than welcome to take pride of place. When they could manage to do so without giving too much offence they preferred to spend their weekends with Jane's family in the little village of Rainford in the flat fertile countryside near Ormskirk. They also gave a great deal of thought and planning to their annual holidays in southern seaside resorts such as Weston Super Mare, in well-run boarding houses where the food was excellent both in quality and quantity. On their return, they loved to relate stories of such luxuries as steak puddings and ham sliced thickly off the bone, and as my father would sometimes remark acidly: 'You'd think they'd been bloody well starving themselves for th' other fifty weeks o' th' bloody year!'

When I think of Norman I hear his voice, a mellow, resonant tenor both in song and speech, with a slight touch of East London which seemed inexplicable until one remembered his six years of service in an army whose rankers frequently adopted a generalised cockney lingua franca. With his tall, spare frame, dark hair, light speaking voice and long, gentle face, his fair Anglo-Saxon brothers tended to regard Norman as the cuckoo of their brood, but not long ago I studied a photograph of the grown-up sons of William, their father's eldest half-brother, and was intrigued to see Norman's features replicated no less than four times, so it seems that these are the true Taylor features and the rest of us may be the Sharrock cuckoos.

Norman's short-sightedness was notorious. One day as a fourteen-year-old I was bowling along Station Road on my Dawes Dalesman racing bike when a lanky figure in a flapping gabardine raincoat stepped off the kerb in front of me. I braked hard but thoroughly skittled the careless pedestrian and shot over the handlebars to join him on the tarmac. He recovered his composure before I did and scooped me up tenderly with an exclamation of apology.

'Hello, Uncle Norman', I murmured with dazed affection.

Not a great pub man, Norman played darts and billiards at the Social Club belonging to the neighbouring Sacred Heart Roman Catholic Church in Springfield Road. When the parish priest was present it was the custom for men ordering drinks to include him in the round. Norman, never one to throw his money around and almost never one to use a swear word, went up to the bar:

'Pint of mild, please.'

'And one for the Father?' prompted the bar man.

'The Father can buy his bloody own.'

HAROLD

Harold served an engineering apprenticeship and eventually became a fitter with the elite firm of Walker Brothers, though he passed through some challenging times before he arrived at that eminence. Childless after a number of miscarriages, and loving children, he and my aunt, yet another Edith, née Harrison, were undoubtedly my favourite relatives while I was in single figures. A fraction short of six feet tall, broad of shoulder and narrow of hip, immaculately dressed even in overalls, he had a solid masculine presence and even an under-stated arrogance which my mother admiringly said was typical of the species she classified as 'Walkers' Man'. I did not question this characterisation until I noticed exactly the same features in the bearing of my son Richard, who also resembles Harold physically, and concluded that they are genetic rather than acquired.

Though generous and often amusing, Uncle Harold was one of the mainstream of moody Taylors, being afflicted on occasions with a combination of imperiousness and absolute certainty which could be very irritating. In fairness I have to add that my brother Stephen and I have been known to plead guilty to the same charge. During the depression of the 1930s Harold, like so many others, was laid off work. Long before Norman Tebbit invented the phrase he got on his bike and set off to seek the heaviest and roughest labouring jobs wherever they might be found. He worked as a navvy on the Mersey Tunnel and stayed in some interesting 'digs'. Himself a clean and fastidious man, one night, having scrubbed down after work, he woke up surprised to find himself sharing a bed with a collier who was still in his pit dirt. Unlike my own parents, Harold and Edith appeared to enjoy each other's company and to share a taste for the kind of zany humour my mother and father would have dismissed as 'stupid'. When I arrived one day at their little terraced house in Higher Ince, where the kindling was chopped with her father Enoch's Boer War bayonet, my aunt asked me solemnly:

Harold and Edith Taylor

'Do you know that we have a Hollywood film star living next door?'

'What?' I exclaimed, my eyes becoming large and round.

'Honest injun. And his mum's just about to call him in for his grub.'

Right on cue, a female voice cried: 'Alan! Your tea's ready! Come on, Alan, lad.'

Edith, a secretary at Coop and Son where Annie and great-aunt Edie had begun their tailoring careers in the Victorian era, was a tall, pretty, shapely woman with languorous eyes that belied her vivacious personality. In middle age her luxuriant hair was still so long that when I released the pins that held it in place it would cascade so far down her back that she could sit on it. She was a Sunday School teacher at the bustling little Ashton Street Primitive Methodist Church in Higher Ince and often took me to its various festivals, 'walking days' and 'sermons', which always starred one of my favourite characters. In addition to having a name reminiscent of one of the better-quality jams, Hartley Seed, the Sunday School superintendent, played the harmonium for all the hymns. A good-looking young man in a snappy knife-edged suit, with crisp curly hair, flashing teeth and glittering gold-rimmed spectacles, Hartley could wring every possible nuance out of the instrument and, under his talented hands, *Sankey's Sacred Songs and Solos* really swung.

On fine Sunday afternoons I would walk in Borsdane Wood or the Haigh Plantation, loitering with my aunt as we foraged for conkers, acorns, oak apples or other treasures, while my uncle plodded patiently ahead with his hands clasped behind his back.

'Look,' she would nudge me, 'owd mon Taylor!'

It was she who introduced me to comic verse, through the works of Marriot Edgar, author of such immortal works as *The Lion and Albert* and *The Battle of Hastings*, in which my uncle's vanquished namesake sat sadly

> ... with an eyeful of arrer,
> On 'is 'orse, with 'is 'awk in 'is 'and.

Day trips to Southport with Harold and Edith were always a great treat. First there was the adventure of the train ride itself and then there were fairground attractions, paddling pools, donkey rides, Punch and Judy, and cockles or ice creams from the promenade kiosks. Southport Beach was vast and almost never saw a tide high enough to cover it. Cars were often driven onto neighbouring Ainsdale Sands and one of my earliest memories is of 'helping' to push a friend's Austin Twelve which had sunk up to its rear axle. One summer day, soon after my fifth birthday, while I was crossing the beach with Harold and Edith, an incident occurred which they recalled with amusement ever afterwards. Another child had built an impressive sand castle with keep, towers, moat and causeway. I took one look at it and deliberately jumped onto it with both feet, squashing it flat. Harold and Edith, thoroughly embarrassed, remonstrated with me about my bad behaviour and instructed me to apologise to the child whose castle I had wrecked. I turned to the boy with a look of entirely bogus concern and said:

'I'm sorry, love. It was an accident.'

Harold, struggling to keep his face straight, tried to explain that the situation called for penitence rather than blatant hypocrisy, but I am afraid I was a lost cause.

It was in Harold and Edith's nature to take responsibility. My own parents were essentially generous but completely disorganised and as a child I yearned for the order and predictability which characterised their daily life. My mother, understandably jealous that I preferred my aunt's house to my own home, sneered that Edie made her meat pies with 'tinned steak' but I was charmed by the fact that her mealtimes were regular, peaceful and unaffected by the emotional storms which in our house could dictate that lunch arrived at three and tea at nine. My father and my mother were earning good money; the food in our house was plentiful and of the highest quality; birthdays and Christmases meant expensive presents, usually bought on hire-purchase, but laying aside money for a future event was unheard of. In 1962, when I was in the Lower Sixth at Wigan Grammar School, my mother rashly agreed that I could put my name down for a school trip to Bacharach in the German Rhineland. When the time came to pay, the kitty was, as usual, empty. Bill disclaimed responsibility but my mother humbled herself to ask Harold for help. Harold duly paid the forty pounds, a very substantial sum in those days, characteristically making it clear that this was a gift and not a loan. I was relieved and grateful but the incident was to resurface a year later with unfortunate consequences for my relationship with my uncle and aunt.

Harold's own house was immaculate and throughout my childhood it was he who saw to maintenance and repairs at 169, unless the problem were electrical, in which case my father Bill would take a hand. Harold had once let slip that in filling in his tax return he claimed for Annie and great-aunt Edie as 'dependent relatives', which infuriated my mother, who as a nearer neighbour was always the first port of call for the old ladies in any immediate crisis. Bill was also periodically nettled by Harold's high-handedness and a long-term resentment smouldered which on one memorable occasion put me squarely in the firing line.

Harold had sold his pristine midnight-blue Austin 10 in 1945 after the war and thereafter never owned a vehicle, so when repairs at 169 required the transportation of tools or materials our family car was pressed into service. This occurred on three Sundays in 1963 when my father and I drove in our Vauxhall Velox from our house in Pemberton to pick up Harold in Hindley on our way to Whelley to carry out whatever job was necessary. By the fourth successive Sunday the job was over but Harold had become accustomed to the arrangement and assumed that he would be picked up as usual. Bill, in one of his more awkward moods, decided not to turn out at all and not to inform Harold of his decision. Arriving much later at 169 by bus, I encountered a very irate Harold who made some very forthright remarks about Bill's irresponsibility. While I privately sympathised with him, I felt that it was inappropriate for a tirade about my father to be directed at his seventeen-year-old son, and I said so. My grandmother, not normally one to cross Harold, agreed with me. Harold was mortified and accused me of ingratitude for his many kindnesses, which was certainly not the case. The incident blew over but never again would we have the same easy relationship we had always enjoyed. Harold was ever one to stand on his dignity and confrontation tends to make me freeze with an embarrassment which is not easily thawed.

When great-aunt Edie died, Annie went to live in Hindley with Harold and Edith. I would visit her there until her death in 1969 but after that, with a new marriage and a new career to build away from the Wigan area, I gradually lost touch with my uncle and aunt until my brother Stephen and I went to inform them of our father's premature death in 1983. Harold's reaction, which I realised was partly due to shock, sounded typically judgemental:

'Well, he always smoked and drank too much.'

At my father's funeral the four of Annie's boys who had survived the Second World War were together for the last time. Afterwards the family crammed into the living room at the Pemberton house in the desultory manner of such occasions, all of us, apart from my mother, wondering how soon we could decently take our leave. My son Will, less than a year old, was impervious to the sad atmosphere, a small, chortling blond figure who shuttled busily around our feet intent on his own pursuits. Harold's eyes met mine. He smiled and I knew that we were both remembering.

JACK

When I am absorbed in a book or in listening to another person I sit with my head bent to the right. Annie would smile and push it gently into the vertical position.

Wedding of Jack and Harriet (Dolly) Taylor

'Put your head straight!' she would say with affectionate exasperation. 'Our Jack always held his head on one side just like that.'

My grandmother said I had been sent to her by God to replace Jack who had been killed when his Wellington bomber had crashed in 1942, but I have never been able to see much similarity either physically or in terms of character. Deeply involved in the life of St Stephen's, the new church which had grown out of St David's, Jack had been a chorister and later a sidesman and a member of the parochial church council, so we do have all of that in common. Even as a child, he had tremendous self-confidence and as a Wigan Grammar School boy he was capped for Lancashire at both football and cricket, while I have never been either talented at or much interested in sport. But there must have been something there because elderly friends of my grandmother on meeting me for the first time would start and stare:

'My God, Annie! He's your Jack!'

Perhaps it had more to do with mannerisms and body language. My favourite photograph of Jack shows a strikingly handsome, square-jawed blond young man sitting on a stone wall in the sunshine with a castle in the background. Like Will, my younger son, his great-nephew, he has a timeless young Robert Redford beauty which makes the 1930s clothes seem the last word in style. I wish Annie could have met Will, who is physically so much like my photographs of Jack and has his charm, his easy elegance and his skill at games.

On 11 November we would meet in front of the school war memorial to commemorate the dead of two world wars. As a child of the 1960s I had reservations about what liberals called 'the glorification of war'. As a Christian I felt deeply uncomfortable with the hymn *O Valiant Hearts*, which described each death in battle as a little Calvary. I even told my Dad, to his spluttering indignation, that in any future conflict I might choose to be a conscientious objector. Since that time my views have changed, though I still admire those who, like the most decorated soldier of the First World War, chose to carry stretchers rather than a rifle. Jack had not waited for the official call-up. A founder member of his works Home Guard unit, he had also been one of the first to volunteer for active service with the RAF. It was not from a boyish spirit of adventure. More than any of his brothers at this stage of their lives Jack was a man who had thought about his reasons for fighting.

In spite of my own reservations I was always moved by the brief Armistice Day ceremony. All wore poppies, the Headmaster read out the names of the dead and I felt a particular frisson when he came to my own name, John S Taylor. It was not of course my name but that of my namesake, my father's brother Jack. We stood motionless for the two minutes silence, which ended with Binyon's words:

> They shall grow not old
> As we that are left grow old.
> Age shall not weary them
> Nor the years condemn.

'When they brought him home the coffin was closed. We were told never to open it. At his funeral it was draped with a Union Jack. St Stephen's Church was full. Mr Wilding the organist played the *Nunc Dimittis*.'

> Lord, now lettest Thou thy servant depart in peace
> According to Thy word ...

'Then the bugler played the *Last Post*. I've never been able to listen to it since. I never go to church on Armistice Day. I can't look at an aeroplane in the sky.'

Although Annie often talked about Jack's boyhood and his young manhood when he alone of her sons could sometimes quietly best her in an argument, she could hardly bear to mention the accident which had ended his life and she always hushed Aunty Edie if she started to do so. I now suspect that she had completely blanked from her memory any information she had ever possessed. Occasionally she would tell me that when Jack came home on leave he would speak enthusiastically of flying above seemingly endless fields of white clouds bathed in sunlight, and once he had chilled her by saying that if an aircraft had the misfortune to fly into an 'air pocket' death would be so instantaneous that the crew would know nothing about it. This fiction became her comfort: Jack, riding in the sunshine above the clouds, had flown into an air pocket and felt no pain. Forty years after listening to this explanation I decided to find out for myself and, as so often, the Internet was my tool for doing so.

The Commonwealth War Graves Commission maintains a website listing every soldier, sailor and airman killed on active service in the Second World War. I knew that Jack was buried in St David's churchyard with his father Fred, so the location of his grave was not in question. What I needed was his service number and the date of his death and the CWGC provided both.

In Memory of
Sergeant JOHN SHARROCK TAYLOR
1024292, Royal Air Force Volunteer Reserve
who died age 28
on 10 February 1942
Son of Annie Taylor, of Whelley; husband of Harriet Taylor, of Whelley.
Remembered with honour
HAIGH (ST. DAVID) CHURCHYARD

Jack's service number enabled me to apply to the Royal Air Force for a copy of his Service Record, which gave me details of the squadron with which he had been serving at the time of his death. In order for the RAF to release the document I had to make a declaration that I was the next of kin. After a moment's thought I realised that, with all of his generation now dead, I was in fact Jack's closest surviving relative, as he and Harriet had not had time to start a family.

I discovered that in early 1942 Jack's squadron had been part of a training establishment flying Wellingtons from Steeple Morden Airfield in Cambridgeshire. A visit to the Steeple Morden website revealed that Jack's name was on the War Memorial there. This in itself gave me a slight jolt, in that my son Richard had been born very close to Steeple Morden and I had often passed the airfield on my way to or from work without knowing that it had any family significance. The service record itself was a fairly stark document but the officer in charge of records was kind enough to write me a personal letter outlining what had happened on the night of 10 February 1942.

Jack had been the Second Pilot of Wellington Mk1C X9905. The aircraft had been on a night-flying exercise from Steeple Morden. The Wellington's engine-driven generator and consequently its radio had failed. It was a murky night and although there had just been a Luftwaffe raid the crew were unable to fix their position in the blackout. The pilot, flying low to look for landmarks, had stalled and nose-dived the aircraft into the ground. The next stage was to find the exact location of the accident. Since Civil Registration began in 1837 every birth, marriage and death has to be registered and the appropriate certificate issued. Thanks to the efforts of a dedicated group of volunteers, millions of such entries have been transcribed from the original records and the indexes for each year and each quarter are available on a search engine called Free BMD. Finding 'our' Taylors among the millions of Taylors listed on any genealogical site has always been something of a challenge but in searching for Jack I was greatly aided by his unusual middle name. Locating a name and an event on Free BMD provides the researcher with the district in which the event occurred, together with a volume and page number. One can then apply for a copy of the certificate.

Jack's death certificate revealed that his aircraft had crashed at Leytonstone, Essex, in busy outer London. Without surprise I discovered that the London Borough of Leytonstone has a website with a section on which interested people post reminiscences of times past. I posted a message asking if anyone had any information about the Wellington bomber crash on the night of Tuesday 10 February 1942. A few days later I received an email message from Joyce Bell, who had not only lived in Leytonstone at the time but actually saw Jack's Wellington crash. She wrote:

> I was eleven at the time. We were at my grandparents' house. The all clear had gone but we could hear a plane flying quite low. My mother decided to go home. I opened the door as the plane hit the ground. The impact threw me along the hallway. Some hours later we came out. The sky was red. The smell was awful. The whole street was covered with fire hoses. Last year I got this PC which gave me the chance to try and trace the six young men that died and just by luck I saw your message. I would be very interested to know about his family.

The Wellington crash had been even more horrific than I had suspected. The aircraft had struck Trinity School, then being used as the Harrow Green ARP depot, and then burst into flames, and in addition to Jack and his five colleagues who included two Canadians and an Australian, five Civil Defence workers had also been killed, a major tragedy for this small, close-knit East End community. Four of the victims were buried in the same grave in Manor Park Cemetery and the local newspaper for 21 February 1942 gives this touching account of their farewell:

> Crowds, including many Civil Defence personnel, lined the footpaths as the cortege of four hearses, followed by the mourners' carriages and the Mayor's and borough officials' car, left the depot and proceeded at walking pace along Beachcroft Road and Harrow Road. Hundreds more people were present at the cemetery, where a guard of honour of Civil Defence men and women awaited the arrival of the cortege.

I was able to respond to Joyce's message by sharing with her some of my stories about Jack, Annie and Jack's wife Dolly. From our later email correspondence it seemed that in spite of the traditional North–South divide which inclines us northerners to think all southerners are rich and effete, we came from very similar environments. Joyce told me:

> Most of the houses where I lived were built in the 1900s. Folks were poor but very proud. Doorsteps were washed and fronts were swept. The high road ran right through the town. Till 1940 you could buy most things. By the end of the war the shops just closed. They had nothing to sell. Food was a problem but gardens were turned over to vegetable plots.
>
> Windows were never there for long. We had a gun anchored on a corner not far from us and another that ran up and down the railway line. We ended up with plywood over the windows. It must have been hell for our parents. At one time we had fifty-six continuous day and night bombings. I watched planes overhead firing at each other. Us kids would jump up and down when a plane was coming down. We always assumed it was a German.

Wreckage of Jack Taylor's aircraft, 1942

Collapse of winding gear at Alexandra Pit
© Wigan Archives Service

Clockwise from top left: group photo of Norman, Jack, Bill, Jim and Harold, Bill Taylor, Jack Taylor, Bill Taylor's soldier's release book

> Harrow Green is now a war memorial at the side of the road with seats and flower beds round it. I watched the lorries and troops passing through for the D Day landings. My grandchildren have asked me to write down my wartime story, which I have done. It wasn't all doom and gloom. It was too dangerous to go out of school. In between raids we had to sign in. When there was a lull we would go back.

Though she loved all her boys, Jack was my grandmother's favourite. He had both a charm and a gravity that she found completely irresistible. On one never to be forgotten shopping day she walked the length of Whelley's straggling main street from Great Acre to home. Remarks, whether innocent or intentional, from five successive neighbours confirmed that all her sons had girlfriends hitherto unintroduced to their mother. Annie arrived home in a smouldering temper to confront them. Mixed with the sense of outrage at having been kept in the dark was the mother's natural protectiveness. Who were these girls? Could they possibly be good enough for her beloved sons or were they fast baggages who would bring shame and disgrace? The tirade rose to its final fling:

'And there's not one of you who'll do me any good!'

Norman, Jim and Bill kept their eyes on the peg rug at their mother's feet. Harold stared out of the lace-curtained window, brooding sulkily. Only Jack met her eyes with the level gaze of the future bomber pilot: 'Mother, wait and see.'

Bowing to the inevitable Annie accepted that young men in their teens and early twenties required a social life and that this would mean some relaxation of the regime. Certain traditions were to be observed. The great square lock on the front door of 169 with its heavy iron key had not been used for many years but as each boy reached his majority at twenty-one he was presented with a copy of the brass key to the new Yale. It was a prized possession and my father kept his key, worn smooth and thin with use, for years after 169 itself had disappeared. Every Saturday night before going to bed Annie and Edie would lay out the boys' supper in covered dishes on the dining table in the middle of the front room. The food was accompanied by five bottles of home-made ginger ale. Electric light had recently been proudly installed by Bill, who was apprenticed to Vic Oldfield, a local electrician with his own small business. Above the table was a central hanging light bulb covered by an inverted pearlescent globe suspended on four thin chains. On Sunday morning, as she rousted them out for Mattins, Annie would quiz the boys about where they had been the night before and what time they had finally arrived home. The answers were usually evasive but, as she told me years later, she had her own rule of thumb for confirming the lateness of their arrival: before going to bed on Saturday night she would always unclip the metal safety guards on the stone ginger ale bottles. From long experience she knew more or less how long the gas pressure would take to pop the corks of the bottles. When she and Edie rose early for Sunday morning Communion all five corks would always be reposing neatly in the bowl of the electric light fitting.

Jack's vivacious wife Harriet hated her given name and was always known as Dolly, which was even less appropriate. The least conventional of my aunts, she treated her formidable mother-in-law with affection and respect but was not the least in awe of her, though Annie was exasperated because Dolly kept Jack's pilot's 'wings' even after her remarriage. I remember Dolly in middle-age, a slim well-dressed blonde with a rough smoker's voice and the rare ability of making even a child feel that he was for the time being the centre of her universe. And naturally she always addressed me as 'Jack'. Much of Jack and Dolly's courtship took place on a tandem with which they travelled the lanes I would explore on my Dawes Dalesman racing bike in the early 1960s. On one occasion they stopped at the top of Parbold Hill to talk with a passer-by, the broad sweep of the coastal plain spread out before them. Then Jack remounted and swept off down the long descent towards his grandfather James's birthplace at Lathom, only to find at the bottom that he had left Dolly a mile behind on the crest of the hill.

Dear Jim,

I received your letter some days ago so excuse the delay in writing to you. Things are pretty well the same here, except that you will see from the address that I have moved to another place about three miles from Basingbourne.

This is a new camp and you know how a place is when things are not quite complete, the usual ten-minute walk for a wash and meal and the only light is from an oil lamp. But why grumble, there must be thousands worse off than I am. By the way, Jim, I have been home for a day twice while I have been here. I went a fortnight ago and I went yesterday (Sunday). I only get about 12 hours but it is a good change.

When I was home I went to see Beattie in the sanatorium and she looks quite well apart from being a bit washed out. The thing that seems to upset her most is the fact that she gets very few letters from our Bill.

I even wrote to him 7 weeks ago but I never got a reply. So I was wondering if you would drop Beattie a line or two Jim. Just to buck her up a bit. I wrote to her about a week ago and if she got one from you it would do her good. Just pull her leg a bit, and if I were you I would send it to mother and she will pass it on because they never know when she might be coming out. I know Dolly is always thrilled when she gets a letter from you and I think Beattie would be the same. Every time Dolly gets one she always writes and tells me she has had a letter from another man, but I always know who she means.

This course here will last until about Feb or March next year but I'm hoping to get home for Christmas or New Year even if it's only for a day.

I hope you're able to make it too, so until then best wishes,

Jack.

Although he was the third of Annie's five sons, it is Jack more than any of the others who fills the shoes of the dead father he can hardly remember. On a forty-eight hour pass from Steeple Morden he braves the excruciatingly slow trains and blackouts of wartime Britain and only manages to spend twelve hours in Wigan during which he finds time to visit my future mother Beatrice who is recovering from a brush with tuberculosis in Whelley Sanatorium. She has received no letters from Bill so Jack's visit and a note from Jim will make all the difference. There is also a tender glimpse of Dolly, gently teasing Jack about her occasional letters from 'another man'.

JIM

I am the child of Annie's youngest child, so my grandmother was sixty-five years old when I was born, but Jim's story provides me with a glimpse of her as the handsome, determined middle-aged woman she was in the 1920s and 1930s. Despite her working-class struggles and, later, her undying gratitude to the socialist creators of the Old Age Pension and the National Health Service, my grandmother was a lifelong Tory who readily offered board and lodging to half a dozen paying guests, all of them visiting policemen who protected her father's Lindsay and Alexandra pits during the great Coal Strike of 1923. Even so, her political credentials were once called into question in a way which still provoked indignation forty years later and which makes me smile whenever I think of it.

In the late 1920s Annie was being courted by a family friend, a master-printer who rejoiced in the splendidly Dickensian label of Ezra Sidebotham. This worthy was wealthy enough to possess a car, a bull-nosed Morris Cowley tourer in which he took my grandmother, with Aunty Edie as chaperone, on trips to Knott End on the coast and even further afield. It says a great deal about Annie's powers of attraction that even though she had five children Ezra proposed to her. I do not know if my grandmother was ever tempted by the luxury represented by Ezra's wealth, but when on one of these trips another vehicle struck and injured a dog and, for whatever motive, he swerved to finish the animal off, that was the end of any chance of real sympathy between them. It was a time of high unemployment and my grandmother's distaste for Ezra did not extend to her turning down his offer of an apprenticeship for Jim. Jim learned his trade at Ezra's print shop in Wigan's ancient Wiend but found his master persistently harsh and unsympathetic. Eventually my grandmother felt she had to go and remonstrate. Ezra outraged her Tory sensibilities by calling her 'a bloody Bolshevik' and felt both the rough edge of her tongue and, very unusually for her, the back of her hand. His treatment of Jim was exemplary ever after.

Jim married Maud Gold, a girl from the village, who was the image of Celia Johnson, the star of *Brief Encounter*. An evangelical Anglican Christian, she sang in the church choir and Jim himself also became more actively involved in the life of the Church. Like all his brothers apart from Harold, Jim served in the forces, though he was not posted abroad and spent most of the Second World War as a drill sergeant in various Army training establishments. Discharged military personnel received a substantial gratuity in addition to the famously ill-fitting demob suit, and Jim eventually used this cash grant towards setting up his own small business at Burscough, close to his grandfather James's village of Lathom. In contrast, and to my mother's considerable distress, my father Bill spent his gratuity on a lavish party in his 'local' to which all their friends and family were invited.

Like many working-class parents, Maud was determined that Joan, their only daughter and David, their only son, would have educational advantages that circumstances had denied herself and Jim. Joan's passing the 11 plus examination and subsequent entry into Wigan Girls' High School was regarded as a direct challenge by my mother Beatrice who declared that her son must do at least as well or we would all be shamed. Joan was two years older than me, blonde, beautiful, with blue eyes and golden curls. I was more than willing for us to be friends but Joan was the kind of little girl who specialises in putting down the male of the species at every opportunity and making it feel inept and grubby. On learning that I detested the diminutive 'Jacky', with which my mother had saddled me, the rest of the family readily agreed to call me Jack or John. Not so Joan, who was still insisting on 'Jacky' when I was a grown man with a wife and children who were puzzled and even slightly offended to hear me so addressed. In her early days at Wigan High School, Joan would arrive for Sunday tea at 169 determined to impress us all with the wonders of her new school, and I remember that all of us, from my grandmother downwards, were quietly delighted when she announced in cut glass tones that on some special occasion her form had presented their teacher with a bow-kwet.

David, who in his graphic and artistic ability resembled our great-grandfather John Taylor, had no affectations at all. He attended Merchant Taylor's School at Crosby but subsequently dropped out of university to enter his father's firm. Burscough Printing Company was then under enormous pressure from a huge contract with the Elkes and Fox biscuit company and David's decision found surprisingly little resistance from his mother. His father enthusiastically welcomed both his son's help and his ideas, and in a period when something of a revolution was taking place in printing the small firm eagerly embraced the new technology. As an occasional visitor to Burscough during the 1970s and 1980s it always seemed to me that Jim and David had the kind of comfortable relationship I had never been able to establish with my father.

'Why have you bought a Mercedes, Uncle? You hardly ever drive these days.'

'The Lad likes it.'

And once with mock melancholy:

'You know, John, my Lad has left home.'

'Where's he gone to, then Uncle?'

'He's bought yon house just across the road.'

When I was child an obligatory feature of our weekly clan gathering at 169 was Evensong at St Stephen's Church. Annie and Edie were founder members of St Stephen's, which had been built in 1928 as an offshoot of St David's. I enjoyed its mellow limestone and its faint odour of sanctity and hymn books and to this day Evensong, a uniquely Anglican ritual, is still a favourite experience whether sung in a great cathedral or a village church. Though Annie pronounced that the Vicar, the Rev. Arthur Wiffen was 'a good minister but a poor preacher' this was thought to be no excuse for restlessness on the part of the young, so as we walked to church, Jim would slip into my pocket a small paper bag which, he solemnly announced, was 'Church Toffee' specially manufactured for consumption during sermons. It proved impossible to quiz him on this or any other issue, his standard reply being that the requested information was 'lay holes for meddlers', a phrase which defeats me to this day. A child said to me the other day 'I can't get you to be serious. You make a joke out of everything!' I used to feel exactly the same about Uncle Jim.

BILL

'It was the war as ruined our Billy.' In what sense was my father ruined? Perhaps my grandmother simply meant that as a soldier in the Royal Corps of Signals from 1939 to 1946 he had learned to drink, smoke and swear. William Thomas Taylor, the youngest, smallest and handsomest of Fred and Annie's five sons, was a year old when his father died of pneumonia in 1918. My mother claimed that Billy had been pampered by his brothers and Aunty Edie and spoiled from birth. The truth, as always, is a lot more complicated and like his favourite brother Jack, Bill demonstrated on a number of occasions that he had the power to puzzle his powerful mother. Annie and Aunty Edie lived tidy lives and one of their ruling principles was not to give trouble. When the air-raid sirens sounded they would rapidly move to the semi-subterranean brick and concrete shelter in the yard of 169. Aunty Edie would carry the sandwiches and a flask of tea which had already been prepared. Annie would slide her hand through the loop in their terrier Gyp's lead so he could not escape if startled by the bombs. Her other hand held the leather attaché case containing the life-insurance policies and other important documents. Prayers were said to an Almighty in whom both had complete faith. If He chose Nazi high explosive as a means of despatching them rapidly to Heaven then, Amen, so be it. Both ladies would of course be wearing clean underwear so that if a German bomb ended their lives that night they would be found with both their spiritual and temporal affairs in order. Much to their consternation, when Bill occasionally came home on leave he found it such a luxury to be able to sleep in a comfortable bed that when the sirens sounded he steadfastly refused to retreat to the air-raid shelter and appeared to sleep perfectly soundly with the prospect of bombs falling all around him.

Bill had served in North Africa, Italy and Austria. When I interrogated him about his war he always claimed that it had been undramatic and his stories tended to concentrate on humorous incidents that had been incidental to the conflict. On one occasion he and Bert, another Lancastrian, had been laying a telephone line during an advance. The normal procedure was to attach the cable at intervals to a tree or other fixed point, but the ground they were traversing had been heavily churned up by vehicles and shellfire. Then they came upon a rigid German corpse, arm raised in his last agony.

'Owd that, mate,' said Bert, looping the cable round the deceased's wrist before they passed on in the direction of the battle.

'Did you kill anybody?'

'Not as far as I know. There were times when we shot at German planes that were strafing our positions but I doubt if we ever hit anything.'

'Were you ever wounded?'

'Only if you count desert sores,' he replied prosaically. 'They were nasty things and had to be lanced by the MO.'

While waiting in line for treatment he had been chatting with a commando who stood over six feet four in his socks.

'What are you in for?'

'Boils. And you?'

'I got shot in the arse.'

He went on to explain that this was a continual hazard for tall men. In putting their heads out of danger they would sometimes forget to keep the other extremity out of the line of fire. I remembered this conversation years later when an ex-soldier colleague told me that at five feet seven I was just the right height for an infantryman.

While attached to the Eighth Army, Bill and his RCS mates had particularly enjoyed their battles of wits with the local traders in North Africa.

'It was a game. The Arabs were trying to do us and we were trying to do them. One time we swapped a big cardboard carton of cigarettes for a similar sized carton of eggs. We checked the top layer of eggs and they were fine. When we got the box back to camp we found that all the other eggs had been blown. The Arabs had exactly the same experience with the cigs, which we'd filled with sawdust. Another time we attached an army blanket to one end of a rope and the other to a motorcycle combination. We buried the rope in the sand and waited for a victim. We sold that blanket at least half a dozen times. Those Arabs really impressed us. Some of them hung on for at least a couple of hundred yards.'

Bill was involved in the Allied invasion of Italy and he liked the Italians. He said they were dreadful soldiers who used too much olive oil and garlic in their cooking, but they knew how to live. In unguarded moments he would irritate my mother by referring sentimentally to a girl called Delia Pasquinelli, the daughter of an Italian Colonel, and my brother and I have since wondered irreverently if we might have a half brother or sister somewhere in Italy. Neapolitans irritated him by singing *Torna a Surriento* at every opportunity but in 1944 in Rome he attended a concert by the great tenor Beniamino Gigli, who had just emerged from the most uncomfortable period of his career.

In his memoirs, published in 1957 Gigli freely admitted that he had sung for the Germans, including Hitler and Goebbels. The Germans had been Italy's allies, so why not? The moment Italy repudiated the alliance and found itself at war with the occupying Nazi forces, Gigli, a loyal Italian, had refused invitations to sing for the former allies who had suddenly become the enemy. In the chaos following the Allied occupation of Rome, Gigli, one of the wealthiest men in Italy, found himself targeted by Giuseppe Albano, the sinister Sicilian gang leader known as Il Gobbo, The Hunchback, who had launched a sustained campaign of defamation and intimidation which included the slur that Gigli had been an active Fascist. Eventually Il Gobbo was shot dead by police and the tenor was able to resume his career with a series of concerts for American and British soldiers. Many years later Gigli, whose records I collected avidly, was to be my special subject on TV's *Mastermind* and when I found that my father had heard him in the flesh I was deeply impressed and not a little envious.

'What was he like?' I asked. Bill paused to consider.

'He was good,' he said finally.

'What about the Germans? Surely there were some good ones too?' I used to ask my father.

'The only good German was a dead German.'

I was irritated by this clichéd reply but Bill immediately went on to disown it. During the months after the war he had been involved in clearing-up operations in Austria, which brought him into daily contact with the defeated enemy.

'Most of them were just like us. Fed up with it all and impatient to get home and see if their families were OK. I once had to sit in the back of a truck guarding a dozen of them with a Tommy gun. There was one little Nazi, ex Hitler Youth, who was trying to get my goat and I was shocked to find that I really felt like popping him. But he was the exception.'

Having studiously avoided promotion throughout the war, Bill found himself an acting NCO in charge of a gang of prisoners who were bulldozing ruined buildings in Vienna. They were a well-behaved lot who could be left to get on with the job when he occasionally went off site. In the chaos following the end of hostilities there was all kinds of German military hardware lying around unattended and, strictly against regulations, Bill had acquired his own transportation, a camouflaged Volkswagen scout car which he used for his excursions into town. His 'trusties' had been well-briefed that if the Military Police were to raid the site Bill would be in trouble if they found the car, but they were ready with a cunning plan, and when the redcaps actually arrived the VW had been deftly bulldozed into a crater and neatly covered with rubble.

Bill was highly intelligent. He had failed the scholarship examination for Wigan Grammar School, perhaps because it was taken only a couple of days after he had sustained a compound fracture of his left arm caused by a friend who had cleverly lassoed his ankles with a skipping rope while he was playing football, but he went on to score 100 per cent in the Matriculation Mathematics paper at Wigan Mining and Technical College. Maths came easily to him and he could effortlessly solve simultaneous equations in his head. He was outraged by my slowness at figures and his attempts to help me with my homework invariably ended in frustration on both sides. Both he and my mother, talented sportspersons, were also baffled by my fumbling efforts on the cricket and football fields and, initially at least, disturbed by my enthusiasm for plays, dressing up and music. My repeated requests for music lessons were dismissed out of hand and it was not until I was twenty-six years old that my mother was finally persuaded to come and hear me sing at Wigan Music Festival. I won the Rose Bowl for the overall top performer in the vocal classes and afterwards she turned to me in amazement exclaiming: 'My God, you can SING!'

I am not sure if Bill ever heard me sing formally, but one Easter I received a phone call from a very agitated church organist whose tenor soloist had suddenly fallen sick. I sight-read a fairly demanding programme and afterwards asked the gentleman how he had come across my name. It turned out that he was an acquaintance of my father who had confidently told him that I could sing anything.

When Bill was in relaxed mood he was excellent company and I enjoyed his stories about his village childhood in the decade following the First World War. He used to tell me how the son of his grandfather's next-door neighbour had been his inseparable playmate who had joined him in all kinds of escapades. One Saturday night when I was in my early teens and, on a rare occasion, my parents had gone out together, there was a knock on the door. A well-dressed middle-aged man stood on the doorstep.

'Good evening. Does Bill Taylor live here?'

'Yes he does, but I'm afraid he's out.'

'Oh, that's a nuisance. I used to know him when we were lads but I moved away from Lancashire a long time ago. Well, I'd better come back later. Please will you tell Bill that Francis Thompson called to see him.'

'Francis Thompson! Carrot tops!'

'My God! How do you know about that?'

'Come in and wait and I'll tell you. Dad will be glad to see you.'

This simple story from the 1920s had become part of family folklore. The two seven-year-olds had dug up and eaten Francis's dad's entire crop of prize carrots and had then carefully replanted the tops complete with their feathery fronds.

Bill liked the variety of his work as an electrician, first for the Lancashire Electric Power Company and later for the North Western Electricity Board. He was particularly happy during the years he worked from their Ormskirk office. He enjoyed driving around the neat, well-kept villages of the coastal plain, with his mate Bernard Sampson in their little electric-blue side-valve Fordson van, and meeting the wide variety of customers who needed their services. One of their regulars was Mrs Ogg, a stately lady with a deep contralto voice and a cut-glass accent. They were fond of her because whenever they visited The Piggeries, as they privately called her palatial home, she always treated them with courtesy and invariably fed them like kings. Even so, as Lancashire lads who normally dropped their aitches, they could not resist a bit of discreet fun:

'Good morning Mrs Hogg.'

'Good morning, William, and kindly remember that it's OGG, young man.'

One day Bill and Bernard arrived to reconnect the electricity for a family who had just moved into their new house.

'Where've you come from, love?' Bernard asked the lady of the house.

'Next door, love,' she replied.

'Really? Bloody nomads, then, aren't you!'

All our neighbours knew that Bill was an electrician and hardly a week passed without somebody calling at the house to request help with some crisis. Gruff but generous, he almost invariably dropped whatever he was doing, picked up his tool bag and went off to solve the problem. He was extremely unworldly about money and too embarrassed to name a charge for his services, though even he was taken aback when my hatchet-faced great-aunt Lily compensated him with a packet of cigarettes for three days' work spent chiselling through oak beams to rewire her 18th-century house in Rowbottom Square. In spite of his willingness to be exploited he did expect certain courtesies to be observed by those who required his services. One wet Saturday evening there was a peremptory knock at the front door. Bill answered it to be confronted by a short, squat, heavily bespectacled man in a belted raincoat and an aggressively positioned flat cap.

'Art tha th' lectric mon?'

'No, flesh and blood like anybody else,' my father responded with ominous suaveness.

'Then get thi coat on. Me leets are off.'

This was one of the occasions on which th' lectric mon did not leap to the rescue.

My grandmother frequently said 'Beatie is a good provider,' and although the compliment irritated her as did almost anything Annie said, it was true and significant. It was true because however slender her apparent resources our family was always well clothed and well fed. It was significant because men, not women, were supposed to be the providers, and though he earned good wages Annie knew that Bill was not a provider in the usual sense of the word. When I was away at university Bill was injured in a freak accident. He was replacing a light bulb in the refrigerator which shattered in his hand, cutting deeply into his right thumb. Microsurgery was necessary to reattach the tendon and during his brief stay in Billinge Hospital his pay advice arrived at home by post. It was a continuing source of irritation that he had always refused to disclose his earnings even to Beatrice, so my brother Stephen, fed up with her harping on the matter, decided to find out the truth once and for all. A couple of minutes with a steaming kettle, the payslip was in his hand and my mother had her answer. The weekly amount Bill gave her for all household expenses, food, utilities, clothes, bus fares, children's pocket money, recreation, school lunches and even petrol for the car, was equal to exactly half his salary. He was keeping the remainder for his own beer and fags and she was well aware that he occasionally cadged cigarettes from her and demanded money when he had run short.

Bill's wages were not the only source of family income because Beatrice had worked throughout most of her married life, something she felt she would not have had to do if my father had been better at providing for his family. She frequently reminded him of these facts and berated him for his heavy smoking and nightly visits to the Hare and Hounds where his closest crony was a scrawny individual whom she contemptuously referred to as 'The Weed'. When Beatrice nagged, Bill would retort heavily that he was entitled to these pleasures because he brought in the lion's share of the money. It was an unfortunate choice of image. Stephen, who was in his early teens at this time had a satirical sense of humour. Unlike mine, his way of coping with the constant bickering was to poke fun at the protagonists. Neither of us would have dared to beard the lion face to face but odd, half-heard scraps of calypso would drift at the edges of the battle zone:

> It's only fair that I go to the Hare
> 'Cos I brings in the lion's share.
>
> In order to get the ale I need
> I go to the Hare and I meet the Weed.

Bill died in 1983. During a very alcoholic lunch when I had flown back from Ecuador fifteen years later for Beatrice's funeral, Stephen and I reminisced about those days. He is seven years my junior and like most elder siblings I have always maintained that he had an easier ride than I did because by the time he arrived Bill and Beatrice had mellowed with age and in any case I had already worn down parental resistance, but there were additional factors at work. With little apparently in common and a definite aversion to his sporting interests, I frequently felt awkward with my father. He could be relaxed and informal but there were times in which he would suddenly adopt the tone of the heavy Victorian father in *Hobson's Choice* and these apparent switches of mood both disturbed and irritated me. The ritual reading of the school report was one of those occasions. As a young teacher in the relaxed 1970s I remember being surprised at the casualness with which some of my pupils would tear open report envelopes which were addressed to their parents. As a child I would never have dared do that. Not even my mother would touch that dreaded buff foolscap envelope, which would rest menacingly on the mantelpiece until my father arrived home some time after six o' clock. These were the days of 'positions' not only in the class as a whole but also for individual subjects. As I later discovered these were often arrived at via some rather dubious mathematical processes, but at that time both teachers and parents seemed to think they were vitally important. To prolong the agony, I was sometimes instructed to open the envelope myself and read the report out aloud at the tea table. It seemed to me that my creditable achievements in such subjects as English and History were brushed aside and it was my execrable performance in Maths which always dominated these painful occasions. Seven years later Bill would attempt with scant success to stage similar rituals with Stephen whose academic performance was in any case much more consistent than mine. Imperturbably my brother would open the envelope and begin to read:

'I came top in English, top in History, second in Geography ...'

'Second! Who BEAT you?' our father would interrupt in his best Hobsonian bass.

'Beat me? Nobody BEAT me. Look.' Stephen spread his arms wide. 'Not a mark.'

It was exactly the right response and everybody, including Bill, dissolved into laughter.

Bill resisted my mother's attempts to persuade him into starting a business of his own, preferring the security of paid employment, so I am still puzzled about something which happened when he was in his mid-fifties. For years he had worked for the North Western Electricity Board, starting as an electrician with the old Lancashire Electric Power Company and later promoted through charge-hand to the foreman stage. When

I was occasionally allowed to join him at work on Saturday mornings, before his lunch-time pint became an established ritual and made my presence inconvenient, the respect and affection his fellow workers had for him was palpable. His bosses also regarded him highly and subsequent promotions took him into the areas of sales and marketing, all of which he handled with his usual flair and efficiency. But he missed the hands-on involvement with real electrical work and some of the administrative problems began to prey on his mind. One morning, as he was driving to work and brooding over some issue, his attention wandered while overtaking another car and he struck an oncoming vehicle a glancing blow. Neither car was more than superficially damaged but Bill was normally a superb driver; he had gained 99% in his Army driving test, the odd point being deducted for his 'bloody civvy street cornering'. The shock of making a potentially lethal error unnerved him and that very day he handed in his notice at NORWEB.

Perhaps he thought that another job would be easy to come by, but he was fifty-four and it was only after a lot of anxiety and a hundred or so applications that he secured an interview with the American engineering firm of Kellog International. In the early 1970s computers were still a recent innovation in industry and there was a shortage of programmers. Bill passed an aptitude test and the Kellogs interviewer told him: 'We'll train you to write programs and after six months you'll be making money for the Company.' After not much more than a week, they scrapped the training programme because Bill had learned everything his teachers had to offer. More than ten years before I so much as touched my first BBC desktop, he was programming huge mainframes like the ones on the bridge of the Starship Enterprise.

Bill shared many of the entrenched prejudices of the working-class male, though these often seemed to be riddled with contradictions. When I developed a passion for vintage cars in my teens he stoutly vetoed my purchase of a dilapidated Bentley, not on the sensible grounds that it would have cost a fortune to renovate and run but because it was 'no fit vehicle for a working man's son'. Though he had a massive contempt for the ageing Churchill as a peacetime leader, he had during his military service strongly disapproved of the practice of promoting officers from the ranks, on the grounds that the hereditary 'officer class' knew what it was doing and should be left alone to do it. Unlike many of his contemporaries he had not the slightest taint of racism or homophobia and, although he took the view that the principal domestic responsibility lay with my working mother, he would often clean, cook and wash up without being asked to. Full of bonhomie outside the house, he was frequently irritable inside it, and one evening in the 1950s when he and Beatrice returned to the house after a rare outing together to watch a film he was practically vibrating with anger. I asked why. My mother explained that on emerging from the cinema they had come across an excited crowd of people standing in a ring around a man who was holding a woman by the hair and beating her with his free hand. Without the slightest hesitation my father had released the terrified woman and sent the bully flying with one well-directed right hook. A member of the crowd had laid a restraining hand on Bill's shoulder and told him in tones of righteous disapproval: 'You shouldn't have done that, mate. She's his wife.'

CHAPTER 8

Very Like a Whale

THROUGHOUT MY BOYHOOD and up to my departure for Lancaster University in 1964, my constant refuge from the bickering and unpredictability of the home front was the little terraced house at 169 Whelley, where Annie and Edie seemed simultaneously to be able to inhabit the present and the past. After a period as colliery foreman, their father James Sharrock had eventually become the Overlooker, or surface manager of the Earl of Crawford's Lindsay and Alexandra coal pits, a post he held until his death. Tall, straight, curly-haired, frock-coated and patriarchally bearded, everybody in the villages knew him, but strangers noting his piercing blue eyes and air of quiet authority, frequently assumed that he was a plain-clothes detective. At seventy-one his wife Elizabeth slipped and fell, breaking her femur. In the early 20th century surgeons had not developed the technique of pinning fractured bone and she never walked again but remained chair-bound, her thigh immobilised with sandbags. When she died in 1917 James was still the vigorous and active Overlooker. He died in harness in 1926 but nearly forty years afterwards he was still a constant presence at 169 Whelley, and not only in reminiscence, for in addition to her many other talents, Aunty Edie was psychic. On a number of uncomfortable occasions she had predicted sudden death. Once, much to the relief of the parents, a sick child had taken a turn for the better, but Edie had seen the little girl entering the gates of Heaven and had sadly shared her vision with my grandmother. Within a few days the child relapsed and died. My grandmother, supremely practical in all things, never doubted Aunty's ability to see things which were beyond

Above: Edie Sharrock

her own perceptive range. Her only requirement was that the inconvenient gift should not be displayed beyond the immediate family. As she reached the last stage of her life, Edie grew less reticent, and one day she entered the parlour when my grandmother and I were entertaining a visitor, and observed calmly:

'I've seen my father.'

'Edie!' my grandmother said warningly.

'When, Aunty?'

'Just now, as I was coming out of the pantry.'

In their late seventies both Annie and Edie were still active and took great pleasure in their occasional visits to family members and a few close friends. Their brothers were long gone. Half-brother George Lowe had survived until 1934 but young Henry, named for his repentant grandfather, had not lived to see his eleventh birthday. Their beloved youngest sibling, John, a talented church organist whose cottage piano had a dummy practice pedal-board, had died in 1912 at the age of twenty-eight, less than two years after his marriage to Margaret Alexander, a Scholes publican's daughter of whom they had thoroughly approved, but their elder sister, my great-aunt Mary, born in 1873 and always known as Polly, was not only alive but vigorously kicking. Aunty Polly fascinated me by inspiring in my grandmother both affection and scandalised irritation in roughly equal degrees. Petite, pretty and vivacious, she had been a rebel against Victorian propriety. In particular she had clashed with her formidable mother. Elizabeth Sharrock was also tiny and determined, with abundant, scraped-back dark hair and an air of ill-suppressed energy. Three hours after giving birth she would be on her hands and knees scrubbing the kitchen floor. She stood for no nonsense. Polly, in a state of exaltation and presuming on her future independence as a wife, had spoken back to her mother as she was dressing for her wedding. She had been silenced by a stinging slap and went with a burning cheek to her nuptials at St George's Church in Standishgate. As a child this story appalled me and it still does, but I have since realised that for Polly's parents and sisters this marriage had been fraught with tensions from the beginning. An insurance agent from Staffordshire, George Matthews was handsome, charming and violent, while Polly would never submit tamely to being bullied. In the 1960s Grandmother and Aunty Edie would recall arriving at their little house in Daisy Hill the moment after George had flung the supper pan at her, Polly sitting at the table, her face grim and frozen, and her long hair matted and clotted with pea soup. They had no children and George's early death released Polly from his tyranny. Unlike so many human beings, she did not repeat her earlier mistake. Like the Wife of Bath she had decided that happiness might lie in domination, and Tom Blundell, her gentle, charming second husband, was happy to let her wear the breeches. She continued to scandalise propriety, toddling off with him to the village pub in her clogs and shawl in an age when hardly any respectable Lancashire woman would have been seen in such a place.

I remember Aunty Polly on visits to Daisy Hill in the late 1940s, a widow once more in her eighties with small, round glasses and waist-length iron-grey hair which was usually gathered into a bun. The excursion was always a great adventure because it involved waiting on the tiny platform of Whelley station until the Wigan–Bolton train arrived to enfold us in its cacophony and smell of hot oil and steam. The equally miniature station at Daisy Hill still had brass paraffin lamps and from there we would walk between hedges white with May to Aunty Polly's little stone terraced cottage with its short flight of steps up to the front door. Polly was fond of her sisters but found them and three of my grandmother's four surviving sons too staid and respectable. Bill, my less conventional father, was her favourite nephew and at some stage during the evening she abandoned the rest of the visitors, took his arm and steered him off to the 'local' as she had once done with Tom. On occasion she was amusingly ruthless. My grandmother recalled sitting with her at teatime when the grocer's delivery boy arrived. It was a hot summer day and he had been pedalling a heavy bicycle and delivering packages up and down the neighbouring stone steps. He looked longingly at the laden tea table and said pathetically: 'Ee, Mrs Blundell, my legs are warchin!'

Aunty Polly received this news with complete equanimity and did not extend the desired invitation. Or as my grandmother put it, lapsing into the same dialect: 'Er leet 'em warch.'

My last memory of Aunty Polly is of her funeral. There was no hearse and no black mourners' cars. We walked behind the coffin which was carried from the village church on a wheeled bier down a green summer lane bright with wild flowers, while black and white fragrant-breathed Friesian cows crowded to the fence to watch us pass. Aunty Polly had been determined to live for the moment and my grandmother recalled with wry affection that the fourpence left in her purse did not cover the outstanding newspaper bill which Annie quietly paid before returning to the cottage. The furniture was worn and worthless. Annie slipped into her handbag a little blue and white ceramic clock before bidding farewell for the last time to Daisy Hill and its eternal springtime. The clock stood on the high mantelshelf of 169 Whelley for another twenty years until Aunty Edie's death, when Annie, nearing ninety, moved in with my Uncle Harold. It never went.

I owe an immeasurable debt to my grandmother who was the single most stabilising influence throughout my childhood and adolescent years. In one of his more approachable moments I remember telling my father that he had been fortunate in having such a tolerant and understanding mother. He replied sourly: 'She ruled us with a rod of iron.'

I quoted this exchange to my grandmother, who smiled and said: 'Bringing up five lads without a father wasn't easy but they don't look too badly on it.'

She knew then what I have come to understand since, that tranquillity is usually easier to accomplish with a grandchild than with a one's own children. Though I sometimes had to submit to guidance I cannot remember a single clash with her and I almost invariably behaved far better in her house than in my own.

Coming from a household where tempers were unpredictable and meals, though often excellent, could arrive at almost any time, I treasured the almost unvarying routine of 169. By the time I got up, the old ladies, who rose at dawn, would have washed, dressed, breakfasted and swept and dusted the house. I could choose to have a substantial breakfast or simply toast and marmalade, after which they would settle in their rocking chairs on each side of the parlour fireplace to read the morning paper or some such magazine as *My Weekly*, *Red Star* or *People's Friend*. Extracts would be read aloud from newspaper articles or from the agony column, often with wry comments. Though intelligent and well-educated according to the standards of the late 19th century, Grandmother and Aunty were not great readers of books. From their schooldays they remembered such novels as *Little Women* and could still comment on them in detail. Surprisingly for inveterate Tories, their daily paper was the *Mirror*, while on Sundays, between Mattins and Evensong, they gravely devoured the *News of the World*'s lurid stories of grisly murder and sexual misconduct, the latter inevitably ending with the reporter's pious assurance that he had made an excuse and left.

Aunty Edie's chair was carefully positioned so that she could look up from her reading and observe passers-by through the net curtains. The comments were ritualistic in tone and even the errors and apparent misconceptions were entirely deliberate.

'There's Mr Cottrell.' (My great-uncle Jack)

'It's "Cockrell", Aunty.'

'He would carry me shopping bag for me t'other day.'

'Aye, he's a proper gentleman even if he is a bit of a fusspot.'

'Mind, I can't allus tell what he says.'

'Well, he's a cockney, you know.'

'He's from Colchester, Aunty.'

'Aye, well, it's same as I say.'

A long pause for staring dreamily across the now derelict mine headgear, then, shades of Hamlet: 'Yon cloud looks just like a whale.'

The nuances of spoken English were extraordinarily subtle. It was a society which could easily tolerate a southerner because he couldn't help sounding different, and the genuine gentry, such as the Earl or the Vicar, who naturally 'talked posh' were also exempt from censure. Farmers, colliers and ancients who spoke Lancashire dialect were treasured but those like my father who had been brought up to speak more or less standard English but deliberately 'talked broad' caused some measure of irritation. Heavy satire was directed at those who used affected language in an attempt to mask their working-class origins, and apocryphal stories abounded:

'Did you hear about the collier who asked his snobbish young wife to buy him a billycan and a tommy tin because he'd got a new job at Owd Nat's Pit? She went to Arkwright's shop in Millgate to purchase a William can and a Thomas tin because her husband was to be employed in old Nathaniel's Coal Factory.'

Sometimes I would be present and take part in these linguistic reflections, sometimes I would be off into the fascinating wilderness of the back garden amid the peppery fume of the blackcurrant bushes, where my grandmother's huge half-wild tomcat Snowy lurked sullenly under the rampant lilacs. Snowy had been brought home as a tiny kitten by my father, who thought his mother would enjoy having a pet to replace her beloved Gyp, who had died of old age, but I knew that supercilious, untouchable, battle-scarred old Snowy was tolerated rather than loved.

'Do you like cats, Grandma?'

'Not really, but I wouldn't do them any harm.'

I have often thought about this conversation and felt that it summed up her attitude to not a few human beings.

When I returned from the garden the centre of operations would have shifted. Aunty would perhaps be making up the beds while Grandmother would have taken up her position beside the range in the back kitchen. On each side of her stood a high mahogany stool. The stool on the left carried an enamel bowl half filled with water, the one on the right a wicker basket of carrots and turnips. An old copy of the Daily Mirror was spread on my grandmother's aproned knee and on this the parings fell as she prepared the vegetables. When enough had been peeled, the newspaper was folded and transferred to the coal fire, where its contents hissed and whistled as they slowly dried out and burned. The washed and chopped vegetables were then placed on the fire in a cast iron pan of salted water to simmer slowly until they were ready to be served for lunch, mashed with butter in an earthenware bowl.

There were weekly variations to the daily routine. On Mondays washing was boiled in an electric 'copper' in the glass lean-to behind the house, filling the nostrils with the smell of Persil and hot aluminium. On Tuesdays the ironing was done, with many time-honoured jokes about bloomers and corsets, the solid flat-irons being heated over the coals. A tiny ornate goffering iron stood on the mantelpiece as a relic of the days of detachable starched cuffs and collars.

The early afternoon was a time of quiet through which the old ladies dozed in their rocking chairs and I could continue my foraging in the garden, raid the biscuit tin, drink lemonade from the cool, stone-flagged larder or explore the books and mementos in the ornate Edwardian sideboard or in my grandmother's dressing table: youthful photographs of my grandmother and grandfather, of Aunty Edie and of my father and his brothers; letters and postcards whose stamps bore portraits of Queen Victoria, Edward VII, George V, George VI and even of a strangely crownless monarch called Edward VIII; ornate black-edged funeral invitations and jet mourning jewellery; golden locks of children's hair secured by thin ribbons; cut-throat razors and their strops; moustache cups, a lacquered cigarette box containing a single mint 1860 farthing; my grandfather's battered silver turnip watch with its key in a Victorian silver match-case; a 'dud' Second World War incendiary bomb; my long-dead great-uncle John's harmonium which could still be coaxed into emitting rusty groans; a huge and ancient valve radio which smelled of hot dust, took an age to warm up and then produced only distant ghostly mutterings which seemed to have travelled immeasurable distances from stations called Hilversum and Athlone. In the best bedroom, Landseer's *Monarch of the Glen* stared down glassily from the faded wallpaper. The one taboo was Aunty's cabin trunk, inherited from her aunt Mary, which was reputed to contain a fabulous sum in gold sovereigns.

When I was still at the infant stage, and sometimes long after that, I would agree that I was worn out from my explorations inside and outside the house and would consent to taking a nap in the small back bedroom, whose low window overlooked the coal shed and the garden wall with its tangle of rambling roses. This room was just big enough to hold the Pirate Chest and a small bamboo table carrying a walnut ink-stand with cut-glass pots, as well as the double bed with its cool, clean cotton sheets, squashy flock pillows, warm woollen blankets and multi-coloured patchwork quilt. The faded wallpaper was printed with roses and the sloping whitewashed ceiling was criss-crossed with fine cracks in which I would see patterns of human and animal faces until I drifted off to sleep. I remember that in my early teens it was my habit before falling asleep to review my day and almost invariably to find something to worry about. On increasingly rare occasions I would decide that there were no causes for anxiety and stretch out luxuriously. Falling asleep in my grandmother's house was always like that.

Though its long main street eventually straggled into Wigan's Scholes, Whelley had all the characteristics of a village, with a church, three pubs, a grocer, a butcher, a baker, a doctor and a large, beefy policeman, 'Bobby' Julian, who proceeded in a leisurely manner towards the various points of the compass on a heavy black bicycle inexorably powered by two size fourteen boots. There was also a doctor's surgery, where Annie and Edie, lifelong Tories, could take grateful advantage of the National Health Service set up by the great reforming post-war socialist government of Clement Attlee, but though they had considerable respect for Dr Gerwood they only consulted him when referred by the village chemist whom they considered to be their infallible guide on medical matters. If Billy Gabbott the pharmacist had been able to straighten his back he would have stood at about six feet eight but a degenerative spinal condition had bowed him into a hoop. Children are often repelled by physical deformity but I always liked visiting Mr Gabbott with his long, bespectacled face and gentle voice. In a poor working-class village he spoke with authority of inexpensive generic remedies that would save both the patient's pocket and the GP's precious time.

Like Miss Marple's St Mary Mead, Whelley provided my childhood with a richly varied supporting cast, the most immediate members of which were the neighbours in our little terrace of four Coal Board cottages.

'Grandmother, it's thundering! Shall I go and get Mrs McKnight?'

Annie and Edie's next-door neighbour Mrs McKnight was the recently bereaved widow of the Wigan Borough Transport Manager, whose name was still embossed on the sides of the town's cherry and white buses, their side panels picked out in gold coach-lines and fleurs de lys. Unlike Annie, a pillar of the Church of England, Mrs McKnight was a Roman Catholic, but religious differences were never an issue in their cordial forty-year relationship. Like my mother Beatrice, my grandmother did not approve of 'neighbouring,' the free exchange of visits and cups of sugar that was a characteristic of so many Lancashire neighbourhoods. Mrs McKnight was of a similar mind and though she absolutely detested the summer thunder and lightning she would have gritted her teeth and hidden in the understairs cupboard rather than impose on us. Naturally, Annie had known about this phobia for years and as soon as the thunder began to roll one of us would always go next door to rescue our neighbour. Mrs McKnight's married son and daughter, John and Frances, regularly visited her, and John still kept at his mother's house a large collection of 78 rpm records which Mrs McKnight would lend me from time to time. John's particular favourite was Johnny Mathis, but I was more interested in the light classical recordings such as the *Blue Danube Waltz*. There was even the odd operatic disc, such as John McCormack's recording of Godard's *Berceuse de Jocelyn*, to which I listened with rapt attention.

At 165, on the other side of Mrs McKnight, lived Mr and Mrs Walsh, a childless couple in their mid-thirties. He was a clerk with the National Coal Board and wore a trilby hat and she was a petite secretary who went to work in smart tailored suits, immaculately straight-seamed nylons and neat little mid-heel court shoes. Annie approved of the Walshes, who were well-spoken, busy and kept themselves to themselves. Mr Walsh was a keen gardener whose small patch did not give adequate scope for his passion, so my grandmother was happy to allow him to take over part of her much bigger but sadly neglected holding.

The house nearest to the railway line at the other end of the row of four was occupied by Mr and Mrs Leyland, whose considerable tribe of offspring probably seemed bigger than it actually was because half-clad children of all sizes and both sexes always seemed to be in swirling motion. Though feckless and untidy, the Leylands were essentially harmless, but I did not have to be told that they were 'not of our class'. It was reliably rumoured that their zinc bath was used only for storing coal and the male members of the family kept pigeons and ferrets, laid snares, shot birds with catapults and air rifles, raided nests and orchards and were generally the scourge of the local gamekeepers. In my grandmother's view all of the lads were destined to be imprisoned in the course of their future careers, if not actually hanged by the neck until dead, while the lasses would almost certainly be nursing several unwanted offspring by the time they reached the official age of consent. These were the days when we spoke of girls getting themselves into trouble, as though they were able to achieve this feat by some process of un-immaculate conception. From her ineffectual attempts to regulate this chaos Alice Leyland, permanently aproned, flat-chested and whippet-thin, was old before her time, while Alf, nominally a miner, seemed eternally to be on the sick. With his pasty face and few locks of grey hair straggling across an otherwise bare and bony skull, he certainly looked unwell. He was one of the very few adults my grandmother referred to by his Christian name and I could tell that this was not a compliment.

'Alf's too sick to work but he's well enough to enjoy his pints and his baccy and a trip to the bookie's.'

It was people such as the Leylands who had caused Jack, twenty years before, to urge his mother to move into a better area, perhaps to one of the larger bay-windowed villas on Springs Bank. His mother's favourite, it was one of the few arguments he had lost.

'I don't like the neighbourhood, Mother.'

'Jack, I live *in* the neighbourhood. I don't live *with* the neighbourhood.'

Jack was being snobbish, but when she put her mind to it, my grandmother could effortlessly out-snob him.

CHAPTER 9

The Girl in the Golden Frame

ON THE WALL of the dim, low-ceilinged living room of our farmhouse in Andalucía, with its massive unsquared beams of poplar, hangs a portrait of a girl in a golden oval frame. It is a studio photograph from the time of the Great War, lightly hand-coloured and completely avoiding the rigid formality often seen in photographs of the period. There is even the hint of a smile. The girl has abundant auburn hair, gathered at the nape of the neck and spreading again in feathery tendrils over her shoulders. It is an open, pretty, even mischievous face with bright eyes and a slightly snub nose. Not perhaps the face to launch a thousand ships, but this young woman would never lack admirers. She is my maternal grandmother Beatrice Adelaide Norcliffe, who died in July 1919 at the age of twenty-one the day after giving birth to her only child, my mother, also called Beatrice Adelaide. In the portrait she wears the diamond brooch and gold locket I remember her daughter wearing when I was a child in the 1950s.

In an age of stolidly traditional names such as Mary Jane and Sarah, Beatrice Adelaide's name says a great deal about the Norcliffe family and in particular about her parents Albert and Caroline. Like the Sharrocks, the Norcliffes are an ancient family, but unlike the Sharrocks who, apart from occasional persons of talent who raised themselves by their own efforts, had never been more than minor country gentry, a number of Norcliffes have held titles of nobility and some have even distinguished themselves on the national scene. Our Norcliffes may have been remotely linked to the aristocratic Norcliffes of Langton Hall near Malton in Yorkshire but if they were I know nothing of it. Albert's grandfather

Above: Beatrice Adelaide Norcliffe

Jonathan, born in 1780 at Stainland in the West Riding, was a cloth maker and by 1871 his son Benjamin, usually called Benny, a late child born in 1821, was established as a wool stapler in Morley, with a wife, Mary Clegg, and eight children of whom my mother's future grandfather was next to the youngest. Like thousands of other boys throughout the country he was named after Prince Albert, Queen Victoria's dynamic husband who, debarred from politics by the unwritten British Constitution, had not been content merely to be a consort but had thrown himself skilfully and energetically into many projects for the betterment of his adopted country.

With a growing family to look after, Mary Norcliffe needed help in the house and by the time of Albert's birth in 1866 at Elland, near Halifax, Benny was earning enough to employ both a resident housekeeper and a maid of all work who lived out. In the West Riding it was almost impossible to avoid some contact with the textile trade and as a boy Albert was employed, like his father before him, in various jobs in the mills. I was brought up to equate Lancashire with cotton and Yorkshire with wool, so it was surprising to find that before going into the wool trade Benny had started his working life as a cotton-twister, and the teenage Albert had been a cotton-piecer. Humble jobs in a textile mill may have been all very well for a start, but Albert, like my other great-grandfathers, James Sharrock and John Taylor, was ambitious. In any case, such work was no basis for married life and Albert had marriage in mind.

The daughter of John Corfield, a millwright, and his wife Elizabeth Rogers, Caroline Sarah Corfield was a Welsh girl from the Marches. Caroline, who had previously been in domestic service in Shrewsbury, had been born in 1860 at Church Stoke in Montgomeryshire, but she looked younger than her age and was careful to keep her year of birth secret from her prospective husband. At twenty-four, Albert had thought he was marrying a girl of his own age but in fact his bride had already turned thirty when they were wed on 18 March 1890 at St James's Church, Halifax. This kind of secrecy was not perhaps the best basis for life together and in less than ten years the marriage was over in all but name.

Albert and Caroline had first set up home at 35 Spring Street, Skircoat and it was here that Albert established his first business venture as a grocer and draper. Though of an earlier era, Caroline was as royal a name as Albert and the names of their children would reflect a similar sense of Victorian middle-class consequence. Their first child was born almost exactly one year after they were wed. They called her Florence, one of the fashionable names of the 1890s after the beautiful city in Tuscany, but inevitably, like most girls of that name, she became Florrie. Although Caroline was far from her Welsh home she did not lack for support through her pregnancy and her daughter's birth, because her elder sister Sinah and brother Samuel, both unmarried, had come up from Wales to be with her. Sam found work in a railway goods yard and Sinah as a worsted-weaver in a woollen mill, and their presence and earnings added to the comfort of the Norcliffe home. Albert Edward Norcliffe, named after the playboy Prince of Wales and future King Edward VII, made his appearance in 1893 and Gilbert in 1896. Albert and Caroline's second and last daughter, Beatrice Adelaide Norcliffe, the girl in the golden frame, was born in 1898.

After the breakdown of Albert and Caroline's marriage the children had stayed with their father and Albert had been obliged to engage a housekeeper. Polly Kirton, a single woman in her thirties with a young daughter, became more than a housekeeper but it was only in 1919, after Caroline's death, in the Menston Pauper Lunatic Asylum near Keighley, where she had been confined for twenty years, that Polly and Albert were able to marry. By this time Albert had shifted his business interests to Lancashire; one of these was the corset shop run by Polly's daughter Ida with the assistance of her husband Bill Bennett, and occasionally their son Benjamin. Benny was olive complexioned, as was my mother, his cousin (an Indian friend seeing her photograph for the first time humorously hailed her as a fellow Punjabi) and my father, not for the first or last time putting two and two together and arriving at five, assumed that there was a Jewish connection and indulged in black humour on the theme that it had been necessary for him to fight the Second World War in order to prevent Hitler from converting my mother and her family into soap.

As a child, I found the corsetry shop slightly embarrassing with its flesh pink satins, steel stiffeners and truncated dummies representing the fuller figure, but apart from Aunt Florrie in distant Yorkshire, the tongue-tied Benny and Ida were my mother's only connection with her Norcliffe origins and she also had a slightly shamefaced and completely misplaced idea that these supposedly well-heeled relatives might eventually 'do something', if not for her then for my brother and myself. In fact the business was not at all the goldmine Beatrice supposed it to be, since by the 1950s corsets were definitely passé as a fashion item and the sparse clientele of Norcliffe's consisted mainly of elderly ladies such as my grandmother and Aunty Edie.

The Norcliffes' move from Yorkshire to Lancashire brought young Beatrice Adelaide Norcliffe into contact with her future husband, John Sydney Hart, youngest son of John Shaw Hart, the fourth of my patriarchal great-grandfathers. Like James Sharrock and John Taylor, John Shaw Hart's name was common currency in the houses of my childhood, partly because he and his wife Jane had brought up my mother Beatrice. A short, square, muscular man, with a big moustache and an even bigger laugh, though he relished his pint in the Silverwell at the far end of Darlington Street East John was a much-respected figure in late-Victorian Wigan. In contrast, his father Jeffrey, born on 3 July 1822 and christened at Wigan parish church, emerges as something of a rascal. Jeffrey was a brass founder, working first at the Peppermill foundry and later at his own Millgate brass works where his son succeeded him in the 1870s, but it is not his metallurgical skills which are of prime interest to me. A quick online trawl through the censuses seems to show that my great-great grandfather was married three times. I write that he 'seems' to have been married because in fact one of his 'marriages' turns out to have been strictly informal. Jeffrey's first wife, Ellen Shaw, was the mother of my great-grandfather John Shaw Hart and his twin Margaret Mary who have different, though of course consecutive birthdays as a result of Ellen's midnight labour. Delving into my family's past I was pleased to find that Ellen's father, my great-great-great grandfather Thomas Shaw, had been a schoolmaster a century and a half before I took up the same profession.

John Shaw Hart

Jane Clough
Hart

John and Jane

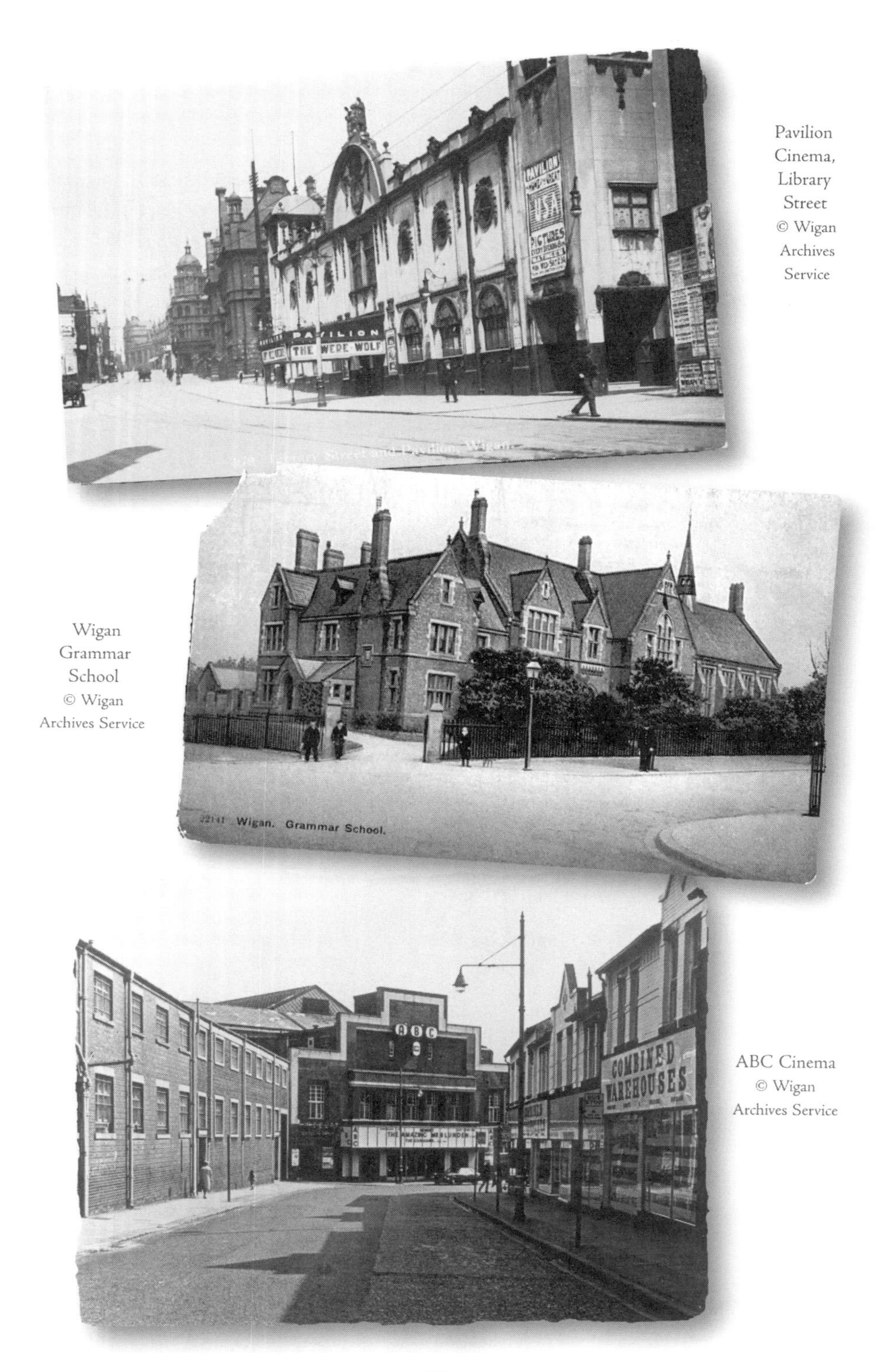

Pavilion Cinema, Library Street © Wigan Archives Service

Wigan Grammar School © Wigan Archives Service

ABC Cinema © Wigan Archives Service

Ellen died of asthma at the age of forty-eight in 1870 and Jeffrey appears not to have wasted much time in mourning, for the Manchester census of the following year shows him, still brass finishing, but with a new wife, Elizabeth, and a stepson, William Bimson in addition to his five Hart children. Bimson is an unusual name, so it is easy to track down Elizabeth in earlier censuses. Born Elizabeth Hallows in Chester in 1833, she had moved to Wigan with her parents when still in single figures, and in 1852, at nineteen, she had married 35-year-old Thomas Bimson, a Liverpudlian railway clerk living in Seddon's Yard. Seeing Elizabeth snugly established in Manchester's Bishopgate with Jeffrey in 1871, I assumed that her husband Thomas had died, but I soon found that this was not so. In fact Thomas was still alive in 1881 fully seven years after Elizabeth, still under her married name of Bimson, had been laid to rest in Wigan cemetery in April 1874. We know that in the 19th century working-class couples in the industrial north of England often cohabited before marriage, but as Jeffrey and Elizabeth had been living 'over th' brush' in a relationship which was not only informal but adulterous, perhaps they had shifted to the anonymity of the metropolis to escape the censure of family and neighbours, though the records show that they soon returned.

Elizabeth's death did not put a stop to Jeffrey's enthusiastic career as a husband, whether informal or sanctified by the church. In 1879 at Wigan parish church he married Mary Ann Kelly, a 43-year-old widow with six children. Mary Ann's husband, Robert Stewart Kelly had died in 1872 and her youngest two Kelly children had been born in 1874 (when Elizabeth Bimson was hardly cold in her grave) and 1876 respectively, which means either that Mary Ann had set a record for human gestation or that Robert was not their father. I suspect, but have not yet been able to prove, that Jeffrey was their dad, though genetic paternity did not appear to be much of an issue for him: he was equally willing to raise his own children and any others who came his way. The fact that Mary Jane's mother, who lived with her and Jeffrey, was a professional midwife, may have been seen as an added blessing.

Jeffrey's son John Shaw Hart was known locally to be something of a Renaissance man, with a well-equipped workshop behind his house in Darlington Street where he repaired everything from shoes through motor cycles to clocks and antique furniture, often turning perfect spare parts on his lathes. A serjeant with the Wigan Volunteers (the 'sergeant' spelling did not come in until much later) he was also a crack shot who, with his broad grin, bristling moustache and round spectacles, looked remarkably like US president Theodore Roosevelt. As a young man his fascination with all things mechanical had brought him into the orbit of Richard Clough.

The Cloughs were a Lancashire family, though Richard's grandfather had been working in Birmingham when Richard's father Charles was born in 1815, the year Wellington and Blücher finally defeated Napoleon Bonaparte at Waterloo. Richard was born in 1839 in the Cloughs' native Bolton and, like his father was an engineer in the true sense rather than merely an 'engine tenter' like my other great-great-grandfather John Lowe. He had originally come to Wigan to maintain the machinery of the Trencherfield cotton mill in Wallgate, now part of the world-famous Wigan Pier Heritage complex, where he lodged with the family of the Manager, James Healey, and, in true Victorian upwardly mobile manner, married the Healeys' daughter Ellen when they were both in their teens. Their first daughter, Jane, born at Trencherfield Cottages when Ellen was barely seventeen years old, did not survive, but a second Jane, the vivacious child who was to become my great-grandmother, arrived in 1861. John Shaw Hart married Jane Clough at St Thomas's Church Wigan on 4 September 1886 and it was a love match which only ended with their deaths within a few months of each other fifty-six years later.

Before the outbreak of the Great War in 1914 two of John and Jane's four sons, Jeffrey and Richard, had emigrated to the United States of America, Jeffrey to work for English Electric in Bridgeport Connecticut and Richard for General Motors in Detroit. I never met Richard but Jeffrey returned to Wigan from time to time to see his sisters, my great-aunts Ellen and Margaret. On one such trip in about 1960, when I was fourteen years old, I was very impressed to learn that he and his second wife Grace had sailed from New York on the *Queen Mary* and were planning to return by air. Quiet, smiling great-uncle Jeff was the complete antithesis of the rich, loud insensitive American returnee of British legend but I was desperately conscious of the huge economic gulf between the two sides of my family. I was fascinated by cars and quickly extracted from Jeff that he drove a Chrysler New Yorker sedan in not one but *three* shades of metallic green. It was of course automatic, and had a huge V8 engine, two-tone leather upholstery, whitewall tyres, electric windows and tinted glass. In contrast, my father drove a 1955 sit-up-and-beg Ford Popular, which, I defensively maintained to Jeff, was far superior in quality to tinny, flashy Yankee creations.

'Show me,' said Jeff tolerantly and I led him to the 'backs' behind our two-up-two-down in Whelley's Bradshaw Street. He gazed impassively at our diminutive fawn 'Pop' with its 1930s styling and red rexine upholstery.

'Lift the hood.'

'Don't you mean the bonnet?'

'Lift it.'

Uncle Jeff stood for a moment regarding the quasi-antique squat, square 1172cc side-valve engine.

'Is that the motor?'

'Yes.'

'My generator's as big as that.'

The two Hart sons who did not emigrate served on the Western Front during the Great War and my grandfather, John Sydney, after whom I was named, still technically a driver in the Royal Field Artillery, was on leave on the day in July 1919 when he registered both his daughter's birth and his young wife's death. After his demobilisation Sydney and his baby daughter moved in with his parents, John and Jane and it was in her grandparents' house that my mother grew up in the years between the two world wars. Before the war Sydney had followed his father's profession of brass finishing but after his discharge from the army, where he had been used to working with the horses which dragged the gun limbers, he became for a time a milkman with a pony and cart, only later returning to engineering. He was one of those fresh-faced young men who always looked years younger than his age and when Beatrice rode with him during school holidays or weekends customers frequently assumed that he was her brother. She enjoyed going on the milk round and she loved the pony, a circus veteran with a tendency to follow any band in the vicinity, and an expert at wheedling carrots and other titbits out of the customers.

If Sydney's customers had looked a little more closely they might have noticed the lines of strain faintly etched on a face which had seen far too much of the horrors of the Western Front. I never knew my grandfather, who died of stomach cancer four years before I was born, but the old black and white photographs tell a story which is as clear as any words could be. In a family group where the other youngsters are skylarking, Sydney stands with his arms tenderly around a frail great-grandmother. Jack and Margaret Cockrell had a happy marriage but it had its stormy moments. In the first of a pair of snapshots taken in about 1930 Jack stands masterfully behind a seated Margaret, every tense line of whose body proclaims that they have quarrelled. In the second snap, Sydney has taken Jack's place and his sister is visibly comforted.

The house where my mother grew up at 71 Darlington Street was only a few doors away from the one where George Orwell lodged when he was researching *The Road to Wigan Pier* during the same period. While staying in Wigan Orwell became friendly with a young man called Syd Smith who ran a newsagents and magazine stall in the Old Arcade. Syd's son Trevor was to be my contemporary at Wigan Grammar School and later developed the business into Smiths of Wigan, which still flourishes in Mesnes Street today, selling a wide range of books and other items. His father was quietly proud of his connection with the author but the famous book was not well thought of in Wigan because it presented a picture of unrelieved deprivation and squalor. Orwell's hosts were dirty, uncivilised and kept full chamber pots under the filthy kitchen table. As in every other Lancashire working-class house I ever visited, cleanliness was an obsession in my mother's childhood home and Jane Clough was a stickler for order and propriety. The interior of the large terraced house was regularly scoured within an inch of its life. Brass oil lamps tinkled with cut-crystal lustre shades. A great bronze clock, whose pendulum consisted of a pair of Watteau lovers spooning on a swing, ticked beneath a gleaming glass dome and the circular mahogany dining table with its eight matching balloon-back chairs shone like oiled silk.

Sydney Hart's youngest sibling Margaret, born in 1900 when her parents were thirty-nine years old, survived to surpass her elder sister Ellen's ninety-nine years by celebrating her hundredth birthday in the first year of the twenty-first century, having lived in the reigns of Victoria, Edward VII, George V, Edward VIII, George VI and Elizabeth II. She remained unmarried for the first eight years of my mother's life and Beatrice grew up to think of her as an adored elder sister who danced the Charleston and the Black Bottom and was the embodiment of the jazz age and the roaring twenties. In 1927 Margaret met an Essex boy who had served with the King's Royal Rifles during the Great War. Jack 's name suited him: a swarthy, dapper little bantam of a man with an assertive beak of a nose, a perky strut and an unruly comb of black hair which had to be brilliantined into submission. Born in Colchester in 1898, Jack first came to Wigan as a result of his sister Lily's marriage to Margaret's brother Jim. Pretty, petite, curly-headed, gamine, in her fringed dresses and swinging flapper beads, Margaret's provincial sophistication was no match for the charms of the suave southerner with the exotic accent, the spats, the wing collars and flowing striped silk cravats. When she told him she was pregnant Jack did what many a man has done before and since. He panicked and bolted. Margaret's brothers, Jack's fellow Great War veterans Jim and Sydney, caught him before the London train had left Wigan's Wallgate Station and returned him under military escort to the arms of his beloved. The group in the wedding photograph is tense. Margaret is unsmiling and Jack wears an air of thin-lipped resignation. Sydney and Jim are determined and Lily looks ready to knit at the foot of any guillotine. Even Beatrice, who has not yet achieved the striking good looks which will arrive in her teens and remain with her into old age, looks bored and quite uncharacteristically gormless.

Wedding of Margaret and Jack Cockrell. Back row L–R, Jim Hart, Lily Cockrell Hart, Sydney Hart
Front row L–R, Beatrice Hart, Margaret, Jack, Gwen Hart

Great-uncle Jim died in 1949 when I was three years old, but Aunt Lily was destined to become one of the extensive cast of characters who enlivened my childhood. She lived in a big, low-beamed 18th century house in the strange little secret enclave of Wigan's Rowbottom Square between the back of Timberlake's garage and Grimes's music shop, and she was handsome, acid-tongued and kept a parrot which delighted in mimicking her saltier expletives. On one occasion, when she was on her best behaviour and entertaining guests to tea with the best china and the lace doilies, this bird convulsed the company by confiding conversationally to the Rector of Wigan that 'Lily's a bugger!'

My mother's cousins, Aunt Ellen's daughter Doris and Aunt Lily's daughter Gwen, were Beatrice's inseparable companions during their teens and early twenties, when they had been thoroughly addicted to films of all kinds from musicals to the macabre. It was during a Boris Karloff movie that Gwen emitted a piercing shriek because Beatrice, crouching behind the seat in front of her and desperately trying to avoid biting her own nails, had bitten her cousin's finger instead. Aunt Margaret, too, was to be a lifelong friend and ally to Beatrice and both she and Jack, who was never subdued for long, were a major influence on the course of both her life and mine.

In 1924, when Beatrice was only five years old, her father Sydney remarried. Alice Gormally was a plain Roman Catholic spinster with a codfish eye and an extended family which claimed all of her attention and much of his. Beatrice felt that she had been orphaned for the second time. She adored her father but the fact that he did not take her with him into his new home at Moore Street East in Whelley was a source of deep sorrow throughout her life. She was immensely grateful to her grandparents, John and Jane, but there was an important sense in which she always felt that she had started life rootless and at a disadvantage, especially when confronted by contemporaries from more conventional homes with two parents. Like her future husband Bill, my mother Beatrice was intelligent but, outside certain clearly defined areas of expertise, very insecure. When one of the partners is like this, a marriage can work. When both are like it, the relationship is destined for some very uneasy moments. One of the fields in which Beatrice was supremely confident was that of swimming, which was to become both an avocation and a career. Her early talent was encouraged by her uncle, Jack Cockrell, himself a powerful swimmer, but she rapidly surpassed him in both style and stamina and by the time she left school in 1933 at the age of fourteen to work at Mark Williams's pork butcher's shop in the Market Place she was already an acknowledged star of the Wigan Ladies' Swimming Team, winning armfuls of cups, shields and medals throughout the North West. Later she was to teach generations of Wigan swimmers at the public baths where Jack was Superintendent.

Beatrice always regretted her limited education and I remember that when she was in her early forties and I was doing my A Levels, she decided that she would study by correspondence for a pre-nursing qualification. She started off well and though she had not written a 'composition' since leaving school at fourteen, the essays she showed me were lucid and well constructed. Suddenly the project was abandoned and I have never known why. She always rose at five in the morning to do her household chores before going to work. Perhaps the additional burden of studying was just too much for her. Perhaps it was lack of encouragement from the rest of us. Though I took a slight interest in her nursing course I was occupied with my own forthcoming examinations and with the business of being a turbulent adolescent, and it would never have occurred to Bill to encourage her in doing anything out of the normal routine. Formal studying was quietly dropped, though Beatrice would later read many of my university literature texts and comment perceptively on them.

'This Fanny Hill's a clever lass, but she's never done a decent day's work in all her life!'

A latter-day Mrs Morell, when I was a little boy my mother would take me onto her knee and tell me gently: 'You will never get married because you see how horrible it is.'

She and Bill had first known each other at secondary school and had later met again when they were both in a sanatorium recovering from diphtheria. They were both exceptionally attractive young people and appeared to be naturally suited, but the compatibility was superficial. Beatrice was both romantic and a natural go-getter, while Bill combined exceptional intellectual and practical ability with a lack of ambition that Beatrice found utterly baffling. Both had tempers and an apparently natural command of invective and it seems to me that throughout my childhood they fought like cat and dog over every conceivable issue. One major cause of conflict was that Bill was content to live permanently in rented accommodation while Beatrice desperately wanted her own home, and it was only in the early 1960s, after they had been married for twenty years that she and I finally bullied him into taking the plunge and buying a bungalow on a new Wigan Corporation development in Pemberton.

Beatrice had been desperate to set up her own home but even before her marriage she had been quietly entertaining second thoughts. Bill had been close to the end of his course at the basic training camp at Prestatyn. He had been given a weekend pass and rather than waste any part of the time on the tedious, slow, wartime stopping train to Wigan and back, he persuaded Beatrice to make the trip to North Wales and meet him when he came off duty on the Friday evening. She arrived only to be told that Bill had gone. He had been posted to Salisbury in the south of England. The news was broken to Beatrice by a young second lieutenant. He was simply fulfilling a duty and was quite unprepared for the effect of Beatrice's perfect heart-shaped face and flawless complexion. She was also smitten. They spent the weekend together and by the time he escorted her to the railway station on Sunday night he had already proposed marriage. Beatrice did not lose her head. As a working-class girl she was aware of the gulf between herself and this scion of the officer class. She told the young lieutenant that feelings engendered by holiday romances were unreliable but if after a month he still felt that he wanted to know her better he should write to her.

Beatrice arrived home full of her adventure. Her mother had died at her birth. Her father had remarried and had never invited her to share his new home. Confiding in her elderly grandparents would have been impossible. She poured out the story to her still youthful aunt, Margaret Cockrell, whom she trusted as an elder sister.

Beatrice Taylor née Hart
(left)

Wigan Baths opening season,
1935
© Wigan Archives Service

Walking Day, Aspull, 1912
© Wigan Archives Service

Textiles factory workers
© Wigan Archives Service

'He never wrote,' she concluded, 'so that was that. I got on with my life and two years later I married your Dad. It was only after the war was over that Margaret confessed that he HAD written.'

In destroying the young officer's letter Margaret had acted in keeping with a tribal taboo which governed working-class society in 1940s England, a taboo which still holds good in rural Africa, India and many other communities to this day: no member shall rock the tribal boat, least of all by forming a liaison with a member of another tribe.

My parents' wedding photographs in 1942 tell a poignant story. Beatrice's father, my grandfather Sydney Hart, has died painfully of stomach cancer a few weeks before. My father's favourite brother Jack, who ought to have been best man, has been in his grave for less than four months. Newly widowed at twenty-nine, Dolly is caught obliquely and impassively by the camera as she busies herself with her duties as Matron of Honour. Of my father's brothers Harold, in a reserved occupation, and Jim, based at an Army training establishment in the United Kingdom, are present but Norman is away serving in Palestine. Aunty Edie looks frankly grim and my grandmother, who adored her beautiful dead son, has obviously screwed her courage to the sticking place. Over eighty, Jane Clough is no longer the confident, bustling, buxom Jane shown joyously fooling around on John's motorcycle in old black and white pictures from twenty-five years before. She is old and frail, her small, pinched face shadowed by her hat, and a grimacing fox fur wound tightly round her neck against the late spring chill. She also has lost a son. At sixty-two my grandmother Annie is still a handsome matron who tops Jane by a head. She has drawn the old woman's arm under her own and holds her gloved hand comfortingly in her own.

CHAPTER 10

Rain & Rexine

My earliest memory is not so much a picture as a sense impression. I am in my pram and it is raining. Outside the world is damp and chilly; inside there are warm blankets and the smell of the pram's rexine lining, which has stayed with me so vividly that the hooded interior of a sports car still brings babyhood flooding back. Later I am standing looking at my mother over the circular top of Jane Clough's mahogany dining table, which she is polishing. The sunbeams coming in through the window behind her are making the dust motes glitter and dance, surrounding her dark brown hair with a nimbus of moving light. And she is beautiful. My eyes are just level with the top of the table.

In the attic, beyond the uncarpeted third flight of stairs, the bare floorboards are layered with soft dust and there are cobwebs and my mother's bicycle. She seats me on the high sprung saddle and we go round and round the room, leaving tyre tracks in the dust. When I become three I have a tricycle of my own which also lives in the attic. The possibilities intrigue me: people go up and down the stairs on foot; why should not a boy ride down them on a trike? My mother picked me out of the wreckage, comforted my tears and stilled my first agonised yells. Dettol, not the cissified modern stuff but the authentic traditional hell-brew that looked like brandy and stung like nettles, was applied to my lacerated hands and knees. This was the last time I descended the attic stairs by wheeled transport. In future more conventional means: banisters, tea-trays, even feet, would be employed. The world was large and unexplored; the possibilities seemed endless.

Above: Beatrice Adelaide Taylor née Hart

Just before the winter dawn I would wake and come to sudden and complete consciousness, as I do now more than fifty years later. Perhaps passing headlights – in my memory they belong always to one of the first British streamlined cars, an Austin A40 Devon – had found a chink in the bedroom curtains. Once awake I would not sleep again but would lie, wrapped in the bedclothes, listening perhaps to the sound of a railway engine moving out of the sidings down Shed Street. Then a different noise: wood and metal on flagstone pavements; a shambling syncopated rhythmic clatter, starting quietly and far away but growing to a roar which filled the echoing cañon between the houses. Then into sight swept an army of flat-capped men in shabby overcoats and mackintoshes. Tommy tins swung from their belts. Their iron-shod clogs struck sparks from the pavement. They were the early shift heading for the colliery. Their white faces shone in the moonlight. Hours later they would head wearily back along the same route towards home. Many pits still had no bathing facilities and the miners returned in their pit dirt to wash in a zinc bath in front of the living room fire. Once as a small boy I surveyed a bus-load of homeward-bound miners with some disapproval: 'What a lot of dirty men!' Then, catching sight of the only clean passenger, I added thoughtfully: 'I suppose your mummy's wiped YOU.'

The wealth that built the town, decked it in Victorian public splendour, raised steeples and monuments, trimmed with ermine the very robes of its civic leaders, stocked its library with books and filled its grammar school with deserving poor boys, was clawed out of the same pits by the ancestors of the same men. In Wigan today there are no working pits and the miners are a memory. Val and I left the town in 1969 and when we returned for family visits during the 1970s and 1980s a few of the pit headgears could still be seen rusting and motionless but the children who played in the deserted fan-housings had no idea that they once contained the machinery that ventilated an underground city.

These memories and impressions belong to the earliest period of my life when we lived in a rented terraced house at 272 Warrington Road, Ince, near Wigan. The house was on the corner of Shed Street in front of the railway engine sheds and had no bathroom or inside toilet. We washed in the brown earthenware kitchen sink and bathed at the Wigan Public Baths. In addition to my parents, Beatrice and Bill, and myself, the family consisted of Judy, our highly intelligent border collie bitch, and a tabby cat named Dusty. Judy was exactly my own age but dogs mature faster than children and she could out-think most of the humans I knew. She walked perfectly to heel and it was never necessary to keep her on a leash. The traffic in Wigan Market Place was directed by a policeman on point duty. One day, as Bill waited the signal to cross with Judy sitting neatly at his side, the policeman walked over to him and my father thought he was about to be rebuked for not having her on the leash. The policeman merely said:

'That's a cracking bitch you have there. She always drops down like that every morning and waits for my signal before going across to the butcher's for her bone.'

Normally Judy was beautifully obedient but she and Bill had a regular Sunday ritual of which both perfectly understood the rules.

'YOU are not coming to Grandma's, you black bitch. You are staying at home.'

Her chin on her front paws Judy would regard him impassively from under her brown eyebrows, the only part of her lithe body that was not either black or white. The family would duly catch the Ince bus to Wigan and the New Springs bus to Whelley and always Judy would already be waiting for us by the fireside at 169. She had a wicked sense of humour and would tease the window cleaner, who was terrified of dogs. When he came for his money he would position his ladder and run up it immediately after knocking at the door. She eagerly awaited coal deliveries because the coalman's handsome sandy dog was her son, and every week they had a touchingly enthusiastic reunion. Her benevolence had its limitations, though, and when roused she could be formidable. In the early 1950s there were still a few gas street lamps and the lamplighter had once struck her and laid her cheek open with his metal pole. After that, however surreptitiously he tiptoed past the house she would growl deep in her throat and the hair would rise along her back. Three years after his attack she knocked him to the ground and stared intently into his face. I do not think she would have bitten him and in any case my father called her off before any damage could be done, but she had made her point.

It was at 272 Warrington Road that I first became aware of the tensions which ran throughout my parents' marriage. Bill liked to round off each evening with several pints of Walkers' 'flatrib' in the convivial atmosphere of the Old Hall Hotel a few doors away from our home. Such pubs were havens of light and comfort for men from the mean terraces. The Old Hall was an Edwardian building, full of bevelled glass, wrought iron, mahogany and deep-buttoned upholstery in faded velvet, fragrant with beer and tobacco smoke, where my father and his friends played darts and skittles and hotly debated the fortunes of Brian Nordgren and Wigan's other great Rugby League stars. I was one of the reasons why my parents seldom went out together. Sometimes they would plan to go to the cinema, but like my son Richard thirty years later I loved the night and I resisted unconsciousness. I used every emotional ploy to keep my parents by my side.

'Please don't leave me!' I would cry, knowing that my mother would not abandon me awake and pleading.

Sometimes she would successfully resort to subterfuge. I loved animals and felt very emotionally attached to my dog and cat. My mother would sing softly:

> Daddy wouldn't buy me a bow wow.
> Daddy wouldn't buy me a bow wow.
> I've got a little cat
> And I'm very fond of that
> But I'd rather have a bow wow wow.

If the ploy worked I would weep and drift off to sleep. If not my father, in exasperation, went by himself to the Old Hall.

I suppose most mothers are vulnerable to the 'Don't leave me!' tactic. Mine was particularly so because I had already been on the verge of leaving her permanently. Asthma was very inadequately understood in the 1950s and the nearest mine came to being diagnosed was the vague statement that I had 'a weak chest'. In fact I was extremely allergic not only to house dust but, among other things, to feathers and cats (we had a budgerigar and our cat had occasional litters of kittens with which, naturally, I played). Both my parents smoked increasingly heavily, another cause of irritation, though at the time everybody seemed to regard it as an inevitable fact of life. None of these causes was diagnosed and, apart from my supposedly delicate constitution, my health problems were ascribed to the dampness of our house and to the general air pollution of industrial Lancashire. On occasions the finger of suspicion was pointed at Judy, but with one rather odd exception I have never had the slightest allergic reaction to dogs. My mother also hinted jealously that my grandmother's frequent 'enticing' of me into dark, poky 169, with its smoky coal grates, was also bad for my chest.

Asthma in itself was bad enough but far more serious was the fact that it laid me open to infection. In winter, the slightest cold would go straight to the chest and rapidly become bronchitis, with my passages congested with thick yellow phlegm. Breathing in was searingly painful and as any asthmatic knows, breathing out was even worse. Under the new free National Health system the doctors prescribed, Mr Gabbott supplied 'bottle' after bottle and I reeked of Vicks and camphorated oil. Useless proprietary medicines cluttered the cupboards and nothing seemed to bring relief. In her anxiety my mother bundled me up in blankets and shawls and carried me the mile or so to the Baths flat and Aunt Margaret, always her guru and her refuge. A scalding kaolin poultice was applied. Surrounded by anxious faces I was put into a huge feather bed in a dimly lit bedroom heated to stifling point by a large three-bar electric fire which smelled of ancient burning dust. A thick feather eiderdown was tucked up to my chin. The next thing I was aware of was the moustached face of our family doctor peering over me through his horn-rimmed glasses. Old Dr Graham had never learned to drive a car and, for both him and his chauffeur to be turned out in the middle of the night, things had to be serious. The killing eiderdown was rolled back, a cold stethoscope was applied and the doctor tapped my chest with the ends of his fingers.

'Take him to hospital.'

I was no more than four at the time and I retain only a vague impression of the yellow ambulance, the red blankets and the kindly ambulance men. At the Royal Albert Edward Infirmary in Wigan Lane my mother and I were put into a single room and my silver-painted bed was covered with a transparent plastic oxygen tent. I must have felt better almost immediately because I caught sight of the steel cylinders standing upright nearby and asked my male nurse: 'What are those things?'

'They're little men who are going to help you breathe better.'

I suppose I must eventually have slept, though I doubt if my mother did as she sat in a hard chair by my bedside. The room was at the front of the building, quite close to the Casualty Department, and it seems to me that for a long time I tranquilly watched the lights of the ambulances tracking backwards and forwards across the ceiling.

Penicillin was the new wonder drug and I responded rapidly to it, though I did not enjoy the frequent injections. As soon as my breathing stabilised I was shifted into Upper Johnson Ward which was full of other children and it was there, strange to relate, that

I spent one of the most enjoyable Christmases of my life. The ward was festooned with brightly coloured decorations and we played party games such as 'Pass the Parcel'. Nurses in starched caps and blue, red-lined capes came to sing carols and when Sister wasn't looking they and the younger doctors involved themselves in a rather incomprehensible ritual involving a sprig of mistletoe. On Christmas Day visiting hours were relaxed and parents arrived with armfuls of presents. Beatrice and Bill, understandably choked with emotion that their only child had to spend Christmas in hospital, were dumbfounded when I thanked them politely for their gifts and told them they could go home. With typical childish callousness I was having fun with my friends and did not wish to be interrupted.

My parents' particular present was much more than an armful. It was an Austin pedal racing car, with the swept tail characteristic of the real racers of that era, and in all respects it was superior to every other pedal car I have ever seen. The bodywork was pressed from the same heavy-gauge steel Austin used in their road cars and painted to the same standard. The detachable curved bonnet was held in place by two thick leather straps and the wheels had proper track-rods and real pneumatic tyres with deep tread. Even the engine looked convincing, with genuine spark plugs and a distributor. All in all, this masterpiece had only one defect, which was soon to emerge. Christmas is not Christmas without a tree and that year Upper Johnson Ward had a beauty, standing about twelve feet high, with dense, glossy dark green foliage and the classic fat pyramidal Christmas tree shape. It had been lovingly decorated by the nurses with tinsel, coloured glass baubles and cotton wool snow, and from its pinnacle a golden angel with a trumpet gazed down the length of the ward. My racing car had caused a lot of interest among the other children and we took it in turns to pedal up and down the ward, though we rapidly discovered that with three or four pushers we could reach a much higher speed than with one child pedalling. The problem was that the Austin was not really intended to travel fast and its brakes were almost non-existent. Seated in the cockpit and fancying myself as Stirling Moss, I egged on my team to new heights of daring. The ward, which looked long from our childish height, proved shorter than we had bargained for. The car struck the Christmas tree head on and for a moment it hung poised at an angle before it crashed down enveloping us in swathes of tinsel and scratchy conifer-scented branches. Ornaments smashed, ricocheted and rolled in all directions. The ward door stood open and I believe one of the baubles even ended up in Lower Johnson Ward. This was the end of motoring as far as the Infirmary was concerned and when my embarrassed parents arrived for their next visit they were firmly instructed to take the Austin home with them.

When I was seven years old we moved from Ince to Millgate, a steep cobbled street close to Wigan town centre. I cannot remember when my fascination with history began, but it was certainly in full flower when I was still in single figures and living in the middle of this ancient settlement. Although much of the town had been rebuilt in Victorian times there were still enough old buildings to stimulate the imagination of a child newly enrolled in the National and Blue Coat Church of England Primary School, which was said to have its origins in a school which had originally met in medieval times in the tower of All Saints parish church. Two thousand years before, Wigan had been a Roman fort known as Coccium. It is not mentioned in the *Domesday Book* but by 1246 it was important enough to receive a charter from King Henry III as one of only four Royal Boroughs of Lancashire. During the English Civil War, the town was staunchly Royalist, which was partly due to the fact that the Earl of Derby, Lancashire's premier magnate and commander of the king's forces in Northern England, made it his headquarters. In 1648 Oliver Cromwell himself besieged Royalists holed up in the parish church tower and stabled his horses in the nave. Over three hundred years later, when I was a pupil at the Blue Coat School, the curate showed us children panels from a medieval stained glass window which had been hidden in the false back of a vestry cupboard to save it from destruction at the time. The Battle of Wigan Lane, the last engagement of the English Civil War was fought outside Wigan on the banks of the River Douglas on 25 August 1651. A local worthy, Sir Thomas Tyldesley, was killed. His monument still stands in Wigan Lane and I remember sketching it as part of a school project. The Earl of Derby, James Stanley, was subsequently arrested and executed at Parliamentarian Bolton. His headless body lay in state at royalist Wigan's parish church. By deserting Richard III during the Battle of Bosworth Field the Stanleys had been instrumental in ensuring the accession of the Tudors. The Civil War was one of the few occasions on which they found themselves on the losing side, though the monarchy was restored in 1660 and with it the family's fortunes and those of Wigan, which was presented with a jewelled ceremonial sword by the new king, Charles II, as a mark of its loyalty.

When I lived in Millgate in the 1950s I had no idea that my great-great-grandfather, brass founder Jeffrey Hart, had lived there ninety years before. The 1861 census presents an extraordinarily rich tapestry from an age in which, despite the industrialisation of heavy industry, individual craftsmen still held their own. Millgate in the 1860s was the setting for a Dickens novel. In addition to the main street, sloping from the Wiend gently towards the Market Place and steeply in the other direction towards the River Douglas, there were pubs such as the Ship, the Albion, the Horseshoe and the Mitre and numerous 'yards' where, in addition to the predictable spinning, weaving and mining skills, Jeffrey's neighbours plied such trades as blacksmith, whitesmith, cooper, sawyer, washerwoman, clogger, tallow chandler, nurse, police constable, chemist, jeweller, tripe dealer, master bricklayer, cabinet maker, pawnbroker, brass lamp maker, upholsterer, flock dealer and cup seller. At number 30 Millgate lived the patriarchal Elias Glencross, silk and woollen dyer, whose daughter Jane was to marry Jeffrey's nephew William Ashurst, orphaned by the early death of his parents Richard and Mary, who ran a boat chandlery near Scholes Bridge. The Glencross family was clearly of considerable wealth and consequence, and one of Elias's grandsons, John James Dix Glencross, who died in 1893, has an exquisitely beautiful and surprisingly well-preserved gravestone a few yards inside the gate and just to the left of the main thoroughfare of Wigan cemetery. As if the romance of all this bustling commerce were not enough, a few doors away from Jeffrey lived Thomas Higham, Bellman and

Sword Bearer to the Corporation of Wigan, while at number 64 Millgate Samuel Lorne, a comedian from Birmingham, and Wallingford musician John Francis lived with Elizabeth and Louisa, their 'theatrical' London wives. It gives me a small thrill of pleasure to think that when I lived at 62 Millgate, the home in 1861 of the Misses Green, provision dealers, I was only a party wall away from these colourful Victorian ghosts.

There were still three pubs. At the top, near the Market Place, stood the faded mahogany and bevelled glass elegance of the Ship Inn, where forty years previously my grandfather Fred had enjoyed his weekly couple of pints on the way home from Haydock Park Races. At the bottom, beyond the Bath Hotel and the Horseshoe, Scholes Bridge spanned the murky waters of the River Douglas. From there the road rose steeply again along length of Scholes, crowded with crumbling terraced houses, shops and pubs, past Norcliffe's corsetry shop to the villages of my Taylor history, Whelley, Aspull and Haigh. Two blocks to the west, in Darlington Street, lay my mother's childhood home, the house of Aunt Margaret's father, my great-grandfather, John Shaw Hart. One side of Millgate was dominated by the Baths and the rear of the imposing Edwardian brick and terracotta edifice of the Wigan Mining and Technical College. The other, our side, was lined with old houses interspersed with alleyways which gave on to 'closes' of dwellings, each grouped around a central court. Some of the names, such as 'Jews Yard', recalled a Wigan long gone.

Number 62 Millgate was a tall, narrow, three-storey mid-19th-century brick terrace house whose airy high-ceilinged living rooms boasted bevelled picture rails and substantial sash windows. The bedrooms were warmed in winter by decorated wrought-iron fireplaces. In its time it had been the home of substantial independent tradespeople whose servants had occupied the third floor, but by our time it was well past its heyday and the dusty and untenanted attic with its flaking distempered walls held only a rusting iron bedstead on which my father had installed a home-made radio aerial consisting of a large square board wrapped in coils of wire. One night the whole family woke in the small hours, transfixed with terror, to hear a ghostly harp twanging plaintively from the empty room. I remember my father's silhouette on the wall as he nervously climbed the third flight of stairs brandishing a poker. With a dramatic crash he threw open the door of the attic room to reveal the source of the phantom music: my large skewbald pet rabbit Peter happily bouncing up and down on the radio antenna and clearly enjoying the racket he was making.

Although Wigan, and Millgate, had changed a lot since my great-grandparents' day some things had remained the same, though they have since given way to what we used to call progress. The macro age was far in the future and we still did our shopping in a variety of stores. The nearest thing we had to a supermarket, and in fact its forerunner, was the Co-operative Wholesale Society's store, known in Wigan as the Co-op and always pronounced in a distinctively Wigan way. From the age of about ten it was my task before Saturday dinner to take my mother's list to the Darlington Street 'Kworp' and stagger back with the weekly 'order' in two loaded shopping bags. I frequently had to 'change hands' on the journey and would just as often protest to Beatrice that it would be a lot simpler to shop at Toppings in Harrogate Street.

'Aye, and a lot dearer an' all, with a penny or tuppence on everything in them little shops. Th' Kworp's better and cheaper and you get divvy an' all,' she would retort, and my barge-toting and bale-lifting would continue for yet another week. It wasn't a totally wasted experience. In those days there was no such thing as pre-packaging and I was fascinated by the wrapping skills of the white aproned shop assistants. Hams and other cooked meats were sliced with a whirring, razor-sharp wheel and deftly enveloped in grease-proofing. Sugar was poured onto the thin blue paper to which it has given its name and squarely wrapped with hospital corners. Sweets and smaller quantities of dry goods were cascaded into paper cones. Unlike with modern packaging there was no wastage and the discarded wrapping could be re-used for fire-lighting or even a child's drawings. An old-fashioned grocer's in Delhi still follows the same system, though Indian supermarkets are now joining their western counterparts in polluting the planet with pointless plastic tat.

Sometimes I would be sent on errands to other neighbouring shops. Walshes sold fragrantly smelling leather soles and all kinds of brads and nails by the pound from deep bins in front of their long zinc-topped counter. Hunters the chemists in the Market Place had mahogany-fronted drawers labelled 'Ipec' and 'Pot Nit' and coloured glass jars in its 18th-century gob-stoppered bow window. Bakers cleaned, repaired and even made clocks and one of their grandest long-casers stood in the shop, its dial chased with gold and its silver-clad weights and pendulum resplendent behind gleaming bevelled glass. In Library Street a few hundred yards from our front door, was Timberlakes, not exactly a shop but Wigan's oldest and most prestigious motor dealers, into whose showroom window I gazed with longing. Apart from the Dewhursts at the corner tobacconists (an ancient yellow-windowed Morris Ten after their new Hillman brake had presumably been repossessed) nobody in Millgate had a car and owning one would have seemed the height of luxury. Like all small boys I liked the new models, the Austin Somersets and Atlantic convertibles, but I particularly lusted after the earlier classic models of the thirties and forties, a few of which Timberlakes always seemed to have in stock. The cars of this era not only looked like cars with their spoke wheels, running boards and walnut dashboards, they also smelled like cars, a rich combination of petrol, oil, wax and old leather. In vain I tried to interest my parents in investing in a sage green Alvis Fourteen with twin Windtone horns or a powder blue Armstrong Siddeley Hurricane sports tourer with a sphinx badge crowning its slatted chrome radiator grille. Beatrice was all for the idea but Bill was cautious. Eventually he agreed to buy a midnight-blue 1939 Morris Ten which was in absolutely stunning condition. The man from Circular Garage in Poolstock was due to deliver it on the very morning we were to set off for our holiday at the Cockrells' north Welsh bungalow and I was beside myself with excitement. When he finally arrived he was driving not the Morris but a much less attractive Standard. He told us some cock and bull story about not having known that the Morris had already been spoken for when he sold it to us, but he had obviously taken an extra tenner or two from some other customer. Clearly we were expected to settle for the Standard, but Bill, unsurprisingly, told him graphically what he could do with it. We were all disappointed and, a child of eight or nine, I wept bitterly, but it was not until several years later that we were to own our own car.

My fascination with post-vintage cars has since surfaced at odd, usually inconvenient times, and I have been known to claim, not entirely convincingly, that while supposedly reading for my BA I sacrificed the chance of a first-class degree to the demands of various mistresses, including a 1936 Riley Merlin, a 1939 MG TA and a 1948 Triumph Roadster (later to be the chosen transportation of Sergeant Bergerac, the TV detective). When I was fifteen I owned a share in an ancient Morris Eight which my friends and I drove untaxed, uninsured and totally illegally in the country lanes near Haigh. It went well but had a tendency towards the palsy because of worn kingpins. We bought it for seven pounds ten from a fly-by-night dealer on one of the slum-clearance lots down Prescot Street, where the air was richly perfumed by Gallaghers glue factory. It was a fascinating area, full of multi-coloured pre-war wrecks with bald tyres, mildewed upholstery and sagging springs and when I later read Steinbeck's *The Grapes of Wrath* it all came flooding vividly back to me. When in later life I have succumbed to the allure of yet another elderly charmer I always tell Val 'It could be worse. Some men spend all their money on floozies, not flivvers.'

Living in Millgate in the 1950s also meant that we were close to Wigan Public Baths where my mother worked as a swimming teacher, and to my mother's closest living relative, her Aunt Margaret, who was married to my great-uncle Jack, the Baths Superintendent. They lived with their fat spaniel, Kep, in a large, sprawling flat on the Baths premises a couple of hundred yards from our front door. Aunt Margaret and Uncle Jack Cockrell's fascinating flat was part of the Baths complex, which also included function rooms and, in winter, a dance hall with a polished wooden floor installed over the larger of the two pools. Downstairs there was a small living room and a poky kitchen-galley, but a narrow twisting staircase led up to another level, to my aunt and uncle's ornate high-ceilinged double bedroom where I had once nearly died of pneumonia, and my uncle's austere dressing room with his single bed and his walnut dressing table with its silver-backed hair brushes. Beyond this was another enormous room, virtually a ballroom, with a broad bay window set into an Edwardian candle-snuffer turret. This room, known as 'The Lumber Room' was full of discarded furniture and treasures. Here in drawers and cupboards long unopened I discovered the spurs my grandfather John Sydney Hart had worn as a driver in the Royal Field Artillery, my great-uncle Jack's spats from Twenties, the Hornby Dublo train set once played with by their now grown-up son Jacky, and the family Bible which had sketchy reminiscences of Hart births penned in John Shaw Hart's shaky copperplate. In the window seat stood a mahogany and brass music box almost a yard across. Though this creaked and wheezed a little when wound with its great brass lever, it still resonantly played twenty or so classics: the *Minute Waltz*, the *Anvil Chorus* and so on. At this stage in my life I was becoming enraptured with such melodies and I would sit for hours coaxing the machine through its repertoire, oblivious of exhortations from below to go out and get some fresh air.

Beyond the Lumber Room there was another flight of stairs which led to a pleasantly furnished flatlet where we had lived for a few weeks before moving into our new home across the road, and beyond that a door that opened into The Cafe (pronounced Caffy), which was let for functions and receptions. This pleasant, carpeted room at the top of the building was one of my favourite resorts. It was seldom used during the daytime and its double doors were heavily padded to exclude noise from the pools below. It had an old upright Bechstein piano which smelled of port wine. I remember going there stealthily with a purpose one day in my fifteenth year. I had become fascinated by the human voice and in spite of having always been to shut up whenever I had joined in the folk songs at school, I had started to think that I might be able to teach myself to sing. My voice had broken some time previously and I had asked a musical friend at school to define a note I ought to be able to sing. He had indicated the F in the middle of the tenor range and so at the first opportunity I had climbed stealthily to The Cafe to try possibilities. My footsteps were hushed on the thick carpeting, the Saturday sunlight muted by the net curtains at the high windows. Tentatively I approached the Bechstein and lifted the lid to expose the yellowing ivory keys. I found middle C and slid my finger hesitantly down the scale to the white note on the left of the group of three black ones. I pressed it and the old piano spoke, soft, plangent and ghostly in the quiet of the afternoon. Breathily, hesitantly I tried to match my voice to the sound. No good. Perhaps I was indeed tone-deaf as everyone had insisted. Yet my ear was good enough to tell me that the note I had produced was different from that I had struck from the piano. Try again. Still wide. Another idea: clatter up and down the keys; make a barrel-organ skirling, awful in the hitherto silence, to forget the erroneous pitch I had produced; walk around the room to relax; come back to the piano and just sing a note, any note, sustain it, then try to find it by running my fingers up and down the keyboard. Yes! Eureka! The noise I was making with my voice perceptibly coincided with the noise made by pressing one of the keys. Which? The black one to the right of the white note above my original F: A flat. More than forty years later having been a principal in several hundred performances from *The Messiah* to *The Marriage of Figaro* I remember my first solo note, and the sense of triumph it caused, as if it had been yesterday.

Another major advantage of moving to the centre of Wigan was the fact that there were six cinemas within a quarter of a mile of my home: The Court, the Princes, the County, the Empire, the ABC Ritz and the ornate Pavilion in Library Street, where John Shaw Hart's eldest daughter, my great-aunt Ellen, worked as a cleaner, not because she needed the money but because she enjoyed the company. During the school holidays you could watch an afternoon show at the 'Pav' for six old pence. The 'Road' films starred Bing Crosby, Bob Hope and Dorothy Lamour, who looked rather like my younger Aunty Edie would have done had she gone in for swim suits and sarongs. I watched *The Road to Bali* five times and each time the giant octopus came slithering aboard our heroes' sailing ship I covered my face and hid behind the seat back in front of me. I also enjoyed Bob Hope's performances in *Paleface and Son of Paleface*. As always, he played the amiable sap who had to be rescued from trouble by his more competent partner, in this case the splendid Jane Russell, a crack shot cowgirl with a firm, square jaw and a heroic bosom artfully lifted into maximum prominence, though not, according to her own statement, by Howard Hughes's legendary cantilever bra. Although it was Jane who routed the bad guys, it was Bob himself who located the treasure by accidentally shooting the moose's head in which it had been concealed, and thereby releasing a shower of gold into his startled lap.

Another duo I liked was that of Dean Martin and Jerry Lewis, and I never forgave Dean for ending the partnership. My favourite films were, and still are for that matter, costume dramas in which swashes, whatever they might be, were well and truly buckled. Of all the subsequent versions of the Robin Hood story, serious or light-hearted, the 1952 Disney film with Richard Todd gave me tremendous pleasure and still continues to do so. Richard Greene's 1950s TV serial had its points, notably Alan Wheatley as a silkily villainous public-school cad of a Sheriff, but by its very nature its writers had to keep inventing new stories which were not in the original saga. The Disney version closely followed the various medieval ballads, including Robin's quarterstaff confrontation with Little John (a twinkling but rather miscast James Robertson Justice). Above all, in Elton Hayes, it had a ravishingly convincing Allen-a-Dale who really could play the lute and had a voice that makes me think of old ale and polished conkers. To my mind, Hayes, with his luminous eyes and long, pointed face, even looked medieval.

Adults often argue about whether or not films and TV influence children's behaviour. I can state with absolute certainty that they do. *The Black Shield of Falworth*, a truly dreadful 'medieval' epic starring Tony Curtis, complete with famous 1950s haircut and Bronx accent, fired my imagination more than many greater works of art could have done, and I was determined to replicate its bogus deeds of derring-do. One of the amenities provided by the Baths was a machine which dispensed a particularly sickly and obnoxious hair dressing called Brylcreem. This concoction arrived in shining five-gallon tins which looked very similar to the jousting helmets in the Curtis epic. A few minutes' business in the Baths workshop with a hacksaw and a pair of tin snips and my helmet had an eye slit. A couple of judicious taps with a hammer and punch produced a socket in the top of the helmet into which a plume could be inserted. It was summer and my mother had placed an arrangement of brightly-dyed dried tropical grasses in the best room's fireplace. These provided the plume. Finding a shield was no problem. There were several in the Baths lumber room left over from the Coronation decorations of 1953. I chose a white one with the red cross of St George and quickly added a rope hand-grip. A broom handle, or brush steel as we called it, was pressed into service as a lance. Now for the charger: in those days Wigan town centre lads used to build 'trolleys', engineless wooden go-karts with pram wheels from Joe Calderbank's scrap yard down by Central Park. The large back wheels were on a fixed axle. Steering was provided by a loop of rope attached to the crossbar which turned on a central nut and bolt and carried the smaller front wheels. The contraption, which had no brakes, went like a rocket downhill but needed a team of pushers uphill or on the flat. Conservative riders sat upright and controlled direction with the guide rope, while the more adventurous assumed a belly-down position steering with hands on the crossbar. The disadvantage of this pose was that if you encountered a hard obstruction the face got there first.

Medievally accoutred with crusader shield and Brylcreem tin helmet I mounted my trusty steed, set my lance in rest, and pushed off along the pavement down Millgate and veered right into Hewlett Street. Plume fluttering bravely in the breeze and gathering speed I swept majestically around the wide curve into busy Library Street with its bus stands. Here disaster lurked. It was late afternoon at the end of the working day. The New Springs Bus was late and its queue had straggled across the pavement right in my path.

'Look out!'

'What?'

'No brakes!'

'No what?'

No evasive action was possible and in any case, knights are expected to sweep ladies off their feet and carry them away astride their destriers, and this is exactly what I did. In my case the lady was not young but she was undoubtedly a lady, though in the event neither her language nor her behaviour were exactly ladylike. In those days old ladies still dressed like old ladies in feathered bonnets and tailored two-piece suits with frilly blouses and lace jabots. It was an old lady dressed exactly like this and carrying an ancient rolled umbrella that I scooped aboard my charger and into my lap in my frenzied passage through that rapidly scattering bus queue, showing her bloomers to the fascinated multitude. Except for her outraged dignity she was quite unhurt and extremely vocal. Calling down well-deserved maledictions upon my person and my knightly ancestry she attacked my helmeted head with surprising vigour and also her rolled umbrella.

At Christmas my mother or my great-aunt Margaret would take me to the Hippodrome theatre in King Street to see a pantomime such as *Babes in the Wood or Aladdin*. The palmy days of the 'Hip' were behind it and it was only later that I learned that its faded plush auditorium had once resounded to the voices of the great pre-war Covent Garden tenors such as Heddle Nash and Walter Widdop, home-grown film stars such as George Formby and Gracie Fields and Shakespearean 'heavies' like Frederick Valk, whom my future mother-in-law would remember as Othello in the 1930s. But my fascination with live theatre was still some way ahead and for the time being it was still the cinema which gripped me.

On Saturday mornings the ABC Ritz cinema in Station Road ran the 'Minors', a club for school-age children, which showed a combination of short films, serials and cartoons. One series which riveted us to our plush seats was *Flash Gordon*, starring Larry 'Buster' Crabbe as the eponymous hero and Jean Rogers as Dale Arden, his beautiful and scantily clad companion. The series was based on a 1934 comic strip and the ambience was both kitsch and camp, with Art Deco spaceships which looked like horizontally mobile Chrysler Buildings and appeared to be powered by Fifth of November sparklers. We enthusiastically cheered Flash's exploits and noisily booed his arch-enemy, Emperor Ming the Merciless, played with silky menace by Charles Middleton. Over twenty years later a new generation of children had been introduced to the same characters by the TV cartoon series and the 1980 feature film with Max von Sydow in the role of Ming. Like the original Ming, he wore a Mephistophelian beard and moustache, with the upper cheeks shaven. I had hoped my own beard and moustache, grown for a production of Shakespeare's *Twelfth Night* had more of a Van Dyke appearance, but apparently not, because the day I took up my new post as Deputy Headmaster of Queen Elizabeth's Grammar School, Gainsborough in Lincolnshire, I was immediately hailed as the Emperor Ming, a title I proudly held until I left to take up my first headship four years later.

Roy Rogers was a cowboy star whose short movies I enjoyed at the Minors. He had a handsome, high-cheeked Slavic face, wore a white Stetson and, when he was not singing ballads about the joys of the open prairie, chased black-hatted plug-uglies on a beautiful palomino stallion called Trigger, accompanied by a clever Alsatian named Bullet. Unlike Wayne and Stewart, who frequently got themselves muddy, dusty, bruised and even bleeding, Roy was a dude who spoke like a college professor and wore well-pressed pants, expensive high-heeled boots and a two-tone shirt with an immaculately tied bandana. His nickel-plated twin Colts were mother-of-pearl-handled and the bullets in his belt always seemed to be made of silver, as if he were in permanent pursuit of vampires. In some episodes he had a beautiful female companion, Dale Evans, his real-life wife whose on-screen relationship with him was left vague to avoid antagonising his youthful admirers. I do not recall that they ever kissed and I am sure if they had done so the theatre would have erupted in one of the cacophonies of stamping, booing, whistling and seat thumping we reserved for such soppy displays of sentimentality. Roy was an engaging personality but probably not one of Hollywood's greatest actors, though he was undoubtedly one of its shrewdest businessmen and many younger readers who have no knowledge of him on the screen will be familiar with his name from seeing it on the chains of motels and family restaurants he founded throughout the USA. As for Trigger, when he died Roy could not bear to part with him and had him stuffed.

The Wild West invaded our everyday lives much more than medieval Hollywood ever did and most of us, including Anne Dewhurst, the street's only cowgirl, played games of Cowboys and Indians. For Bobby Sherrington, the grandson of Old Bob, the landlord of the Bath Hotel, being a cowboy was less a game than a way of life. At weekends and every evening after school, he dressed in the full outfit, including cowboy boots, checked shirt with red bandana, soft leather waistcoat and wide-flared chaps, all topped off with a Hopalong Cassidy high-crowned Stetson. Bobby always spoke in an American drawl and of course he went armed to the teeth. Not for him the flimsy plastic which was creeping into our lives via Japan and Hong Kong. His twin six guns, which fired satisfyingly noisy percussion caps, were of heavy die-cast metal, his suede bandoliers held weighty bullets which looked exactly like the real thing, and for long-range work he carried a heavy replica Winchester repeater with a solid wooden stock. It was this fine weapon which on one memorable occasion got him into serious Injun trouble.

The whole gang was present on the 'Brew' which was what we called the vacant lot close to my home, and we had built a very satisfying stockade out of discarded cartons and other miscellaneous rubbish. This fort was being defended by the cowboys against a circling horde of yelling Indians armed with improvised spears, bows and arrows, tomahawks and deadly plastic scalping knives. For some reason I was always quite happy to be an Indian and in this role I led an enthusiastic charge against the cardboard ramparts of the white-eyes. We had all seen movies in which the desperate defender, his ammunition exhausted, reverses his empty rifle, swings it by the barrel and brings the butt crashing down on the head of some hapless brave. In his excitement and thirst for realism this was exactly what Bobby now did to me. The bloody cut on the scalp and the subsequent bruising, were of less importance to me than my fury with this idiot who could not tell the difference between play and grievous bodily harm. My expression must have said it all, because Bobby took one look at my outraged face, abandoned the fort and ran for his life, pursued by a savage hell-bent on revenge. We pelted down Millgate, panting heavily, with Bobby heading for the sanctuary of the Bath Hotel. The short flight of stone steps up to the ornate Edwardian entrance made him stumble but he had pushed open the heavy door with its engraved glass panels and polished brass fittings before I managed with a last desperate effort to fling myself full length and grab him by a trailing heel. He came down on the coloured tiles of the lobby with a satisfying crash and I was comfortably seated on his chest and getting into the rhythm of pounding his skull into the tessellated pavement when his father, Wilf Sherrington, fortunately arrived to declare the match a draw and haul his shocked son off to the bunkhouse.

The Bath Hotel featured in our lives in various ways. Its name reflected not only Wigan's Edwardian Public Baths, which stood on the opposite side of Millgate, but also an older mineral spa which had existed long before Peter Platt received the Rector's permission to sink the first coalmine on the same site in 1619. In the 1950s the landlord of the Bath Hotel was Old Bob Sherrington, a kindly Falstaffian figure who was the grandfather of Bobby the Kid. Old Bob was a good friend of the Baths Superintendent, my great-uncle Jack Cockrell, and I suspect that he was also a fellow Freemason. On occasions I remember visiting the pub out of hours with Uncle Jack, when I was allowed a bottle of pop while the two of them drank strong Mazzawattee tea laced with navy rum. Old Bob's daughter-in-law, Bobby the Kid's mother Madge, was from Preston, only a few miles away, but she spoke rather differently from us. My father said it was because she was trying to sound 'long-curtained and bay-windowed' and she certainly had a tendency to drop names, telling us she had been at school with both the great footballer Tom Finney and the trumpeter Eddie Calvert, both of them distinguished sons of her native town.

A major Millgate occasion centring on the Bath Hotel was the coronation of Queen Elizabeth II on 2 June 1953. My father and the other young men worked hard to decorate the street with coloured bunting and painted royal insignia of lions and unicorns. Only the Sherringtons had a television set and all of us children sat cross-legged and fascinated throughout the ceremony from Westminster Abbey, as the Archbishop of Canterbury anointed the young Queen with the holy oils and placed the heavy crown on her head. She smiled, apparently completely at ease, throughout the long service and afterwards drove through the streets of London in a golden coach between ranks of cheering crowds, many of whom had travelled from every corner of the world to be there. Of all the dignitaries in the procession, the huge, smiling Queen Salote of Tonga was one of the most popular with us children. In her open landau she was accompanied by a small equerry and when Noël Coward was asked who he was he replied, mercifully off-sound, 'I think he's her lunch.'

After the telecast we had our own procession, with several of us togged up as pages in satin-knee breeches and Anne Dewhurst as a regal Queen Elizabeth in a simulated ermine robe and a convincing cardboard crown with jewels made of coloured glass. As at a church fete, there were organised games and the Glynn brothers, burly young miners who lived at number 58, challenged all comers to an improvised wrestling match on a cardboard square laid out on the Brew. It was at these times that I was proud of my father Bill who, though small, was in his physical prime, and much lither and faster than his lumbering opponents, and easily ran rings around them.

Soon after the coronation the new young Queen herself, with her high, girlish voice and brilliant smile, came on an official visit to Wigan accompanied by her tall, handsome husband, and we Blue Coat children were taken to see her drive through the centre of

Bill and Beatrice's wedding car. The Bath Hotel stands in the background

town in what would now be described as a Rolls Royce 'queenmobile'. I immediately fell in love with her and was convinced that amongst the seething crowds in Market Street she had smiled directly at me. In the early 1950s 78 rpm records were just giving way to twelve-inch LPs and seven-inch EPs. Still very much the innocent, the joke exchanged by two of my older friends passed straight over my head:

'What's the Queen's favourite record?'

'I don't know. What IS the Queen's favourite record?'

'Magic Moments, on Philip's seven incher.'

It is inevitable, I suppose, that one looks back through rose-tinted spectacles. My grandmother and great-aunts almost invariably emphasised the positive aspects of their Victorian childhood and compared them unfavourably with what came afterwards. When I listen to news reports of child murder and molestation and the slaughter of the innocent for political ends I tend to do the same. There were murders in 1950s England, and as we shall see in a later chapter, one of them came very close to home, but it was an era in which even careful parents like mine felt comfortable with the fact that during the school holidays their children might wander widely, come home when they were hungry, and sometimes not even then. One hot summer, stripped to the waist, I fried a couple of pounds of sausages over a fire in the Bottling Wood sector of the Haigh Plantation and I can vividly remember discovering that it would have been a good idea to prick them first. One of our favourite Millgate games, which could go on for hours, was Skilly, involving rival teams hunting each other through the yards, ginnels and alleyways which surrounded our ancient street. Sometimes the game would spill over into neighbouring streets, though the 'all-round-town-jumping-on-and-off-buses' version was only tried once before it was firmly vetoed by parents. On Sundays when the Baths was closed, I even managed to sneak in my friends to play in the huge labyrinthine building. On one occasion we tied Colin Dewhurst to a pillar in the dance hall, wandered off and forgot him when we went home to tea. Very belated apologies, Colin, if you ever read this.

Any reader who has managed to stay with my story this far will be in no doubt that I enjoyed most of my childhood, but for many years my parents were the major aspect of my early life which was not surrounded by a rosy nostalgic glow, and I am convinced that their twenty-five years of guerrilla warfare was the major cause of the thread of anxiety which has run all the way through my adult life and still bedevils it from time to time. One day during the early 1990s, reading *Death of a Salesman* with my International Baccalaureate class in El Salvador, I asked them:

'How many of you have said "I'm not going to make the same mistakes my parents made"?'

All the hands went up.

'We all say it,' I told them. 'Now tell me something a little more profound.'

Alicia smiled and said 'I'll make different ones.'

While I hope I have avoided repeating most of my parents' mistakes there is no doubt I have made some of my own. Writing this book has helped me not only to come nearer to understanding some of the errors Bill and Beatrice made but also to appreciate the ones they avoided. Like all children who are not getting their own way I would sometimes whine.

'It's not fair!'

'It's not that,' my father would agree infuriatingly. 'Th' Fair comes only once a year and tha doesn't like noather coconuts nor black-eyed peas so I don't know why tha moiders abeht it.'

I sometimes wonder if fairness is overrated. Purely by accident, with a plywood skimmer (the word 'frisbee' was still far in the future), I broke the plate-glass window of Walsh's hardware shop in Millgate, confessed immediately, and got clouted for it by my father. It wasn't fair but I got over it and filed the experience away to emerge later when I was dealing with my own children's mischief. Once during the summer holidays I decided to provide a picnic for my friends. My parents were at work and our house was locked, but I slipped up the sash of the kitchen window and climbed in to raid my piggy bank for the money to buy the picnic supplies. My great-uncle Jack Cockrell later heard my mother berating me for wasting my money, got hold of the wrong end of the stick and confined me to barracks for burgling our house. When I tried to explain that the handful of small change had been saved out of my weekly pocket money he refused to listen and I abandoned my protest. It wasn't fair but I was confident in Jack's affection for me and I knew the affair was a storm in a teacup. It did, however, occur to me that no good came of saving money if you couldn't spend it as you wished, an idea which became a cast-iron certainty when my mother withdrew the small balance in my Trustee Savings Bank account in order to purchase my brother's pram in 1953. Children do learn from their parents, but what they learn is sometimes unpredictable. I like the story of the man who was determined to toilet-train his pet monkey, so every time it messed on the floor he smacked its bottom and threw it out of the window. Eventually the monkey learned. Whenever it messed on the floor it would smack its own bottom and jump out of the window.

Margaret Cockrell née Hart

Jack Cockrell was one of the pillars of my young life and on one occasion I was the agonised and unwitting cause of a temporary breach between him and my father Bill. Although for much of the time they co-existed peaceably, both were volatile and frequently irascible little men who could easily rub each other up the wrong way. The Cockrells had a timber holiday bungalow on a hilltop with spectacular views of the Vale of Llangollen and the two families would often spend holidays there at Easter time, in summer or in the October half-term holiday. In the years before we acquired our first car in 1960 I vividly remember the excitement of boarding red Ribble and green Crosville buses for the expedition to Garth Ucha via Warrington, Frodsham, Chester, Wrexham and Ruabon, carrying not only our suitcases and rucksacks but also my great-aunt Margaret's weighty pre-transistor 'portable' valve radio. Having arrived at the Garth bus 'terminus', a finger-post at the intersection of four fields, we still had to portage our goods and chattels over several rough meadows and stiles until at last the white-painted gable of Bowen Bungalow hove into view. In those days the Bungalow had no electricity and water was fetched from the farm well in large galvanised buckets. We washed in rain water. Cooking was done on paraffin stoves and in the evenings we played dominoes and Ludo by the mellow light of hurricane lanterns. The house was fronted by a veranda with views far into Denbighshire, Shropshire and the English marches. It even had a metal post box with the inscription 'US MAIL', which I vaguely connected with Aunt Margaret's two emigrant brothers, but though as a small child I would check from time to time, letters arrived from neither Michigan nor Connecticut. In the daytime we would roam the heather- and bracken-covered hills, talk to farmers who spoke halting English, watch shepherds shear their sheep, pick wild mushrooms, whinberries and mountain strawberries and visit castles which had been fought over by Owen Glendower and King Henry IV.

Towards the end of one of these holidays, with the inevitable awkwardness of pre-adolescence, I seemed, against my will, to get myself into an increasing number of scrapes. Early on the last morning I made myself a bow from the ash coppice below the bungalow. Repeatedly warned about the dangers, I insisted on shooting recklessly until I managed to hit Kep, my uncle's poor, inoffensive spaniel in the face. I can still hear his indignant yelp and was much relieved to find that he still had both his eyes. I abandoned my bow and went into the house in search of other pursuits. Emerging again I took the four verandah steps in one bound. My great-uncle, stripped to the waist, was taking his morning wash in a bowl on the grass. He was short-sighted, had unwisely left his spectacles next to the bowl and I landed on them with a sickening crunch.

'My God! You've smashed my bloody glasses!'

Bill, who habitually used worse language than that, immediately accused Jack of 'cursing' me, which was not, and never would have been, the case. A full-blown row escalated which ended in the Cockrells and the Taylors packing and leaving the Bungalow in separate parties and heading off down the path to the distant bus terminus with me galloping backwards and forwards between them in a vain attempt to effect a reconciliation. Fortunately it was only a temporary rift. We continued our Welsh expeditions and Val and I even spent our honeymoon at the Bungalow in 1968.

CHAPTER 11

Flash Cards & More Murder

WHEN I HAD TURNED FIVE my parents had enrolled me in the National and Blue Coat School, the Church of England primary school attached to All Saints, the parish church of Wigan where they had been married ten years earlier. Beatrice and Bill had had the option of sending me to school a year earlier, in the Nursery class, but this had been precluded by my frequent health problems. Although I later came to enjoy quite a lot of my school experience, especially in the Juniors, I mostly detested the Infants and would frequently distress kindly dinner ladies by asking them: 'How many hours are there till home-time?' Especially in the cold, damp, air-polluted Wigan winters, my chest still played up occasionally and I was always delighted when I had the excuse to miss school. In the early days, when Beatrice had not yet returned to work, this meant she would mollycoddle me at home. Later she would either leave me with Annie at 169 or take me with her to the Baths, where I usually recovered rapidly enough to explore Aunt Margaret and Uncle Jack's Lumber Room or get under the feet of the cashiers or the mechanics in the cellar workshop. Real life was so much more interesting than school and I am still puzzled as to why I eventually decided to become a teacher, especially as I have always been convinced that most, though not all, of the important things I have ever learned came my way outside the formal education system.

Bronchitis and pneumonia had left me with some residual problems and during my first year in the Infants I was able to escape from school on a weekly basis to attend physiotherapy sessions at the Royal Albert Edward Infirmary. It was even more of a

Above: John Sharrock Taylor, author

pleasure because my escort on all of these occasions was my grandmother Annie, and the day always involved a visit to 169, which was ever my haven from the less pleasant aspects of the world. It was in 1952, during one of these hospital visits, that something quite momentous occurred. We were in the waiting room chatting to the nurse when a young doctor, complete with stethoscope and white coat, came in and said quite conversationally: 'The king's dead.' I was profoundly shocked because it had never occurred to me that kings could die. This king was King George VI, the father of Elizabeth II, who has reigned through most of my life, and at that early stage I knew nothing about him, though I have since come to respect him as a man who was obliged to take on a heavy and unexpected burden when his feckless brother decided to drop his responsibilities in order to marry a twice-divorced American tart. When I was in my teens my mother still spoke sentimentally of David, Prince of Wales, and his romantic sacrifice in favour of the woman he loved, but his younger brother Bertie has always seemed to me to have possessed true grit, like John Wayne, another of my heroes. Like myself, and for similar reasons, Bertie struggled with a stammer and, years later, I listened with interest to him conquering this impediment in the recording of his most famous Christmas broadcast:

> I said to the man who stood at the gate of the year 'Give me a light that I may tread safely into the unknown.' And he said 'Put your hand into the hand of God, for that shall be to you better than light and safer than a known way.'

Shortly after this, while I was buying a comic a customer came in and said to our kindly newsagent: 'It's just been on the radio. Stalin's dead.'

'Oh, good,' said Mr Caterall.

I had no idea who Stalin was but I gathered that he had not been nearly as popular as our king.

The only thing I remember about my first day in Mrs Smith's Reception class was that I knelt sloppily in prayers and was made to stand behind the blackboard to teach me to show better manners to the Almighty. This, I am afraid, was an indication of things to come, and I never came to like Mrs Smith, with her loud voice, red face, stout, sensible shoes and elastic support stockings. In those days the idea of treating pupils as individuals was a long way in the future, and many teachers regarded children as so many loaves, to be browned, or browned off, all at the same time. (In passing, whereas Americans talk of 'The Class of 2007' Indian schools, influenced by British ideas of fifty years ago, still refer to 'batches' of students.)

I was slow at anything to do with numbers, though I caught up rapidly when, as an adult, writing sensible budgets and controlling cash-flow meant the difference between my independent school's solvency and bankruptcy, but from the beginning almost anything about language utterly fascinated me. I write 'almost anything' because in the Infants there were certain linguistic rituals which both bored and puzzled me. In one of them the teacher would hold up a large 'flash' card on which a word was printed together with a picture. She would then intone, for instance 'V-A-N, Van' and the class would chorus the sounds back at her. I emphasise that she did not make the mistake of saying

'Vee-Ay-En' which is quite useless (and the kind of brick our Indian primary teachers used to drop before my wife Val persuaded them out of it). No, she was using perfectly correct phonetic pronunciation 'Vuh-Ah-Nnn'. The only problem from my point of view was that I had no clue that this exercise was intended to teach us to read, and the reason the ritual mystified me was quite simple: I already read, fluently and voraciously, everything from books through comics to the French on the sauce bottles, the latter with pronunciation à la Wigan. It was only when, sixteen years later, I married an infant school teacher that all became clear.

Pupils in my primary-school days were not expected to break ranks either by lagging behind or forging ahead of the rest of the class. If you failed to learn something, either because you were slow on the uptake in that particular academic area or because you were absent from school, it was quite likely that you would continue not knowing it. Conversely, if you finished your 'Janet and John' book before your classmates did you were told to re-read it rather than going onto the next one. Both my future wife and I got into trouble at our respective schools for forging silently ahead in the class reader and not knowing the place when our turn came to read aloud, but a teacher who could dramatise a story could keep us both spellbound. Mrs Pegg in Standard Three was particularly good at this and introduced me not only to such treasures as Richmal Crompton's 'William' books but also to Arthur Ransome, whose novels I still occasionally re-read. Today such stories, with their children who attended boarding schools and had cooks and nurses to minister to their needs, would be frowned upon as non-PC, and even then I was aware that these middle-class children were different from me and my friends, but some of Ransome's plots also included working-class characters whom he depicted realistically and never patronised. At this ten-year-old stage in my school career I was laid up in bed with yet another bout of winter bronchitis and Aunty Edie, who had been detailed to nurse me, was despatched with a list at nine o'clock most mornings to the Children's Library in Station Road. One afternoon, returning to the Library just before closing time with another list and the three books she had taken out the same morning, she was irritably informed by one of the snottier assistants that I was supposed to *read* the books with which I was issued, not just send them back and forth. She replied firmly that I *had* read all three books from cover to cover, that I sometimes read all night, and that it was one body's work keeping me supplied with reading material. After this I was allowed to take out four or even five books at a time. Almost everything I read, whether by Ransome, Enid Blyton or Frank Richards, was about 'adventure', which was something which apparently happened on remote islands, in locations such as the Lake District or the Norfolk Broads, and occasionally in odd places called public schools. I prayed each night that I too might have adventures and in spite of the pram fiasco I saved up my pocket money in a large jar so that I could eventually buy a sailing dinghy and sail off in search of them. When the total reached almost five pounds I bought instead a cricket bat from JJ Broughton's sports shop (which eventually became the basis of the chain owned by John Bradburn who would occasionally teach us for PE when I became a pupil not at Greyfriars but at Wigan Grammar School).

I realised long ago that Blyton's middle-class child heroes and heroines were rather cardboard creations but Ransome's characters were certainly drawn from life and presented in such detail that I even knew some of the books they had on their shelves at home. Whether their tastes ran to other kinds of reading material I have no idea but my own certainly did. The weekly arrival of the *Beano*, the *Dandy* and the *Hotspur* was eagerly awaited and I revelled in the exploits of Desperate Dan, Dennis the Menace and Dennis's dog Gnasher, who were also to become favourites with my son Richard many years later. In addition to the strip cartoons, comics in the 1950s also included features on such diverse subjects as science and history and my reputation with my primary school teachers for 'general knowledge' rested largely on information picked up from publications they would probably have despised as utterly trivial. My enthusiasm for trivia has stayed with me all my life. At Lancaster University, almost exactly ten years after I left the Blue Coat School, I was part of a singularly incompetent *University Challenge* team which was annihilated under the benevolent gaze of Bamber Gascoigne by Oxford's still all-female St Hilda's College, and almost exactly twenty years after that debacle I scored a respectable twenty-eight on Magnus Magnusson's *Mastermind*. My pleasure in this small achievement was slightly dented by a friend's comment that not only did I have a habit of collecting useless information but that I then used it to enter stressful quizzes where there was no money to be won.

It was at the Blue Coat School that I discovered that however general my knowledge might be I was not much good at the things my parents held dear. And it was not only sums which were a struggle. Anything involving physical co-ordination, from country dancing to physical education, was a nightmare. It was not that I despised these activities. I simply couldn't do them. I loved the tunes such as *Bonnets So Blue* and the intricate patterns of the dances, but my feet always seemed to get in the way. When we did gym I gazed with awe at Joan Barrow's apparently double-jointed ability to contort herself into any shape she chose, but both forward and backward rolls were, and remained, quite beyond me. I even joined in the lunchtime scratch games of football and cricket, but was always the last to be picked for teams. During one school match, on one of our rare summer visits to the Rectory field, I was given the opportunity to attempt bowling at Tony Settle's wicket. By some miracle my first ball was dead on and Tony, who was holding the bat wrongly, ended up with bloody fingers. The next year I attempted to repeat my feat and my full toss hit Tony squarely in the middle of the forehead and raised a bump the size of a pigeon's egg. This was more or less the end of my school cricketing career, though I continued to be cannon fodder in our informal matches on the vacant lot close to home. Much later, for a brief period as an Intermediate at Wigan Grammar School, I was skinny and mobile and discovered that I could run reasonably quickly and somehow bundle myself over the high jump bar without knocking it off. My House Captain, John Ritson, who the following year was to be a highly respected Head of School, told me one day: 'Chaps like you are the backbone of the House. You're no particular good at anything but you'll have a go at everything.'

Oddly enough, this backhanded compliment has always pleased me more than accolades received for things I could really do. Though for many of my adult years I have been a keen follower of professional tennis, which, to the puzzlement of my literature students, I sometimes used to compare to Shakespearean Tragedy, I could never match the burning enthusiasm both of my parents felt for rugby, except for those times, still far into the future, when my sons would be playing. The notable exceptions were the two rugby league finals my family attended at Wembley, where I felt fiercely partisan in support of my home town. As we returned on the train from overcoming Workington in 1958 I composed a victory song which received an enthusiastic reception from what I suppose must have been one of my earliest audiences. We were all immensely proud of our team and Wigan gave them a tumultuous reception when they returned from Wembley. It was about this time that somebody defined the longest pass in the history of rugby league: Ashton to Boston, three thousand miles. Eric and Billy were not the only great names we had to conjure with in those days. The great Joe Egan was still coaching Wigan and although I never saw him play, for he retired in February 1946, five months before I was born, I came to know the legendary Jimmy Sullivan, who was not only part-owner of a garage near my home but also a friend and close neighbour of my future parents-in-law. By this time Mr Sullivan was partially incapacitated by a stroke but gained the admiration of all who knew him by his determination not to succumb to his limitations. With the left handle of the garden shears strapped to his body he could do a neater hedge-trimming job than most of us managed with two fully functioning hands.

Art was another subject at which I had only modest ability, though I greatly enjoyed it and later won a national prize when my stiffly controlled pen and ink sketch of Wigan Grammar School appeared on children's television. I was too inflexible to be good at the freehand drawing but I excelled at all kinds of ships, though I occasionally sacrificed realism to symmetry, as when I drew a steamship with the smoke from the two funnels spiralling in opposite directions. Most of my classmates were quick to pour scorn on the error, but Beryl Derbyshire, who had a sweet face and a luxuriant mass of black curly hair tied back from her face with a red ribbon, stated firmly: 'Well, I think it's lovely. And when we grow up John and I are going to get married. Aren't we, John?'

'Yes,' I replied, grateful for the moral support but absolutely dumbfounded by the only proposal of marriage I have ever received.

Mathematics was my particular bugbear, but there was one area of it which I functioned quite efficiently and I still remember the delight I took in my first contacts with money when I was allowed to count it for the Baths cashier. Not that I was a particularly mercenary child, rather the opposite in fact. It was the look and feel of it that I liked. The biggest denomination I ever saw was the white fiver with the portrait of the queen, several lines of copperplate script and the scrawled signature of a mysterious and powerful figure called L.K. O'Brien, Chief Cashier of the Bank of England, who 'Promised to pay the Bearer' the fabulous sum of Five Pounds. It was an improbably huge note and I could well understand how the Owl and the Pussycat had been able to wrap up their loose change in it. As I was never the bearer of one of these wonderful documents I never had the opportunity to test Mr O'Brien's good faith, but on such occasions as birthdays and Christmases I did become the proud recipient of fabulous wealth in the shape of a ten-shilling or even a pound note. In some ways, coins were even more fun than notes because they were a history lesson in themselves. Early in the reign of Queen Elizabeth II there were thousands in circulation bearing the effigy of her father King George VI and substantial numbers showed the bearded face of her grandfather King George V. There were even a few from the reign of her great-grandfather King Edward VII and, almost impossible to think of in the 21st century, the occasional worn specimen with the faint imprint of her great-great-grandmother Queen Victoria, who had died in 1901 when my own grandmother was scarcely out of her teens.

This was long before the simplicity of decimalisation but the currency we grew up with seemed to us to be perfectly straightforward and logical. Forty years after my first experiments with it, one of our primary teachers in El Salvador asked me to explain it to her Year 4 History class. I found that I could recall it without difficulty and even reproduce the addition, multiplication and division sums I had done as a child at the Blue Coat School. The initial difficulty, soon overcome, was the fact that the sums had to be worked in two bases. There were twelve pennies in a shilling and twenty shillings in a pound. There was a satisfyingly heavy silver coin, improbably called a florin after a medieval Italian coin of almost the same name, which was worth twenty-four pennies, which meant that there were ten of them in a pound. There was an even more gloriously heavy silver coin called a half crown, which was worth two shillings and six pence, which meant that they were eight to the pound. This was slightly baffling because though there were half crowns there appeared to be no such coin as a crown. I learned later that though such a coin had at one time been in general circulation it was now only issued as a keepsake to commemorate special occasions. The shilling was familiarly known as a 'bob' and in addition to the larger coins already mentioned, there was the sixpence, or 'tanner', a hexagonal 'thripenny bit', a halfpenny, pronounced haypenny, and even a farthing, the smallest copper coin, worth a quarter of a penny, with a wren, the smallest British bird, on its obverse side. The pound itself was a 'quid', which is the only one of those old slang terms to have survived into regular modern usage. In the same way that thirty bob was never thirty bobs, the plural of quid was also quid and it was axiomatic that foreign spies might betray themselves by offering 'twenty of your English quids' for classified information.

The newest coins were no longer minted in silver or copper but in harder-wearing alloys, though the surviving pre-1920s specimens still had the weight and ring of the real stuff. Most threepences were modern alloy creations with the portcullis device on them. The small, exquisite silver three pence coins were gradually being taken out of circulation and when we came across one it was jealously hoarded to be stirred into the family's Christmas pudding. Ship ha'pennies with the monarch's head and a galleon on the obverse were collected at school in aid of missions to other countries. It was well before the era of political correctness and at the Blue Coat School, as we dropped our ha'pennies in the box, we still sang hymns such as:

Over the seas there are little brown children,
Fathers and mothers and babies too.

The older high-value coins carried the abbreviations 'Fid Def' and 'Ind Imp'. The first of these, Fidei Defensor, was the title bestowed on King Henry VIII by Pope Leo X in 1521 in recognition of his staunch support of the Roman Catholic faith. Not long afterwards Henry, who wished to divorce his wife Katherine of Aragon and marry his mistress Anne Boleyn, thumbed his nose at the pope and declared himself Supreme Head of an independent Anglican church. Being utterly shameless, however, he kept the title Fidei Defensor and so have his successors. Indiae Imperatrix was the title adopted by Queen Victoria and subsequent monarchs up to George VI to signify that she was Empress of India. Even Winston Churchill, normally prescient in historical matters, thought that Britain ought to have ignored Gandhi, Nehru and Jinnah and hung onto India beyond 1947, but the tide of the times was against him and the inscription does not appear on coins after this date.

Like 'peso' in Spanish, the names given to coins were sometimes originally measures of weight, and modern British currency retains the stylised capital L as a pound sign, though few may now know that it stands for the Latin 'libra', the astrological sign of the scales. A pennyweight, the weight of a 'bun' penny, was still an accepted imperial measure in early Victorian times. When I was a child we calculated money as LSD, meaning libri (pounds), solidi (shillings) and denarii (pence). This was before those initials came to be associated with perception-altering drugs and *Lucy in the Sky with Diamonds*. Since 1971 it has only been pounds and pence, often referred to as 'pee', perhaps because of their increasingly piddling value. Unlike the least formally educated of my Spanish campesino friends, the British of the 21st century have decided that they cannot cope with subjunctives, object pronouns, ships having feminine gender or plurals not ending in 's', so increasingly on my visits to England I am offered 'one pence' change when I buy one of those articles irritatingly priced at four pounds ninety-nine, as if I am too stupid to work out that this really means five of our English quids.

In an era when most primary schools took music seriously, the Blue Coat was a particularly musical school, and as well as folk-dancing we had frequent singing sessions. In addition to the Headmaster, both Mr Hedley and Miss Faulkner played the piano outstandingly well. Our standard song book was the *New National*, but Miss Faulkner's playing went far beyond the sparse accompaniments Charles Villiers Stanford had provided, and such surprisingly erotic ballads as *The Raggle Taggle Gipsies* fairly zipped along.

In his Memoirs, Beniamino Gigli, later to be my operatic hero, asserts that the one musical skill which is completely unteachable is 'the instinctive timing of a musical phrase', a view with which I heartily concur. The Blue Coat School gave me ample exposure to great songs, such as Purcell's *Fairest Isle*, which were full of perfectly formed phrases, and my teachers' insistence on proper breathing provided the basis for sound vocal technique. True, the Blue Coat School never recognised my potential as a singer because even before the early change of my voice to tenor I was an alto rather than a treble and persistently inclined to pitch an octave lower than my contemporaries, but I knew I could sing and many awards and concert appearances in the subsequent fifty years have confirmed that conviction. It is of course a hereditary talent. My grandfather Fred was a fine tenor and as a treble my father Bill was a *Messiah* soloist and would have made an exceptional bass had he chosen to develop his man's voice. Thirty years after I sang with Miss Faulkner my five-year-old son Richard came home from school and announced: 'We learned a new song today.'

I had a cassette recorder on my desk and I pushed the buttons surreptitiously and said 'Sing it.'

I still have that childish recording of *My Ship Sails from China* with its perfectly curved phrases and intermittent sniffs (Richard had a heavy cold). Five years later, when I was a lay clerk in the choir of Newcastle Cathedral and Richard and his brother were choristers, we all sang in the Royal Maundy ceremony in the presence of Her Majesty the Queen, who at the end of the service on the way back from the High Altar, touched Prince Philip's arm and smilingly drew his attention to Will, at eight the cathedral choir's youngest red-cassocked probationer, diminutive, blonde and singing with tremendous concentration in spite of a notable lack of front teeth.

By the time I reached Standard Three I was a strange mixture of confidence and diffidence, which I suppose is true of many children, and I remember being quite fascinated by our Headmaster, Charlie Yates, who was one of the only two male teachers in the school. With his tweeds, ruddy complexion and matter-of-fact way of speaking, Charlie looked like a farmer, but he played the piano exquisitely and introduced us in Assembly to the folk song recordings of Kathleen Ferrier, the lass from Higher Walton who had become an international opera star and died of cancer in her early forties. On another occasion, he brought into school the perfect corpse of a snowy owl which had perished by crashing into an overhead power cable. My respect for Charlie even survived the fact that he taught us for 'Hand Work', or Craft, which involved such pursuits as bookbinding, where my lack of physical co-ordination was a definite handicap. I remember how, using a metal tray and coloured oils, he made the swirling patterns which were to be pasted on the insides of the hard covers. Charlie's mitred corners were naturally perfect, which mine were far from being.

One of my most vivid memories of Charlie Yeats is connected with an incident which occurred when I was nine years old. The 1950s in England was certainly one of the safest decades for children to grow up in, but there were exceptions. One of these occurred at the beginning of the school year of 1954 when Wigan suddenly realised with a shock that it had a serial child killer in its midst. Billy Mitchell had been playing near the Leeds and Liverpool Canal when he was grabbed by a stranger and stabbed in the chest. Billy struggled, escaped, survived his injuries and was able to give the police a description of his attacker, 'a man with blonde, almost white hair'. Billy had been fortunate but the next victim was not. Eleven-year-old William Harmer was not a pupil at the Blue Coat School, but he lived quite near to it. In late August of 1954 his body was found on waste ground having sustained eleven stab wounds, all inflicted with a small penknife. After a lull of more than seven months the murderer struck again, stabbing to death ten-year-old Norman Yates on the Easter Monday of 1955. Once again, witnesses spoke of seeing a white-haired man running away from the scene of the crime. Parents were naturally terrified that their children were at risk and while the murderer remained at large even pupils who lived close by were escorted to and from the school. At home we had a large and very blunt sheath knife which I secretly strapped across my chest under my jacket each morning before setting off for school with my mother, foolishly confident at eight that I could see off any assailant. As soon as William Harmer's murder had hit the press headlines, Charlie Yates made a very emphatic speech in Assembly, which ended with words to the effect that:

'Until this man is caught NOBODY is allowed to leave school premises at any time except in the company of a parent or a teacher. I will CANE any child who puts a foot out of bounds.'

I clearly remember asking myself 'I wonder if old Charlie really means that?'

At break time I walked down to the main school gate, which happened to be open for some delivery or other, and stood looking up at the window of Charlie's study. When he eventually looked out, I firmly planted my right foot out of bounds. He meant it and he duly carried out his promise. My hand stung for a while but I honoured him for his resolution and thought the three strokes a reasonable price to pay for such a definite answer to my question.

Soon after Norman Yates's killing, 25-year-old Norman Green was arrested for the murders, and it was clear that Charlie's concern had been fully vindicated, for Green lived locally and had even on occasions played football with us at lunchtimes on the vacant lot next to the school. When confronted with the forensic evidence he admitted killing both boys. At his trial in Manchester in the summer of 1955 he pleaded insanity but after four hours of deliberation the jury found him guilty and he was hanged at Walton Jail in Liverpool by Albert Pierrepoint on the morning of Wednesday the 27 July 1955.

Our teacher in Standard Four, the Eleven Plus year, was Mrs Yates, the Headmaster's wife whom we called Fanny, though I am fairly sure this was not her real name. Like Tennyson's Maud, Mrs Yates was tall and stately, though of course she was considerably older than Maud's not-seventeen. She wore smart two-piece suits and had abundant grey hair pinned up in a French pleat. Unlike Charlie, she had the kind of voice our parents called 'refined' but like her husband she stood for absolutely no nonsense, though her discipline was experienced and effortless and I do not remember her ever having to hand out a punishment. Mrs Yates had a certain gift for the dramatic and 'Ian Wadsworth, I warn you that if you continue to irritate me I shall go up the wall in a flash of blue light and hang there by my fingernails' was a fairly typical threat which we found both impressive and amusing.

Unlike Miss Marland in Standard One or Mrs Pegg in Standard Three, Mrs Yates was neither motherly nor of romantic interest, but whatever her system was it got a substantial number of us working-class children through the Eleven Plus examination. When the results arrived they were accompanied by a graph of our individual achievement in four areas, which I seem to remember were English, Arithmetic, Verbal Reasoning and General Knowledge. Predictably I had done well in English and General Knowledge and fairly well in Verbal Reasoning, but, more to the point, I had scraped through the Maths part by the skin of my teeth (seven years later three out of four of my brother Stephen's scores would coincide with the top axis of the graph) and was destined to follow in the footsteps of my Uncle Jack and enter Wigan Grammar School where I would continue for a further seven years my school career of disorganisation and confusion enlightened by occasional flashes of lucidity. My mother Beatrice was of course delighted that I had let down neither myself nor her by failing my 'scholarship'. The reaction of the Millgate gang was more surprising. We were all sitting in a ring on the Brew admiring my new bicycle and discussing the state of the world. It had already been established that a couple of my friends who were the same age as myself would be going to secondary modern schools when the summer holiday was over. Not wanting to brag, I had kept my own counsel, but with the shiny new Dawes Dalesman in view the subject could not be avoided.

'Why did your mum buy you the bike, Jack? Is it your birthday?'

Note that only mums bought presents. Dads were far above such childish considerations.

'I got it for passing the Eleven Plus,' I responded with bashful pride and was quite unprepared for the gale of ribald laughter which met this revelation.

'Come off it,' said Alan, wiping the tears from his eyes. 'Come August, we'll be seeing you at All Saints like all the rest of us.'

I didn't protest. Millgate kids did not go to grammar school. Come August they would find out.

I have already mentioned that from a very early age I was reading everything I could lay my hands on and when I was in the Juniors this included the literature texts which had survived from Jack's and my parents' school days. By the time I was in my eleventh year I could make a reasonable stab at much of the Prologue from Chaucer's *Canterbury Tales* and declaim by heart several scenes from *Julius Caesar*. The lean and hungry Cassius was my favourite character. Except for the occasional Christmas pantomime, my parents would never have dreamt of attending a theatre performance but when I learned that Wigan Little Theatre was to present *Caesar* I spent my pocket money on a ticket and took myself off to see the show. Apart from shows such as *Babes in the Wood* it was my first experience of live theatre; I was immediately hooked and have remained hooked, through many Stratford seasons, ever since. A fascinated small boy in a school cap, shorts and an over-large gabardine raincoat, I must have presented a quaint figure and I remember being puzzled and slightly irritated by the indulgent smiles of two women who sat near me in the theatre's intimate auditorium. It was a strong cast and Robin Cooper, the actor playing Cassius, bronzed, and lean almost to emaciation, was particularly brilliant. He had a beautiful light baritone speaking voice and absolutely crystal clear diction of the kind I later learned to associate with RADA. Imagine my delight when I arrived at Wigan Grammar School in the August of 1957 and discovered that

Mr Cooper was to be my Form Master. He also taught me for English and I particularly enjoyed his readings from Jim Corbet's *The Man Eaters of Kumaon* which is to this day a favourite with my son Will. Thirty years after teaching me at WGS, Robin was to be my clerk when I adjudicated the Speech section of Wigan Music Festival, and during the coffee break he asked me what had first interested me in the idea of teaching English. I was able to reply quite truthfully.

'It's all your fault, Cassius.'

Throughout my time at the Blue Coat School it was impossible to forget that I was part of a Church of England institution even if I had wanted to. The calendar we followed was the Church's Year and every day began with a full school assembly at which we invoked the Lord's protection in the words of the third collect from the service of Mattins in the 1662 Prayer Book:

> O Lord our heavenly Father, Almighty and everlasting God, who hast safely brought us to the beginning of this day; Defend us in the same with thy mighty power; and grant that this day we fall into no sin, neither run into any kind of danger; but that all our doings may be ordered by thy governance, to do always that is righteous in thy sight; through Jesus Christ our Lord. Amen.

The parish church, only a few hundred yards away at the other end of Hallgate, was both a physical and a spiritual presence. We went there in crocodiles for special services and its clergy flitted in and out of the school in their long black cassocks and their Canterbury capes and hats. On one occasion one of the curates arrived in a state of great excitement to tell us that a vestment cupboard in the Vestry had been discovered to have a false back in which fragments of a medieval stained-glass window, preserved at the time of the Cromwellian depredations of the 1650s, had been hidden. These were the last palmy days of High Anglicanism in Wigan, when the Sanctus Bell in the medieval tower of All Saints rang each weekday and Sunday morning to inform all within earshot that the Mass was being offered for the whole town and not merely for the congregation present in the church. In addition to the Rector there were three curates and even a community of Anglican nuns who occupied All Saints Mission House, where Val and I were to live in an upstairs flat during the first year of our marriage.

By 1968 the nuns had long gone, but our bathroom door still carried the inscription 'Sister Bridget' in faded gothic lettering. The Rector, Canon Finch during my schooldays, lived at Wigan Hall, a huge echoing Victorian mansion standing in several acres of wooded grounds diagonally opposite the school in New Market Street. The hall was much too vast for one family, so the school used a big attic room for gym classes and one wing was occupied by Jack Hopwood Sayer, the Wigan coroner. Later, when Val and I lived in the neighbouring Mission House, Mr and Mrs Sayer, then aged about eighty, invited us to supper and we discovered that Jack Sayer and Val's grandfather Will Fairhurst had both entered the same chambers in 1907, Jack as a barrister and Will as a junior clerk. In his black jacket, wing collar and pinstripes, 'Hoppy' as everybody called him, was for many years a favourite Wigan character and lived to be Britain's oldest coroner, permanently eschewing tape recorders and shorthand writers and taking his own notes at a stately pace with a gold-nibbed fountain pen. I always think of him as the Lord Chancellor from Iolanthe and a wing-collared sepia photograph of him as a young man, affectionately addressed to Val's grandfather, Will Fairhurst, looks down benevolently at me from my little Andalusían study wall as I write this.

Wigan Hall has an impressive gatehouse through which all visitors were obliged to pass and here the parish church's kindly and long-serving full-time Verger, Billy Cowan, lived with his wife and his son John, a parish church chorister and later to be a fine cathedral baritone. It was one of Billy's pleasant tasks to show visitors round the church and tell them something of its history. When I was in the men's choir in the 1960s the then Rector, Canon John Park, overheard Billy in full flow and later gently reproved him for his outrageous exaggeration and sheer invention.

'Eh, Rector,' said Billy, 'they love it. Especially the Yanks.'

Digging into ancient parish records, Billy thought he had discovered that one of his predecessors had held the post for fifty years and he had hopes of surpassing this achievement. Taking a second, closer, look in about 1970 he realised with a jolt that his target was nearer sixty years. When he told Mrs Cowan she exclaimed: 'Ee, Billy, lad! You'll never do it!' – but I hope he managed it after all.

Given that several of my friends were members of the Parish Church choir during my time at the Blue Coat School, it may seem surprising that I never became a boy chorister. Indeed, though I have sung in several church choirs and directed three of them I never sang in one until I joined as a callow tenor in 1962. The reason is not far to seek: as I have already mentioned, with my deep alto voice I tended to sing the higher passages an octave lower, and probably for this reason I was classified as a 'groaner' when school singing classes were scouted for potential chorister talent. And during the 1950s there was no shortage of applicants for choristerships, for the boys' section of Wigan parish church choir was at its absolute zenith under the brilliant and demanding Kenneth Long. The choir has had a distinguished history and several church musicians who later achieved national fame, such as Sir Walter Parratt and Sir Ernest Bullock, have either led or sung in it. During my boyhood and throughout my membership of it up to 1970, one of the leading soloists was the baritone Frank Heath, who had sung as a boy under Dr (later Sir Edward) Bairstow, who had left Wigan in 1902 en route for York Minister via Leeds parish church. Even at eighty Mr Heath sang with an excellent tone, though organists always had to allow for the extra beat he insisted on adding in the middle of the Stanford *Benedictus*. By 1960 the choir had fallen into disarray, but it was rescued by the arrival of David Cutter, and by the middle of the decade it had regained much of its former glory. David, who is godfather to my son Richard, was an organ pupil of Sir Francis Jackson, himself a pupil of Sir Edward Bairstow, so there is a pleasing sense of the cyclical nature of time.

Clerical garb was not the only kind of fancy dress we saw at the Blue Coat School and church music was not the sole aspect of parish life which eventually came full circle. In those days the government of the emergent nation of Malaya, which was to gain its independence as Malaysia in 1957, the year I transferred to Wigan Grammar School, used to send its most promising teacher trainees to complete their education at Edgehill College in Ormskirk. Our school and Wigan Grammar School were regular teaching practice placements for these students and in my last primary school year one of them delighted us by coming in national costume complete with the Kris, the characteristic Malay wavy-bladed dagger. More than thirty years later when I was an international school Principal in Johor Bahru and Will was working his gap year on a coral island resort in the South China Sea, I met a very elegant Tamil lady, then in her sixties, who told me that she had done her teaching practice at the Blue Coat School.

The walk home from school to Millgate was an adventure in itself because it took me through the very centre of town. In the early days my mother or one of my other female relatives would meet me and bring me back by the direct route from Hallgate via Bishopgate and the Market Place but later, when I was trusted to go to and from school on my own, I would take a more indirect route along New Market Street, through the busy Market Hall and up one or other of the arcades.

There were two arcades. The Old Arcade, now sadly disappeared along with so much of Wigan interest, was a narrow medieval thoroughfare. In addition to Syd Smith's newspaper stall it boasted a chair dangling by thick chains from a huge cast iron weighing machine, where brave customers could be very publicly weighed against a combination of great buttery yellow brass weights. The delicious smells of roasts and gravy and meat and potato pies from Gorners' Café are wafting across the nose of memory as I write this and so is the smell of beer from the Legs o' Man, Wigan's longest pub, which straggled behind practically the whole length of the arcade so that customers would talk of entering it by the 'top Legs' or the 'bottom Legs' according to which end of the arcade they approached it from. The Makinson Arcade, which has thankfully survived the depredations of the improvers, was also a feast for the senses. Makinsons themselves fragrantly ground coffee beans and sold an exotic variety of teas. Meesons hand-made the most sumptuous chocolates and toffees and it is mostly to these and the humbler spangles, smarties, fruit pastilles and gums that my Indian orthodontist owes his luxurious twenty-first-century lifestyle. Most working-class families in Wigan seemed to regard teeth as a phase to be got through as quickly as possible. As my great-aunt Margaret put it:

'Teeth are a nuisance. It's painful getting 'em and it's painful getting without 'em.'

My younger aunt Edith looked after her teeth and my grandmother Annie had hopes of my doing the same, but sweets and faulty brushing made it an uphill struggle necessitating many visits, always after school, to Ralph McGuire's dental surgery in Dicconson Terrace. Mr McGuire may or may not have been a good dentist but he and his staff had no concept of child psychology. Appointments were frequently overbooked and I waited in increasing anxiety as adult after adult jumped the queue. The intercom summoning patients for treatment would come to life with a loud click which would throw me into a rigid state of tension only to subside again if another victim were called. Frequently by the time I was called it was almost the end of the working day and an agonising session under the drill would end with a temporary dressing being inserted. The dangers of missing the next appointment were not explained and by the time I arrived at my middle teens my back teeth were a total mess and I was in a state of intermittent agony. At this point my father remembered that his 'difficult' wisdom teeth had been dealt with by a certain Mr Hegarty in Wrightington Street. Mr Hegarty duly injected me with a syringe which might easily have been used on horses, extracted a molar and promptly retired, passing me onto his young partner, Ian Thom, who carried out such a brilliant restoration of my remaining gnashers that his work has been praised by every dentist I have visited since, including a consultant in the USA, which was truly praise from a dental Caesar. These days I am a fanatical brusher and flosser who avoids sweets except on very rare occasions, but I still remember the heady scent of Meesons in the Makinson Arcade.

The old Market Hall was a warren in which literally anything could be bought. The modern Galleries may be prettier but they have nowhere near the same character. It is the smells of the place which I remember best. When I shopped there with Beatrice on Saturdays Mrs Leyland's cheese stall was a favourite venue and there was always a generous sample for any passing child. Beatrice, who in her later years would try anything from squid to risotto and curry, was a complete chauvinist about cheese. If in my twenties or thirties I was out shopping with her and mentioned the word 'cheese' she would almost unthinkingly correct the term to 'Lancashire cheese', and although I enjoy most of what Spain, France and Italy have to offer in the way of Manchego, Brie, Gorgonzola and the rest, Lancashire Tasty, with its clean, astringent smell and crumbly texture, is still one of my favourites. Another unforgettable smell was that of the flowers in Waterworths shop. When I was taught at the Blue Coat School by the equally fragrant Miss Marland and Mrs Pegg, I would buy freesias at Waterworths, ostensibly for the nature table.

Lunds floor coverings offered a different range of interesting odours. Years later, when I worked in my university vacations at Witters linoleum factory at Heapey near Chorley, I was to remember one of the characteristic smells of Lunds. They also had a warehouse in the Wiend where there were carpets ranging from humble cords to AO quality Axminsters and I know of few smells more pleasing than a new good-quality carpet. Tom Lund, the effective boss of Lunds, was something of an idol to Beatrice. Born to his mother Sally Williams in 1915 when she was eighteen, he had been adopted by Arthur Lund after he and Sally married the following year. In the early years when they were building up their haberdashery business Sally and the teenage Tom would 'stand' Ashton Market with a handcart. By the 1940s, when Beatrice became a regular customer, the business was well established with its main outlet at Seven Stars Bridge in Wallgate. It was well known that you could get anything from carpets to overcoats and washing machines from Lunds on very reasonable credit terms. If they didn't stock an item they gave you a note to a company who did. On Friday evenings, Tom Lund and his brothers Charlie and Bill were the 'tallymen' who went around collecting the instalments from customers. The other two were sharper on the surface but Tom could always get round the defaulters with a combination of charm and persistence. Once he arrived home late on a Friday evening, his suit faintly spotted with white, because he had come upon an elderly customer struggling to paint a ceiling and had stayed to finish it for her.

In common with most women who knew him, Beatrice adored Tom Lund, though he only had eyes for his petite wife Ethel. When in my teens and early twenties my mother became aware that I was seeing some girl, she would make it clear that nobody would be good enough for her son, with two possible exceptions. A certain businessman called Tom Lund had two delightful convent-educated daughters whom she had occasionally glimpsed at one of the Lund outlets or shopping with their mother. I became sick and tired of hearing about the Lunds' paragon daughters but one day in 1967 when I had just begun to teach at Wigan Grammar School this conversation occurred:

'Who's this latest floozy, then?'

'She's called Val. She sings in the Gilbert and Sullivan Society. I'm afraid she's one of your Tom Lund's oh-so-perfect daughters, but I'm determined not to hold that against her.'

Beatrice didn't actually say 'My cup runneth over' but I could tell she was close to it. Of course she recovered from her adulation and though she always got on well with her daughter-in-law she was sometimes a little taken aback by my wife's increasingly firm application of Kipling's doctrine of 'Daughter I am in my mother's house but mistress in my own'. We both treasure her final words on the subject of our relationship:

'It's a good thing you two found each other when you were young uns, because you'd definitely have spoiled another couple.'

CHAPTER 12

Sod the Lodgers

Remember, remember the fifth of November
Gunpowder, treason and plot.
I see no reason why gunpowder treason
Should ever be forgot …

THE 5TH OF NOVEMBER, Bonfire Night, was always an eagerly awaited event for which preparations started many weeks in advance. Bonfire Night, or Guy Fawkes Night, is an essentially English festival which officially began as a celebration of the survival of King James I and his parliament of a Catholic assassination plot in 1605. James, a protestant king with a Roman Catholic mother, Mary Queen of Scots, had hinted at the time of his accession in 1603 that he was prepared to allow English Catholics to follow their religion without harassment. He had not kept his promise and a group of Catholic gentry, headed by Robert Catesby, decided to blow him and his Lords and Commons sky high when parliament met for its state opening on 5 November 1605. A Yorkshire soldier of fortune, Guy Fawkes, was given the honour of detonating the explosion of fifty large barrels of gunpowder secretly placed in the cellars beneath the House. If the plot had been successful, the column of smoke would have been so high that it would have alerted a Spanish invasion fleet lurking just over the horizon. But the plot was doomed from the outset. The conspirators were disorganised and talkative and one of them even wrote to a relative in the House of Lords telling him to avoid the opening ceremony. Even without this tip-off, it is inconceivable that the plot could have succeeded, because Robert Cecil, the king's chief minister, whom his own father had dubbed 'The Deep Dissembler', already had most of the conspirators under surveillance, and it is even likely that he had secretly encouraged the plot in order to have an excuse for smashing any underground Catholic resistance. Guy Fawkes was caught red-handed in the cellars with his lantern and his tinder box and he and his colleagues were tortured and executed. Instructions were given for an annual Gunpowder Plot celebration and up to Victorian times a special service of thanksgiving was included in the *Book of Common Prayer*.

Early Guy Fawkes celebrations were quite elaborate and began with a spectacular torchlight procession in which huge effigies not only of Guy Fawkes but also of the pope and other Catholic dignitaries were paraded through the streets before being burned on a bonfire. Similar processions, with many of the marchers in 17th-century costumes, still survive in such places as Lewes in Sussex and Edenbridge in Kent, where my family spent a year in the lodge of an Elizabethan mansion from 1990 to 1991. During the reign of King James's grandson, Charles II, the celebration in London at least, became an even more spectacular event. This was ironic because Charles was suspected of being a Catholic sympathiser and, far from being a demonstration in favour of the royal house, London's Guy Fawkes parade was used by his political opponent Lord Shaftesbury as a threat to the king himself. The highlight of the procession was a troupe of Oliver Cromwell's Ironsides veterans leading a riderless horse representing Cromwell himself. The message was clear: Behave like a good Protestant or there could be another civil war and, like your father, you may lose it by a head.

Most of us children in Millgate in the 1950s had only the vaguest notion of the origins of Bonfire Night, though in my tenth year I easily managed to win the five shillings' worth of fireworks offered by my class teacher for the best account of the Gunpowder Plot. I still have some twinges of conscience about this windfall because I have an uneasy feeling that my pastiche of Uncle Jack's old history text book may have been near enough to the original to count as plagiarism. Our own celebration consisted of building the biggest bonfire possible on the Brew, the vacant lot close to my home in Millgate, and collecting as much money as possible to buy fireworks. The pretext for this collecting was always the effigy we would build of Guy Fawkes himself, clad in old clothes and stuffed with rags or newspapers, his face and beard represented by a crudely drawn mask. We would parade this scarecrow around the streets of the town, accosting the citizens as they went about their business and harassing them with shrill cries of 'Penny for the guy!' None of us was particularly artistic, competition between rival bonfire gangs was rife, and we always felt dissatisfied with our efforts at creating a convincing guy, until Graham Ellis had the idea of using a real person as the basis for our effigy. So we togged up Jimmy Harrison in our selection of ratty old clothes and covered his face with the mask. Jimmy's half-brother Kevin, always something of a tender conscience in spite of a couple of Borstal holidays, objected that replacing the effigy with a living person was not exactly in the spirit of the game, but Graham ruthlessly quashed all opposition, pointing out that we all knew Jimmy was a dummy whether or not he was disguised as one, so what was the difference?

My parents had their own embarrassed reservations about the whole 'penny for the guy' scenario, which they regarded as little different from begging, and my father, who got though at least couple of packets of Players every day, added that in any case fireworks were a criminal waste.

'All that money going up in smoke,' he would growl sententiously.

When I was about eleven years old I suddenly discovered that I agreed with him. It was a record year for loot and the town centre passers-by had done us proud, not only with dozens of pennies but also a few threepenny bits and even a couple of tanners. So we forgot about fireworks and spent the lot on pie and chips at Thurston's Café. But before we arrived at these serene heights of epicurean wisdom there were still some battles to be fought.

With the possible exception of Kevin, who in any case was highly articulate and preferred to solve disputes by negotiation rather than by combat, we Millgaters were not a tough lot. In contrast, the gang from nearby Harrogate Street could always field an impressive array of seasoned street fighters who would easily have made the younger Krays look like church choristers. This was partly because, in addition to home-grown talent, they could draw upon the services of the kids from the Royal George Model Lodging House, a hostel for homeless families, who were hardened graduates of what were later to be called the School of Hard Knocks and the University of Life. It seemed that whenever we were enjoying ourselves in a quiet game of cricket on the Brew these plug-uglies would inevitably materialise at the run, screaming like banshees, while stumps and players would scatter in all directions as they hurled the ball over the Tech and shattered the bat on some convenient straggler. The despairing cry of 'The Lodgers!' would send us scurrying for cover and I for one deeply resented the repeated humiliation and was determined to do something about it. The Guy Fawkes Night of 1956 provided just the opportunity.

Bonfires were built on a street by street basis and for weeks before 5 November different gangs of children feverishly collected and stored combustible material: cardboard cartons, orange boxes, garden rubbish, threadbare sofas, mattresses and old railway sleepers soaked in years of train oil. Worn-out car tyres, though outlawed by the Borough Fire Brigade, were highly prized because they would burn for hours. None of the gangs had anywhere to store their combustibles and the stuff was piled up on the bonfire site until zero night. Rival gangs would not only strive to outdo each other in terms of the size of their bonfires, but would also try to raid their opponents' sites and steal their combustibles. We Millgaters did not have the muscle power to confront the Lodgers in such a raid and get away with the spoil unscathed, but it occurred to me that the next best thing would be to burn their bonfire in situ and leave them with nothing to bake their potatoes with on the big night. Logic would seem to have dictated climbing out of the bedroom window after lights out and sneaking stealthily round to Harrogate Street under cover of darkness with a box of Swan Vestas, but this was too simple, and in any case I was hoping to count a more spectacular coup. I explained my plan to a Council of War in our tar-paper headquarters on The Brew.

'The Lodgers'll never let you get away with it,' Kevin, always the voice of common sense, warned cautiously.

'Sod the Lodgers. We're gonna do it.'

As the privileged great-nephew of the Superintendent I had access to the workshop in the cellar beneath the Baths. From a thick softwood board I used the fretsaw to cut out a solid rifle stock, to the top of which, after sanding it smooth, I stapled a three-foot length of copper tubing to act as the barrel of my new invention, Jack's Non-Patent Rocket Launcher. I then spent all my week's pocket money on the largest Brock's sky rocket I could lay my hands on. Thus equipped and with arson in our hearts the Millgaters set out in the November dusk for Harrogate Street, death or glory. Jimmy and I had already rehearsed our attack in dumb show. On the word of command he would go down on one knee and I would rest the Rocket Launcher on his shoulder before striking the match, lighting the blue touch paper and not retiring. A rocket of this enormous size, launched into the heart of the opposition's bonfire, would set it on fire without the possibility of error. It seemed foolproof and all might have gone well if the Lodgers had not taken it into their heads to mount a simultaneous raid on our own bonfire site. Deployed in open order and shaking with nerves, we had reached the mid-point of Harrogate Street within two hundred yards of their bonfire when they suddenly debouched from a side alley in a shambling column and converged on us at their usual whooping run. It was still too far for a feasible attempt on their piled-up combustibles and I knew that if they closed with us they would probably murder us, so I took a split-second decision to take a pot shot not at their bonfire but at them.

'Kneel!' Like a seasoned artilleryman Jimmy coolly went down on one knee.

'Ignite!' I fumbled for a moment with the matches. A sputter. An agonising moment as the tiny flame hesitated, caught the wick and grew into smouldering life. A fizz, then a glorious whoosh as the rocket leapt from the launcher. If I had known anything at all about ballistics I might have been aware that a projectile loosely fitted into a tube will seldom fly accurately, and that Congreve's early experiments had done as much damage to the British as to Napoleon's troops. Although it was aimed at the Lodgers, the rocket fortunately did not fly straight, or a tragedy might have occurred. Instead it veered off left at knee height at an angle of forty-five degrees, struck the wall of the nearest building in a shower of sparks and smoke and rebounded back to ricochet off the opposite side of the street, repeating this performance several times before finally exploding harmlessly in a storm of coloured lights, by which time the Lodgers had been shocked into a cowering immobility which allowed us to make our escape.

Kevin had warned us against possible reprisals, and as the obvious author of the outrage I was now a marked man. Only few days later I was walking two dogs on the lead, Judy, my border collie bitch, and Kep, my great-uncle Jack Cockrell's fat, lazy golden spaniel, when we were waylaid by a party of Lodgers, still smarting from their defeat and looking for trouble. The strategic situation was perilous. I was alone. I was encumbered with two dogs. The enemy was between me and my home-base. To the left of me as I faced down Millgate was Jews Yard, the courtyard which contained the painter and decorator's shop, Sherburn's glaziers and the big rambling house where Jimmy and Kevin lived. The Yard was separated from Millgate by a covered entry, wide enough to admit a large vehicle, which actually ran underneath part of Jimmy and Kevin's house. Today, as usual, the big double gate with its faded blue paint was locked but pedestrians could enter through the small postern. I quickly hustled the dogs through this and peered apprehensively through the gloom. The yard was a dead-end. The door of Jimmy and Kevin's house was locked, so there was no help available there. I turned to face back the way I had come and found the postern crowded with triumphant plug-uglies who were clearly planning my imminent dismemberment. The blood was pounding in my head and the dogs, in their different ways, were also agitated. Tubby old Kep stood panting noisily, his large brown eyes bulging and his mobile brow knitted into a pained expression. He hated any kind of confrontation and was so completely unaggressive that once, as he rolled over in his sleep, a mouse which had been enjoying the warmth of his long, silky coat, shot out with an indignant squeak. Though he still loved a sedate romp in Bordsane Wood, where he could splash along the brook, he suffered from a touch of arthritis in his paws, detested walking on the hard Wigan pavements and would seize the first opportunity to get back to the comfort of his basket. Judy was already crouched and growling deep in her throat, her hindquarters tensed for a spring. The gentlest creature imaginable with those she considered to be her friends, she had a ferocious reputation for defending her own and she never forgot an injury. The obvious strategy was to slip her off the lead and let her make short work of the besieging Lodgers. Somebody would certainly be seriously bitten, though the thought of lacerating a Lodger or two worried me less than the possibility of having Judy put down as a dangerous dog.

'If I let this dog off the lead, it'll probably kill somebody.'

The roar of derisive laughter which greeted this warning left me with no alternative. I bent down and released the catch and the dog hurled itself forward, its jaws slavering with anticipation.

Like Lady Macbeth's dinner guests, the Lodgers stood not on the order of their going but went immediately. The ring of grinning faces at the postern gate just dissolved, as for the second time in as many weeks the battalions of the enemy rushed headlong for home, pelting down Millgate in abject flight, shirt tails flapping like the banners of a routed army, boots and clogs clattering hollowly on the uneven pavement. I reached the postern and poked my head out just in time to see the slowest of them sprinting past the Baths as if pursued by the Ancient Mariner's grinning fiend and not daring to look over his shoulder. If he had done so he would have seen Kep, intent only on reaching home, swerve sharp right into the Baths Yard, paws skidding, ears flying like battle standards en route for his comfortable basket by the kitchen fire.

The Lodgers had successfully been repelled on this occasion but, like Soviet Russia, they remained as uncomfortable neighbours and I continued to brood on dangerous and impractical schemes for outwitting or even annihilating them. The house two doors lower down Millgate from ours was occupied by Mr and Mrs Heyes, a retired couple whose large brown and white cat sat on their windowsill and gazed benevolently at passers-by from his one bright green and one bright blue eye. The Heyeses had one son, James, who was several years older than the rest of us and, in addition to playing the tea-chest bass in a skiffle group, was extremely knowledgeable about science. James was a natural teacher and willing on occasions to share his expertise with us younger children. He had converted the spare bedroom of his parents' house into a laboratory cum workshop, a place I regarded as a paradise. The Heyes house had a green door and I always associated Frankie Vaughan's hit song of the same name with its fascinating and dimly understood secrets. In James's lab we fiddled with small radio sets, made salt crystals and were allowed to rub a little jeweller's rouge on the lens he was grinding for the new telescope he was building for his backyard observatory, a miniature Mount Palomar with a dome revolving on tramlines. In an unguarded moment James let slip that he had once made gunpowder. He absolutely refused to give us the formula, warning us that in mixing the ingredients we would certainly burn off all our hair and eyebrows even if we were not blinded, but my imagination was already working overtime. Bombs! The ultimate deterrent to the Lodgers!

Upstairs in the Baths flat I had already discovered a large single-volume engineering dictionary. Could it possibly contain the required formula? It did. The ingredients were innocuous in themselves but I was acute enough to realise that if I walked into Hunter's chemists and asked for all three of them the assistant would promptly give me what some of my Hollywood idols called the bum's rush, so I deviously shopped for them in three separate locations. Remembering James's warnings about unexpected explosions I was very careful about combining them in one of my mother's large mixing bowls using a wooden rather than a metal spoon. Once the gunpowder was made I packed it carefully into small Robertson's marmalade jars, using a sharp nail to make a pinhole in each lid, through which I threaded a length of the quick potassium fuse used to ignite the 'Jetex' motors of model aeroplanes. The resulting bang was much more impressive than the biggest firework and demolished quite a large part of a derelict lavatory on the Brew. I was fortunate not to be shredded by the fragments of a *Golden Shred* jar, but the pure scientist does not worry himself with such details. It is even more fortunate that I was distracted by another idea before I had time to try my bombs on the Lodgers, though in fact the new idea was almost as dangerous as its predecessor.

At the back of the wardrobe in aunt Margaret's spare bedroom, along with the engineering dictionary, I had discovered her son's ancient airgun. I bought a pound of lead pellets from the sports shop at the top of Millgate and several of us were soon taking turns to pop at tin cans in the Baths yard, with the vague idea of eventually bagging a Lodger or two. It didn't end at tin cans, though fortunately we never got round to shooting at the Lodgers. Thirty feet away, propped up against a wall, there was a sheet of corrugated iron which formed a sort of rough shelter. Being a foolish child who had not yet absorbed the simple rule that a gun, whether loaded or not, should never casually be pointed at anyone, when it was my turn to shoot, I recklessly swept the barrel round towards the three or four friends who were with me. I had no intention of shooting at them but they were not to know that and they rapidly took cover under the corrugated iron sheet. I squeezed the trigger and there was sharp CRACK! followed by a satisfying PING! from the iron. My friends started to emerge to disarm me, knowing that I had trouble 'breaking' open the breech of the gun to reload it, but I cunningly managed the job by placing the end of the barrel against the cobblestones. My friends retreated again in horror and disarray. CRACK! PING! and it was only the intervention of Arthur Spooner, Assistant Manager of the Baths, that ended what might easily have turned into a nasty accident. After that the air rifle disappeared into oblivion. So did the engineering dictionary, which is why I never got to try that interesting formula for nitro-glycerine.

While not as naturally equipped for delinquency as the Lodgers, with their rich heritage of misbehaviour, it will be obvious to the reader that we Millgaters had our moments. None of us would have vandalised occupied property, but empty houses scheduled for demolition were fair game and their windows exploded with a satisfying crash. Equally satisfying was the pleasure of annoying Mr Sherburn, whose glazier's shop occupied an old house down the yard behind Kevin's and Jimmy's house. Mr Sherburn piled his glass offcuts directly opposite his front door against a wall which divided his yard from the 'entry' behind my house. He was easily provoked to red-faced rage by calculated cheek and several of us lurked out of sight on my side of the wall while Derek prepared to light the biggest 'banger' we could find. Fizzz ... !

WHO'S THAT FELLER WITH THE BIG BALD HEAD?
SHERBURN! SHERBURN!
WHO'S THAT FELLER WITH THE BIG BALD HEAD?
SHERBURN! SHERBURN!

Bang! Crash! went the glass pile, shards flew in all directions and Mr Sherburn's face would appear like an irate purple chad from the other side of the wall. We were reasonably safe from retribution because the glazier was much less agile than we were. His anger cooled rapidly and although he could easily have shopped me to my mother, who would certainly have clouted me for my insolence to an elder, he never did so. Our local bobby, PC Hughes, was much faster on his feet and we had some narrow escapes when he chased us after some of our more outrageous episodes. When I think of the Wigan Borough force of my childhood I am reminded of the book of Genesis, for there were giants in the earth in those days. Even the WPCs were strapping specimens and the most formidable of them all, Big Amy, chased young Ethel Fairhurst, my future mother-in-law, the length of Library Street for disobeying her instructions when on point duty at the top of Wallgate. Even so, legend had it that there were areas in Wigan, such as Caroline Street, where the police dared walk only in twos. Sometime in the 1970s I mentioned this to long-retired Sergeant Joe Wood, who at seventy-odd still had muscles like Popeye, and was rewarded with his big booming laugh.

'Many's the half-crown I've earned from that piece of nonsense,' he told me. 'Coming off duty I'd call in one of th' pubs at top end of Caroline Street. I'd not be wearing me helmet or a uniform cape but I'd leave th' neck of me mac undone and let th' top silver button of me tunic show. Somebody would always notice it and say summat daft like

"Hey, bobby, I bet thee tha dursent walk down th' street on thi own with thi mac off." Of course I'd allus do it and nowt would happen. Th' bad lads knew me, tha knows, and they wouldn't maul wi' me.'

I mentioned to Mr Wood that my friend's father had been a Wigan policeman at the same period as himself.

'John Benn? Aye, of course I knew him. He made Inspector. Mind you, *he* was a *big* man.'

I looked at Joe's barrel chest and towering frame, still only slightly stooped. 'He must have been,' I said.

CHAPTER 13

Romance & Reality

IT WAS IN MY GREAT-UNCLE'S FLAT at the Baths that I first became aware of the enchantment of women. Jan, my second cousin, great-aunt Lily's younger daughter, who was at college, had brought home her friend Anne Salisbury to visit. I must have been no more than two years old, because I remember Anne as a softness and a fragrance rather than as a face. I lay on a sofa with my head in her lap and as she bent down to kiss me her long feathery hair brushed my face. It is well over fifty years ago and I trust that she is alive today, a contented woman with a lifetime of achievement behind her and a host of children and grandchildren. I met her once as a softness and a fragrance and I shall never forget.

'I had a girl whose name was Anne'. Do you remember the Spinners' song? 'Had' is not at all an appropriate word. This Anne, who came into my life seven or eight years later, was eleven years old and so was I. She was thin and flat-chested with a shock of sun-bleached hair cut pageboy style and freckles across the bridge of her nose. Her father was a policeman and had already risen to the rank of inspector. He even had a car, something only one family in Millgate possessed. I was acutely aware of the gulf between Anne's home, a small modern suburban semi, and our crumbling, rented terraced house. I watched her covertly in class but hung back when there were kissing games at school parties. The only time I ever touched her small-boned, dry hand was during our infrequent country dancing classes, when my incompetence and apparent lack of any rhythmic sense vied with a heady sense of the sensuousness of the rustic music,

Above: Bill and Beatrice Taylor with bridesmaid Jean Clayton

of the proximity of the girls' warm fragrant bodies and especially with my consciousness of the nearness of Anne.

Sometimes at school we sang folk songs from the *New National Songbook*. In me they often evoked intense feelings of longing for something I could only dimly define. Even at eleven, though I had never heard the word, I realised that some of them were intensely erotic. Why did the lady run off with the *Raggle Raggle Gipsies?* Obvious! The amazing thing was that my contemporaries, many of them much readier than I with a ripe expression or a youthful innuendo, stood there raptly carolling, their rosy faces entirely innocent of the sex which dripped from the lyrics.

All in the merry month of May
When green buds they were swellin'
Young Jemmy Grove on his deathbed lay
For love of Barbara Allen.

I knew about swelling, an embarrassing phenomenon that could take one unawares at the most inconvenient moments. We told jokes about young men who employed lengths of chain in the doomed effort to pass impossible tests in eastern harems. We reacted covertly to the different and seductive swellings in the front of Dorothy Wilson's blue school pinafore dress. We were already aware that girls, while not necessarily thinking exactly as we did about these matters, could be intensely conscious of their power to disturb. No wonder Jemmy Grove was in such a miserable state. Barbara Allen had cut off his swellings! When the girl finally visited him the only words of comfort she had been able to muster had been a callous statement of the blatantly obvious: 'Young man, I think you're dyin.' We knew Barbara personally: there were at least three of her in Standard Four, beautiful, self-possessed ice-maidens who were not about to lavish their favours on any of us. Oh, I know that in the final verse Barbara took to her bed determined to die of remorse. But I bet anything that she didn't do it. Meanwhile Anne was my ice-maiden, not an imperious Barbara Allen, but remote, secret and absorbed in the business of being that incomprehensible creature, a girl.

If I left my house in the dark winter evenings, perhaps to visit cousins in a neighbouring street, I would walk home in a parabola through the back alleys to ensure that my final approach to home would take me towards, rather than away from, Anne's house on the other side of town. I went to sleep with a prayer for or to her. Once in the summer holidays I walked across town with two friends to the field behind her house with the romantic notion, culled from books, of serenading her with a zither I had found in The Lumber Room and which I could not play. We ran away when her mother came to hang out the washing; three scruffy sunburned little boys. In all of this I was conscious of nothing but an undefined longing. Jealously I guarded thoughts of Anne from the taint of mundane speculation. From conversations in the playground and with older youths on the Brew I was aware of the existence of sex, but like many an idealistic youth I did not associate this mysterious activity, at once seductive and distasteful, with the object of my adoration. Nor, of course, did I associate it with my parents.

We sat in a circle in our cardboard-floored den. The grass was high, our hiding place invisible to the outside world. As usual somebody made a knowing reference to sex and there was a snigger. Kevin, a year or two older than our average, admonished us gently. In spite of a chequered career and Borstal training he had, my mother often pointed out acerbically, the best manners of the lot of us.

'There's nothing dirty in sex,' he told us firmly. This was news to me and I gave him my full attention.

'You have to do sex to make babies.' This was more news and I stared at him incredulously.

'My Dad had to shag my Mum to get me.'

I thought this was the oddest piece of news of the lot. Who would have thought that Kevin, who looked eminently normal, had had such a strange start in life? I thought about Mr and Mrs Rasburn involved in this remarkable and bizarre activity which I imagined as taking place standing up and with a least six inches of space between them, rather like the miniature refuelling of an aircraft in flight.

'Derek's Dad had to shag Derek's Mum to get him.'

Not surprising, this. Although nobody had ever seen Derek's dad, who was reputed to live in Leicester, we all knew Derek's mum, a brassy, well-upholstered redhead with a swinging social life and a string of admirers who drove highly polished Lanchesters and second-hand Jaguars. I secretly rather approved of Derek's mum and certainly would have put very little past her. I grinned at Derek's evident discomfiture.

'And Jack's dad shagged Jack's mum to get him,' concluded Kevin, to my unspeakable horror.

Somebody, I think it may have been Graham Ellis, had a copy of a magazine called *Health and Strength* which included black and white photographs of athletic-looking girls artfully posed so that very little was visible except breasts which looked rather like fried eggs. These, I was informed, were 'nudes' and I was told that there were even theatres, such as the Windmill in London and the Folies Bergère in Paris, where the nudes were 'live'. I never got to visit either place, though on a school trip in 1962 I did eat a meal in the self-service restaurant of the Moulin Rouge, and it was good, very reasonably priced and not at all erotic. As a youngster I savoured the word 'nude', which had a satisfyingly rounded sound to it. A few doors away from us lived a devout Roman Catholic family called Almond, whose three sons we referred to as Bumbly One, Bumbly Two and Bumbly Three because of their supposed resemblance to Michael Bentine's family of aliens in the TV series. The elder two boys, David and Francis, were altar boys and the Almonds had over-protective parents. Their children were seldom allowed to play with us rough lot, a fact we tended to resent. Some time after poring over *Health and Strength* I peered through the Almonds' back fence and yelled the rudest word I could think of: 'Nude! Nooooooooooood!'

The Eleven Plus divided Anne and me, though there is no need to express it so pathetically, for we had never in fact been together. I went to the town's ancient Grammar School, she to the newer Girls' High School. Sex at this early adolescent period was manifested by another Anne; one who was far less remote because she lived in my street, was the sister of two of my friends and because, though I have no reason to suppose that it meant anything, accessibility was part of her style. She was fifteen, had painted toenails, an easy smile and a generous bosom which was either triced up hard into sharp cliff edges when she went out in the evenings or rolled around severally in a loose pink sweater when we saw her around the house in the daytime. I was physically stirred by her but she was several years older than myself, which normally represents absolute impossibility at that age. Perhaps because of this I found it easy to talk with her and she once said to me: 'You are the nicest boy I ever met!'

I am still not sure whether this was a back-handed compliment or even a message which I was too gormless to comprehend. She pleased me but she only disturbed me, very slightly, in an obviously biological sense because I was not in love with her, and although this story properly finishes with my departure from the Blue Coat School en route for Wigan Grammar School in August 1957, this chapter only ends four years later with when I met a girl who seemed to encompass both the celestial and the earthly Annes of my childhood.

The youth club met on Monday evenings in the basement of the Queen's Hall Methodist Church, a large, domed Victorian structure in the centre of town. On this first occasion I had taken the bus from my outlying suburb down to the Market Place and then walked slowly in spite of the grey chill with my overcoat collar turned up against the rain. Friends from school had encouraged me to join the club but, though not timid, I was bleakly apprehensive at any prospect of meeting strangers in numbers. I particularly distrusted those of my own age who would probably play ping-pong and 'dig' Beatles numbers and who, before they had got the message that verbally I was more than capable of demolishing most, if not all opposition, might be disposed to mock either my reserved and conservative style or my taste for tailored suits and fancy waistcoats.

I paused uncertainly at the top of the wide flight of stairs which led down to the unknown. There was a vaguely ecclesiastical smell compounded equally of polish, dust, disinfectant and old hymn books. At the foot of the staircase two girls stood talking in a pool of bright light which spilled from the open door of a side room. One of them, though she was pretty, I merely registered as unimportant stage dressing. The other was slim, shapely, compact, in a short slightly flared skirt, medium high heels and a dusty-pink mohair cardigan worn open over a white Peter Pan blouse sprinkled with blue forget-me-nots. A heart-shaped face was framed in a mass of coarse chestnut waves which shone glossily in the side-lighting. She was completely unconscious of my existence and I had the immediate and totally ridiculous sensation that I loved her. Later when I knew her I came to understand that for me the special piquancy of her attraction came at least in part from the harmony of contrasts I had perceived in this first moment of seeing her. It was both physical and spiritual, but initially I was conscious only of the physical: her short hair was abundant, rough-textured, coarser than I have ever known in any other human being, rich in colour and to the touch exactly like an Airedale's coat. Her dark brows were heavy over eyes which reflected the forget-me-not blue of that first blouse. She was slim and small-breasted but her little hands were square and practical, her calves sturdy, muscular and well-shaped like an Italian peasant girl's. Her features were small and fine-boned, her complexion white satin tinged with rose which died to a faint half-flush along her throat.

I do not remember hearing her voice on this first occasion. Afterwards, when I knew its sound well, I came to identify it with the rich chestnut of her hair. Though never loud it was a deep, slightly throaty contralto. Audrey was a fourth-form pupil at the Girls' High School and her speech, like my own, was consciously more attuned to the middle-class norm than to the south Lancashire working class. Like myself she loved music but she was one of the few people I have met in my life who genuinely could not sing in tune. When eventually we arrived at a relationship which would allow this without embarrassment I tried to teach her to imitate simple musical phrases. Though she would occasionally manage to do so, she would prove quite incapable of repeating the feat half a minute later. In church, supported by the organ and the other voices, she managed the hymns at tenor pitch, only slightly off key. I think this intractable tone-deafness would have irritated me profoundly in any other human being. In her it was only an endearing blemish in someone otherwise perfect, though ultimately her inability to share what was to be an increasingly important part of my life was to become a limiting factor in our relationship.

Being in love did not guarantee that love was requited. Audrey was friendly towards me from the first but at fifteen she was her father's girl, a cherished only child who was happily absorbed in school work and family rituals. She had a particular friend, Christine, with whom I had seen her talking on that first occasion, and who monopolised her leisure hours. I also had a friend, James, who, I thought craftily, could be persuaded to occupy Christines' attention while I made some much-needed progress with Audrey. Years later, when she was the headmistress of an Anglican girls' school, her pupils asked her if she had had a boyfriend while at school.

'Yes I did,' she replied, 'and we used to meet in the rose garden of Mesnes Park almost every afternoon after classes.'

Indeed we did, and like generations of Wigan youngsters we would sometimes invite good luck by rubbing the shoe of 'th' mon i'th park', the brooding bronze statue of Sir Francis Sharp Powell, the borough's long-serving Victorian MP.

After 'going out' together for several years Audrey and I, in some ways too much alike, eventually went our separate ways and found our soul mates in gentler partners than ourselves. She and her husband Charles have long lived in Australia, while after years of travelling the world Val and I live contentedly in the hills of Andalucia. James and Christine still live in Wigan and, like us, have been happily married for nearly forty years.

CHAPTER 14

Goodbye to 1969

LONG BEFORE THE TERM was in vogue, the upwardly-mobile Walshes left the village in the early 1960s to move into their newly built bungalow. The elegant, reserved young Mrs Walsh's successor was initially something of a shock. Married less than two years, Sharon was a bouncing, buxom, chatty twenty-year-old.

'What's your new neighbour like, grandmother?'

'She calls me Annie.'

Since her marriage in 1908 hardly anybody apart from her parents, siblings and close contemporaries had addressed my grandmother as anything but Mrs Taylor, and by 1960 almost all of these were dead. She was equally formal in addressing others and I never knew the Christian names of the Walshes or Mrs McKnight. As children will, I had occasionally tried calling her Annie and though her eyes twinkled and the corners of her mouth lifted a fraction she had not commented. She knew how to deal with cheek and in my case it was never with a heavy hand. Suddenly an unrelated girl, young enough to be her granddaughter, was popping in from next door and calling her by her first name.

'How do you feel about that?'

'I don't mind. She doesn't mean anything by it. It's just her way.'

I could tell that she was slightly surprised that she didn't mind it, but as she sometimes reminded Edie, who could be something of a Cassandra, the times were changing and we had better change with them. It was typical of her openness that at eighty she could

Above: Harold and Edith Taylor

take pleasure in the company of this lively youngster and her eighteen-month old toddler and was even up for a spot of babysitting when required.

I was not always at 169. In the late 1950s we left Millgate and moved back to Whelley and, during the school holidays when my mother was still working at the Baths and my brother Stephen was small, Aunty Edie would frequently come to spend the day at our house in Bradshaw Street. Less frequently Annie would come with her, but when she did she would never be content with simply visiting and she too would pitch into any outstanding household task. One day in 1960, at the age of seventy-eight, she slipped while scrubbing the lobby floor, fell heavily and was unable to rise. An ambulance was called and took her away to the Royal Albert Edward Infirmary in Wigan, where a fractured femur was diagnosed. It was exactly the same accident which, forty-three years previously, had ended her mother Elizabeth's mobility and ultimately her life. In spite of Edie's physical vigour, Annie was the presiding genius of 169. My aunts were dismayed.

'What's going to happen to Aunty Edie?' they asked each other pessimistically and eyed my mother speculatively.

Edie was a treasure but she was also a fusspot whose 'moidering' could be extremely irritating. No job was ever allowed to be left pending. If I made a pot of tea and left it to brew she would pour it away and wash up the cup before I had time to drink it. If I put a record on the turntable and turned up the volume to mezzo-forte she would complain that her eardrums were in danger. The one exception was Harry Secombe's recording of her favourite piece, Handel's *Largo*, which could be played fortissimo until the doors of the radiogram rattled. If Annie were to die, as seemed extremely likely, how, my aunts asked themselves, would my mother, admittedly a logistical genius, manage to combine working five days a week with looking after an increasingly wayward Aunty Edie, who, jealous of the attention being paid to her injured sister, had taken to our spare bed and announced that she too had broken her hip?

I remember the atmosphere of tension but at fourteen it did not occur to me that Annie's life was in danger. Fortunately it didn't occur to Annie either. She emerged triumphantly from the operation to pin her femur and enthusiastically recounted her first conversation with the surgeon, who rejoiced in the unusually appropriate moniker of Dr Contractor.

'Mrs Taylor, breaking your hip was the best possible thing that could have happened to you!'

'Really, Doctor? How in thunderation (one of Annie's few expletives, originally invented by her father, James) do you make that out?'

'Because you have one or two medical complications, including quite severe anaemia. We are going to sort all that out for you. Your quality of life is going to be ten times better.' As indeed it was.

During my childhood we saw very few black people in Wigan. The few one met were almost always African postgraduates studying at the Wigan Mining and Technical College. Some of them lodged in the village and Annie would often meet one or other of them on the New Springs bus. If the bus was full, the young man would always be the first to offer Annie his seat. Their subsequent conversation would confirm that the visitor had perfect, if somewhat accented English, perfect teeth and even more perfect manners. In this way Annie reached the conclusion that black people came from a rather superior race and culture and, indeed, when my great-aunt Grace Hart, an elderly southern belle, visited us from the USA round about the same era, she also pronounced impressively, 'My! YOUR nigras certainly are different from OUR nigras.' When Annie emerged from the anaesthetic to be greeted by the handsome, enthusiastic West Indian Dr Contractor it only confirmed an already rooted conviction.

The measured idyll of 169 was resumed and seemed set to go on forever, but nothing ever does. Surprisingly it was vigorous, strapping Aunty Edie who first showed signs of failing, and the change was frightening. Edie's energy had always been legendary. At eighty-nine she still rose even in a winter dawn, stripped to the buff, climbed onto the wooden draining board in the freezing glass lean-to and scrubbed herself from head to foot in cold running water. Years before the term was invented she would jog through the village with a heavy shopping bag. On Sundays, when the extended family gathered at 169, Edie was the architect of stupendous Lancashire high teas which began with potato cakes (still a family favourite) followed by meat pie, sliced cold beef and ham with salad, new potatoes and pickled beetroot and onions. Sherry trifles and mouth-watering combinations of apple, blackberry and rhubarb pies would appear in due season. Even in those days I was an instinctive performer and impresario and those Sundays at 169 provided me with both a cast and an audience. Nobody was spared. Uncles and increasingly portly aunts became theatrical extras. My grandmother and great-aunt Edie took part in boxing tournaments and athletic competitions and competed for gold medals and Lonsdale Belts. A natural extrovert, after years of bringing up nephews and great-nephews Aunty Edie was a seasoned trouper and these demanding events did not phase her. When I was a small child she had read to me for hours. Because I knew my favourite stories by heart she would keep me on my toes by omitting important details or deliberately mispronouncing words so that I could correct her.

'In a house in a hollow oak tree there lived a little GOME.'

Shrieks of protest: 'It's a GNOME, Aunty! A GNOME!'

We shared a love of singing and silly linguistic jokes and she also tried to teach me to dance, which I am afraid was a lost cause from the beginning. She was always ready for any game a child could dream up and when the time came she nagged and irritated me through the disorder of my adolescence as she had done with my father and his four brothers, receiving equally scant thanks for her efforts. When I brought my first girlfriend to 169 Whelley there were hilarious reminiscences of her own courting days and the ingrained choosiness that had ensured that she remained a spinster. The family's living repository of traditional superstition and folk wisdom, she threw salt over her shoulder into the face of the Devil, lamented broken mirrors as harbingers of seven years' bad luck, refused to countenance shoes being put on the table for cleaning and warned us strictly against looking at the new moon through glass. Some of her dicta, such as

'Milk makes phlegm', were sound science, and as an undiagnosed asthmatic I wish I had taken more notice of them. Some were irritating generalisations such as 'Gypsies steal children' or 'The Irish keep pigs in their houses.' Long after we had grown out of them she had a habit of repeating little jingles which had amused us as tots, and my mother would mutter 'If I hear any more Sharrock-carrot-parrot, I'm going to scream.'

'Edie's Eightieth Walking Day' sounds like the title of an epic and, in its way, an epic it was. Lancashire's Whit Walks, those processions of Christian witness which have their origins in medieval times, were still taken very seriously when I was in my late teens in the mid 1960s. I have described in an earlier chapter how Edie and Annie and the other young village maidens used to put on their new Easter dresses and join the whole of their church community, decked out in its finery, to beat the bounds of the parish, accompanied by choir and brass bands. For Edie the walking day tradition started in 1884 when she was a little girl of six and it didn't end until she was an old woman almost at the end of her life. From the beginning, almost to the very end, she walked eighty times and she never missed a single year, though her seventy-ninth was the hardest. It was a blisteringly hot day, quite unusually so for the time of year. It was of course a Sunday and as usual the family was gathered at 169. Since breaking her hip five years previously Annie no longer took part in the procession and on a day such as this she was worried about Edie doing so. She tried to persuade her sister to watch from the sidelines and her sons and daughters-in-law supported her.

'Aunty Edie, it's so hot. You're eighty-six. You've walked for seventy-eight years. You've done enough.'

'She's stubborn, that one,' said Annie, her lips set in a thin line. She'll not listen to a word I say, nor you neither.'

Stubborn? She was that. She didn't argue. She didn't even reply. She'd made her mind up and I privately agreed with her. What she was intending to do was remarkable in its own small way and she was determined to do it. It was a windless day without a cloud in the sky. The sun beat down and the tarmac melted. The procession started at St Stephen's Church and wound out with the brass band playing past the Plantation Gates onto the main road and past 169, where the family watched anxiously. Edie made no concession to the heat. She wore a topcoat, a hat and crocheted gloves. Up the steep hill of Springs Bank, past the Von Blucher and the little boarded-up sweet shop where she had worked to make a few pounds a week to help support her orphaned nephews. Up the hot, dusty length of New Springs to the very end of the parish. Then back. There was still at least half of the journey to be walked. Down Whelley past the George and Dragon where she had taken her jug to buy beer for our shandy treats. Past the Lodge where Old Mr Ramsdale, ten years younger than herself, was sitting on a kitchen chair which his children had brought out to the pavement. Past Naylors grocer's shop at the end of Bradshaw Street and in and out of the side streets around Great Acre. Then back up the weary length of Whelley. The amateurs of the St John's Ambulance Brigade were in attendance but in those days the danger of dehydration was less well understood and she might have needed to collapse before any help had been forthcoming from that direction. As she approached 169 her steps were beginning to weave and she was visibly struggling to keep in column with the rest of the Mothers' Union. But she had done it. At the age of eighty-six, seventy-nine walking days had been accomplished.

That was the year I went to Lancaster University. Every holiday I would return to 169 and for almost three years nothing much seemed to change. Suddenly, shortly after my graduation, I arrived to find Edie morose and withdrawn. No sooner had I sat down than she was asking when I intended to go home. I did not understand what was happening and tried to tease her back into being her normal self, attempts she resisted with utterly uncharacteristic sullen resentment. Annie was as frustrated with her as I was. She herself was eighty-seven but was not at all ready to let go her hold on life. She and Edie had lived together almost continuously since childhood and she was afraid of what was about to happen.

Once she had made her decision, Edie slipped away very quickly. One dawn she refused to get out of bed but literally turned her face to the wall and within a couple of hours she was dead. The unmarried daughter, she was laid to rest in the same plot as her parents James and Elizabeth Sharrock in St David's churchyard at Haigh. She had cared unselfishly for all of us but she had worshipped her youngest nephew, my father Bill, and, according to my mother, spoiled him beyond redemption. Although he protested at her 'moidering' and her attempts to organise him, he felt much the same about her and he shocked me by sobbing bitterly as the clods clattered onto her coffin lid. Like her parents before her, she would never have uttered the word 'love'. She would never have needed to. As a spinster she had merited only honorary membership of the Mothers' Union at St Stephen's Church in Whelley, but all the same she had been an utterly devoted parent to those five fatherless boys and a loving grandparent to me. Not least, after retiring prematurely from tailoring in order to take on her domestic responsibilities, she had made most of our clothes. She often had a sharp tongue and I certainly never heard her utter a sentimental word, but sometimes a far off look came into her eye.

'All them little pants,' she would say quietly, 'All them little pants.'

There was no question of Annie's remaining alone at 169. Harold, her second son, adored her. He and his gentle wife Edith were both retired and there was plenty of room in their large terraced house at Hindley Green. Annie lived there for a further two years, still mentally alert but increasingly frail in body. Although the hip, repaired ten years previously, sometimes troubled her, she was still quite mobile and would go for quite long leisurely walks. Harold and Edith looked after her with complete devotion and were a little anxious about leaving her behind as their summer holiday approached. Typically she brushed aside their concern. She would be perfectly comfortable spending a fortnight with Jim and Maud at Burscough, right next door to her father James's home village of Lathom. In fact she had an excellent time and in new surroundings, with her grandson David and the other print shop workers popping in and out for a cup of tea and a chat, she recovered some of her old vivacity. Jim and Maud were active church members and one of their regular visitors was their young bachelor curate. In spite of the sixty-year age gap he and Annie took to each other instantly and she accepted his invitation to tea in his parsonage. There was a certain amount of teasing from the family that grandma was still able to 'pull' a handsome young fellow at nearly ninety. A few days later she returned, full of stories of her adventures, to Harold and Edie at Hindley and the following Sunday she walked the short distance from church back to the house and drank a welcome cup of tea. Placing the cup carefully in the saucer she smiled contentedly.

'I enjoyed that!' she said, and died.

Although he must have been prepared to some extent, Harold was devastated. He berated himself for going on holiday and leaving his mother to overtax herself with the social whirl of Burscough. He berated his brother for allowing their mother to overdo things. He was being unreasonable, but grief is not reasonable. And of course it was a tremendous compliment to Annie. How often we view the old as a burden and are relieved when the burden is taken away from us. Annie was never a burden to anybody. She had lived a full life, often in the face of circumstances which would have crushed a lesser spirit, and when she left us we wished we had been able to keep her for longer. Could there be a better epitaph? She and Aunty Edie died almost forty years ago but hardly a day goes by without my thoughts turning for a moment to the little house at 169 Whelley, the bedroom with the sloping ceiling and the overgrown garden with its view of brown and white cows grazing hock-deep in the meadow behind.

For many years after leaving Wigan in 1969 it seemed a simple thing to pop over from Lancaster, Cambridge or even Chile to keep in touch with my family and the old home town. Suddenly, or so it seemed, nobody was at home. My parents Bill and Beatrice are buried at St Matthew's Church, Highfield, where for many years my father trained the Sunday School football team. After sixty years they are finally completely at peace with one another. My Harts, Norcliffes and Cockrells are in Wigan cemetery in Lower Ince, a mile from the town centre where they lived and worked. Like all big Victorian necropolises it is a melancholy place, full of black marble and weeping stone angels. Apart from William whose grave overlooks the mountains and the Pacific Ocean five thousand miles away, the earthly remains of my Lancashire Taylors and Sharrocks all lie in St David's churchyard at Haigh. John and Mary Taylor are close by their first daughter, Margaret, who lived for only three days. Aunty Edie Sharrock is with her parents James and Elizabeth, my grandfather Fred, who died in 1918, with his RAF pilot son Jack, who was killed at the age of twenty-eight in the Second World War, and with his beloved Annie who joined him in 1969 after fifty-one years of widowhood. It is a typical English country churchyard, beautiful, peaceful and slightly unkempt, where tall grasses wave between leaning, weathered headstones.

CHAPTER 15

Gold, Frankincense & th' Mayor

'NOT WORKING TODAY?' A hairdresser is allowed to ask questions. It comes with the territory and in any case at four o'clock on a chilly, blustery midweek afternoon the traditional barber's shop near Grimes's old arcade was almost empty and there was plenty of time for a chat.

'As a matter of fact I have been working all day. In the History Shop just around the corner.'

'What doing?'

'I'm researching for a book I'm writing. My publisher has asked me to dig out some old photographs from the archives.'

'So you're an author. How many books have you written, then?'

'This is my first one.'

'What's it about?'

'I suppose it's about me. And Wigan.'

'About you? Are you famous, then?'

'Not at all.'

'But you'll be famous when your book comes out?'

'I very much doubt it. In any case, it's as much about Wigan as about me.'

'Wiggin! What the 'ell can anybody find to write about Wiggin? Do you LIVE in Wiggin?'

Above: the Richard and William of *this* generation, Massachusetts, 1986

'I was born in Wigan and as a youngster I lived in Millgate only a couple of hundred yards from here.'

'Apart from th' Baths there's nowt much in Millgate these days.'

'That's true. If I ever DO become famous they'll have to put my little blue plaque on the multi-story car park.'

JOHN SHARROCK TAYLOR, Author, lived here 1952–1958

'Are you not still living in Wiggin, then?'

'No. I live in Spain.'

'Spain! If I lived in Spain I wouldn't be wasting my time writing about bloody Wiggin!'

'Spain's not all bullfights and Benidorm, you know, and in any case Wigan has its points.'

'Name one.'

I named several but my new friend remained dourly sceptical of the merits of our home town. Neither am I at all sure that he was convinced by my credentials as a working author because Val, who had enjoyed being the proverbial fly on the wall throughout this conversation, later pointed out that I had been charged the OAP rate for my haircut. I hasten to add that I am not at all sensitive about this or about anything else that saves me money. As he brushed me down and helped me on with the faded, darned old 'fleece' which I bought ten years ago in preparation for the chilly Andean nights of Ecuador he had a couple of final questions.

'How long is it since you lived in Wiggin?'

'I left Wigan in 1969, though I've been back quite a few times during the last thirty-eight years.'

'You'll have noticed a lot more changes than yon Millgate car park, then.'

'I have that.'

I met Val, who taught infants at St James's Road Primary School in Orrell, during a Wigan Gilbert and Sullivan Society rehearsal of *The Gondoliers* shortly after I came down from Lancaster University in 1967 and started to teach English at my alma mater, Wigan Grammar School. In spite of the reservations of her formidable mother, who thought things were going too quickly, we were engaged before Christmas and wed in the following August. After a year of married life in a first-floor flat in the old All Saints' Mission House in New Market Street we moved to new jobs in the Lancaster area, though for the next twenty years or so we were frequent visitors to family and friends in Wigan. Because my parents' house was small and my brother was still living there we would usually stay at Val's family home in Orrell. Her adored father Tom Lund had died suddenly in 1970 and apart from Oliver, an amiably crazy dog, and a cat called Lucy who had a small, square black moustache and a personality which suggested that she might be a reincarnation of somebody notorious and teutonic, the household at 12 Milton Grove consisted of her mother Ethel and her aunt Winnie. Aunty Winnie's contralto produced some of the swoopiest portamentos I have heard from any human throat and my mother-in-law had a very acid turn of phrase when she was that way out, so comparisons with the then-popular Hinge and Bracket were inescapable. A central feature of our visits to Orrell during the 1970s was always a ritual duet beginning with the words:

'You know, they're ruining Wigan.'

'The Grammar School's gone.'

'Gone?'

'It's gone ... what d'you call it?'

'Comprehensive?'

'That's it. Comprehensive.'

'Now it's called the Mesnes High School.'

'But the type of child they've got there now can't pronounce hard words.'

'So they call it the Mez-Nez High.'

'The Queens Hall's been knocked down to make way for a new bus station.'

They've just left the small chapel and the foyer in Market Street.'

'But that was the only decent acoustic in Wigan! The Linacre Hall was hopeless when I was at school and it's even worse since they filled it with all that upholstery. At the Music Festival rose bowl final last year it was like singing with my head in a bag!'

'Even burning decent coal is banned. In Lancashire! I ask you!'

'We're in Greater Manchester now.'

'Pshaw!'

'How do you spell that?'

'So even the buses are the wrong colour.'

'You're still bussing it to Wigan every day, Aunty? No thoughts of retiring?'

'What would Winnie do if she retired? She can't even wash up without knocking the handles off the cups. She bashes them twice on the mixer tap. Once coming and once going. At least I keep some interests outside the house.'

'Ethel still fund raises down Pemberton for the Life Boat but half the houses she used to collect from have been knocked down.'

'Never mind. The legions of the Great Unwashed have got to live somewhere and I do my best to track them down to their council flats and part them from their giro cash before they spend it all on filling those brand new baths with smokeless briquettes.'

Aunty Winnie carried on working as a legal executive at Frank Platt and Fishwick in King Street, Wigan's equivalent of High Holborn, until she was eighty-six years old and my formidable mother-in-law continued to harry potential RNLI donors well into the 1980s, but the message of Mesdames Hinge and Bracket was clear: Wigan was no longer the place it had been. I wonder what they would say if they knew that King Street is now better known for clubbing than for conveyancing and even the despised Mez-Nez High has become a health centre.

In the early years of our marriage one of our continuing links with the old town was Wigan parish church, where I was a member of the choir and drove over for rehearsals and services until our move to Cambridgeshire in 1979 made that impossible. In an era when many all-male church choirs, especially those whose town-centre parishes were suffering wholesale demolition, were shutting up shop, the All Saints choir was still thriving under the directorship of David Cutter. Godfather to our son Richard, David is one of the last generation of Keble graduates to speak with the Oxford accent of Huxley and Professor Joad. Thirty-odd years in Wigan did not manage to erode it but it was even more remarkable that he managed to persuade choristers from Delph Street and Gidlow Lane to sing in the cut-glass tones of Christ Church Cathedral. I recall one Grammar School lad who stubbornly insisted on 'gold, frankincense and MARE' until David pulled him up short with 'Listen, Karl, What do you Wiganers call your civic leader? The fellow with the gold chain?'

Karl paused for thought and then broke into a broad grin. 'Th' MURR,' he replied triumphantly.

'That's it! Keep thinking "gold frankincense and th' MURR" and it'll come out just right.'

In addition to the couple of dozen trebles drawn from several local primary schools, the choir of the 1970s had a strong corps of men ranging from youngsters like myself to veterans such as Eric Harris, Jack Hollis, Arthur Prescott, Harry Talbot and the splendidly named William Henry Sumner Taylor Walker, Wigan's answer to Beniamino Gigli. Like his great hero, and to paraphrase the General Confession in the 1662 *Book of Common Prayer*, Sumner had a habit of haspirating where he hought not to have haspirated and not haspirating where he hought to have haspirated, and his memorable performance of the tenor solo in Harold Edwin Darke's beautiful carol *In the Bleak Mid-Winter* inspired our colleague John Benn to pen the following gem:

In the bleak mid-winter
Sumner made great moan.
Thought he was a tenor
(A view which was his own).
Oh, how we abhor him
On this Christmas Day
With his 'hox' and his 'hass'
And his haitches hall hastray.'

Ethel and Winnie's Cassandra-like prophecies may have had a lot of truth in them but one of my visits to the Parish Church during the late 1970s stays in the memory not only because it ended in a scene worthy of *Monty Python* but also because it seemed to sum up my own conviction that the more things changed in Wigan the more they remained essentially the same. The Christmas Midnight Mass had just finished and the richly coloured interior of Th' Owd Church was bathed in mellow candlelight. The Rector said the final vestry prayers and the men's choir prepared to process back to un-robe in the Song Room behind the church. Billy Cowan, the Verger, swung open the heavy gothic door and the lamplight spilled out into the churchyard. It had been snowing for perhaps half an hour and huge feathery flakes floated gently down onto the worn paving stones and onto a young couple who were feverishly making love right in front of the open door.

There was a brief reflective pause, then two of my elderly colleagues delicately lifted the hems of their cassocks and stepped, daintily as duchesses over the prostrate bodies. The couple were so absorbed that several seconds and half the choir had passed before they noticed what was going on. Then they leapt to their feet in embarrassed confusion and fled down the churchyard, the girl covering her face in horror and the young man hopping unsteadily on one leg as he attempted to insert the other into his jeans. He turned and glared fiercely at us: 'What do you lot think you're gawping at?'

Well, I don't think we had any doubt about the answer to that and I can remember supposing that my older colleagues, all round about the age I am now, would be scandalised or embarrassed by the experience.

We arrived in the Song Room and there was another thoughtful pause, then 'Poor kids! To be as desperate as that!

'And snowing too!'

'We used to tek our lasses down th' canal bank to do yon. Dosta remember, Jack?'

'We did that, Arthur, but, my God! Never in December.'

'Well, Merry Christmas, all.'

'Aye, Merry Christmas.'

Return visits were never complete without an evening at one of Wigan's excellent pubs, such as the Old Pear Tree in Frog Lane where the Boddy's was good, the landlady dripped diamante and stood her round and Tommy the Wigan–Irish tenor could provide a 'Danny Boy' that left not a dry eye in the house. Colin Cook, who looked like everybody's idea of Mr Pickwick, was still landlord of the Market, with its unreformed Victorian interior, tobacco-yellowed walls, varnished stools, scrubbed tables and little private booths. The Younger's was superbly kept, the pies were Wigan's best and you could stand a spoon up in the gravy. None of Colin's barmaids was under seventy and they had looked sceptically but tolerantly at myself and Gordon 'Pugsley' Parr, later to be my Best Man, when we made our first experiments in under-age drinking. Nothing could have been further away from the theme pubs which clutter Wigan town centre in the first decade of the twenty-first century, with their garish décor, muscular bouncers, alcopops and fizzy chemical lager.

There were giants in the earth in those days, or at least there were in Wigan. The chef who served the excellent lunch-time buffet at the Grand Hotel, now long gone, topped even John Benn's six-feet-five and could give him at least ten stone. One of the regulars, Norman Bamber, though well below the mighty chef's height, was of similar girth and had a personality to match. Norman's idol was another great Lancastrian, Sir Thomas Beecham, and if you stayed at the Bambers' little terraced house in Richmond Street just off Hallgate it was rumoured that you really did have to sleep with your head on a bust of Beethoven. Norman loved music and he loved beer so his day job as an electricity meter reader gave him the flexible hours necessary for enjoying both to the full. His Wigan Chamber Orchestra rehearsed in the Blue Coat School next door to the flat we lived in during our first year of marriage and we would see the musicians arrive carrying their violins, cellos and crates of ale. They always warmed up with *Eine Kleine Nachtmusik* and on summer evenings we would leave the windows wide open to listen. The sound was warm and magical though the ensemble tended to deteriorate a little after the refreshment break.

Some of my earliest and most pleasant singing engagements were under Norman's charismatic and eccentric baton. We travelled to our gigs in a dilapidated black Jaguar Mark 5 with a dicky clutch, our vocal quartet jammed tightly into the leather-upholstered back seat with Norman's mighty double bass across our knees. He also conducted the Gilbert and Sullivan Society and his directions at rehearsals were a delight, deep, resonant and pure Wigan.

'Tacet. Basses!'

'Yes, Norman?'

'This 'ere is supposed to be pianissimo. That means gie o'er blawtin.'

Tenors are rarer birds than basses and a couple of years after we left for Lancaster Val and I entered the bar of the old Grand one Sunday night after Evensong. Norman, red-faced and more massive than ever, was holding court to an admiring group of young musicians. As we walked in he looked up, caught my eye and pronounced portentously: 'When I were th' conductor of th' Wigan Gilbert and Sullivan Society, I gie'd my tenor section 'ELL.'

He winked, beamed broadly and indicated me with an airy wave of his hand. ''E knows what I mean. 'Cos 'E were IT.'

As parents died and family and friends moved on Val and I gradually lost touch with the Wigan of our childhood and our visits became fewer and further between until in 1991 we flew with our sons to the USA, bought a van and set out on the five-thousand-mile drive to San Salvador and an adventure which has taken us through Latin America, Africa, Asia and still goes on to this day. Although from time to time I had been jotting desultory notes for this book it was only when we returned permanently to Europe early in 2006 that I got down to shaping them into something like a coherent narrative. There is a lot of useful family history material to be found on the Internet but there were many gaps I could not fill in without going back to Wigan itself. Apart from a very few, almost literally flying, visits I had not set foot in the town for more than fifteen years and as I drove my rental car around the places I had known in my childhood and young manhood I realised how much had changed.

The Market has gone. The Ship, where my grandfather Fred Taylor used to drink his weekly couple of pints on the way home from Haydock Park Races, is now, horrendously, called Bambooza, while the Minorca, a name with a wealth of history behind it, is now something so tritely trendy that no matter how hard I try I can't call it to mind. In contrast, the Old Hall, my dad's local in Lower Ince, has re-christened itself as The Coaching Inn and dreams away its days at the corner of Cemetery Road waiting for top-hatted and crinolined passengers to alight from the next Cranford Flyer. I sense an attack of the Hinge and Brackets coming on, so I'd better remind myself that the Crown at Worthington offers good traditional grub and carries at least half a dozen perfectly kept guest ales, while the tatty old Whitesmiths of the 1960s has become an authentic tapas bar where the owner's children are totally bilingual in the languages of Galicia and Standishgate. While staying at Charnock Richard, Val and I drove to Standish to a beautifully appointed Indian restaurant which effortlessly met the demanding standards we had become used to during four years of eating the best food Delhi has to offer. As we chatted with the Cheshire–Bengali owner, who commutes every day from the other side of Manchester, driving home to Hyde in the small hours of the morning, he said with a grin 'I bet you two don't know what this place used to be in the 1960s.'

'I bet we do,' I replied. 'It was Lil's Caff, where all the bikers used to hang out. In fact, Val admits she came out here in those days, though she's cagy about which greasy rocker's pillion she used to arrive here on.'

On a blustery day with flurries of rain spotting the windscreen we drove around the scenes of my childhood or, to be more precise, we drove more or less to the places where those scenes used to be. Scholes and its plethora of pubs had been the first to go, dissolving in the 1960s into tower blocks, to the plaintive accompaniment of the Houghton Weavers lamenting the demise of their 'old two-up-two-down'. My grandmother's house at 169 Whelley fell to progress many years ago, as did number 62 and all that bustling Millgate community where us kids annoyed the neighbours and battled with the mighty Lodgers. Wallgate and Caroline Street, Chapel Lane, Darlington Street, where my mother was brought up by her grandparents, and Lower Ince, where I spent my early childhood, are so changed that at first I struggled to find anything familiar at all. Whole communities, where people were born, married, made love, had children and died, have been razed. Even landmarks such as the great brick bulk of St. Mary's Church, redundant as its parish melted away, have vanished as if they had never been.

'It's a lot tidier than it was in the old days,' I said doubtfully, looking at the neat grass verges that have replaced the sooty fronts of crumbling terraced houses and trying desperately to suppress a twinge of Hinge-and-Bracket.

'It IS tidier ... and cleaner,' replied my wife. 'But it's so BORING. The whole of this side of Wigan is one big industrial estate.'

'You need industry,' I replied sententiously. 'Industry pays for your Shakespeare and your Mozart. Where there's muck there's brass.'

'There's plenty of brass in leafy Surrey but you'll not find this kind of muck in Ashtead High Street. That Home Counties crowd's a lot better at NIMBY tactics than us poor Wiganers.'

'You live in an olive grove in southern Spain on a road to nowhere.'

'That's because I'm not really a Wiganer. I'm from Orrell, where the *naice* people live, as you've so often reminded me.'

As I write, Gordon our Prime Minister has declared his commitment to building three million houses, mostly, appropriately enough, on brown field sites. I hope the idea works and that it does something to regenerate the centres of our old industrial towns because, quite frankly, some of them are scary places after the sun has gone down. Before we were all improved by the planners my dad used to say that towns like Wigan simply grew up 'where the horses walked'. As the motor car grew more widespread, traffic jams became commonplace so pedestrianisation was hailed as the saviour of urban centres but, for reasons we are all aware of, it benefited few apart from the big supermarkets. I have been working with lively teenagers for most of my life but as we walked through Wigan's Market Place in the late afternoon there was a degree of loud aggressive horseplay which made us feel distinctly uncomfortable. No doubt some camera or other was recording it in detail but of course there was not a flesh and blood copper in sight.

In some of those areas where the camera doesn't pry, vandalism appears to go unchecked. We visited St John's churchyard in Pemberton, where Tom, Ethel, Winnie and a host of Val's Lund, Fairhurst and Atherton ancestors are buried. The most recent graves are still intact but row upon row of headstones in the Victorian part of the cemetery have been toppled, smashed or thrown about. What price a culture that makes playthings of its dead?

As we emerged from the churchyard I noticed something brightly coloured on the pavement near the car: a handful of current credit and debit cards which had no doubt been discarded when some thief had looted a wallet of its cash. Driving back into Wigan town centre we looked for the police station which we'd last seen in the Harrogate Street area. It had gone. A passer-by looked at me pityingly.

'Ee, love, there's been no police station in Wigan for years. It's in Newtown these days, somewhere near Robin Park.'

A Metropolitan Borough of 300,000 people without a police station in the main town centre? Somewhere at the back of my mind Dame Hilda and Dr Evadne are muttering acidly that things were different in the palmy days of Stackton Tressel and Orrell Mount.

Though the streets of my childhood had more or less disappeared, we fared better at finding surviving evidence of my roots in the villages to the north-east of town. Haigh in the 21st century is a much pleasanter environment than the smoky industrial village it would have been in my great-grandparents' time and if I ever return to Lancashire,I'd be proud to live in pretty Lindsay Terrace where my grandmother Annie was born, though I couldn't come near to affording one of the half-dozen beautiful homes-and-gardens residences into which Astley's Farm, my grandfather Fred's birthplace, has been lovingly converted. The hall and plantations are much as they were, though the wonderful miniature steam railway of my childhood is no more. The basin on the Leeds and Liverpool Canal where I learned to row is still there, choked with water lilies, though the boathouse itself is long gone. The brewery wind pump, apparently on its last legs in my day, has been restored to postcard picturesqueness.

It does not do to be too Hinge and Bracket about what has passed into history. My great-aunt Margaret Hart Cockrell, who died at the age of one hundred in the first year of the new millennium, never looked back. Well into her nineties, when she had outlived all her contemporaries, she gave the milkman a tongue-lashing for rattling his bottles too early in the morning.

'I lead an active social life, my lad, and I need my eight hours.'

In conducting her funeral service, the Rector, Malcolm Forrest, commented that when Margaret was born in 1900 the average life expectancy in Wigan must have been about twenty-seven years, and when browsing the old burial registers I have continually been moved by the endless procession of premature mortality. Frock coats, carriages and bustles aside, nobody can feel nostalgic about that.

Forty years on from the Royal Enfields and Triumph Speed-Twins doing a ton down Wigan Road to Lil's Caff most, though not all, of the great town centre landmarks are little changed. Mesnes Park is still beautiful, though these days folk walk on the hallowed grass and Sir Francis Sharp Powell's shoe has been worn right though by generations of Wigan children rubbing it for luck. The Duggie is still murky and I wonder in passing how visitors from Wigan's twin city, Angers, think it compares with their famous Loire. Like the redskins of yesteryear, the ABC Ritz, that place of dreams where Roy and Hopalong rode both the range and the silver screen, has finally bitten the dust after spending its unloved dotage as a bingo hall. Crompton Street is dominated by what my Indian friends would appropriately call the backside of Debenhams but there is a plushy Grand Arcade which just fails to compensate me for the loss of the Old Arcade of yesteryear. Potters, providentially, are still making pastilles and Uncle Joe, thank God, goes on manufacturing mint balls. The magnificent Coops building where my great-aunt Edie copied Victorian fashion plates has been saved for posterity by imaginative conversion into flats. Central Park has gone but there is a spectacular JJB Stadium named after my old PE master, John Bradburn. In my youth Wigan Pier was an industrial slum. As I write, the fascinating *Way We Were* exhibition is coming to an end but plans are forming for a new exhibit based on the mighty steam engine at Trencherfield Mill, where my great-great-grandfather Richard Clough was the engineer. Meat and prater pies and Lancashire cheese are as good as they ever were but orchids now bloom where dirt rooks darkened the sky. Strangest of all, I've just read that Chinese textile magnates have decided that Wigan would be an ideal centre for making cotton fabrics. As they probably say in Angers, 'Plus ça change, plus c'est la même chose.'